BODRUM

A TOWN IN THE AEGEAN

SOCIAL, ECONOMIC AND POLITICAL STUDIES OF THE MIDDLE EAST

ÉTUDES SOCIALES, ÉCONOMIQUES ET POLITIQUES DU MOYEN ORIENT

VOLUME III

FATMA MANSUR

BODRUM

A TOWN IN THE AEGEAN

LEIDEN
E. J. BRILL
1972

BODRUM

A TOWN IN THE AEGEAN

BY

FATMA MANSUR

With 2 Sketchmaps and 29 Illustrations

LEIDEN
E. J. BRILL
1972

Le but de la collection est de faciliter la communication entre le grand public international et les spécialistes des sciences sociales étudiant le Moyen-Orient, et notamment ceux qui y résident. Les ouvrages sélectionnés porteront sur les phénomènes et problèmes contemporains: sociaux, culturels, économiques et administratifs. Leurs principales orientations relèveront de la théorie générale, de problématiques plus précises, et de la politologie: aménagement des institutions et administration des affaires publiques.

The series is designed to serve as a link between the international reading public and social scientists studying the contemporary Middle East, notably those living in the area. Works to be included will be characterized by their relevance to actual phenomena and problems: whether social, cultural, economic, political or administrative. They will be theory-oriented, problem-oriented or policy-oriented.

ISBN 90 04 03424 2

To my husband
Münir Coşar

CONTENTS

PART ONE

THE ENVIRONMENT

PART TWO

THE PEOPLE

LIST OF ILLUSTRATIONS

Maps

Photographs

INTRODUCTION

The following study is an account of life in a small town of Turkey. My purpose has been to describe a given situation as factually as possible in a period and in a country where extremely rapid social change is occurring. Thus I have not set out to use the study as a case in the demonstration of a social theory or to situate the study in a comparative framework in Turkey. This, to me, does not detract from the usefulness of this work, for the following reasons.

Field work in the social sciences is relatively new in Turkey and, except for one or two pioneering works, it can be safely said that it is only since the late fifties that communities have been subjected to scientific scrutiny. In the last ten years, a great number of village studies have been carried out, but only one of a small town. This was a study commissioned by the State Planning Organisation, to serve as a guide for future industrialisation. It was conducted by Professor Mübeccel Kiray of the Middle East Technical University in the town of Eregli on the Black Sea. The study was conducted by teams of interviewers led by Professor Kiray and the results tabulated and spelled out in Ankara. When I decided to work on Bodrum, I opted to work *in loco* and by myself. This book is therefore the second study of a small town, but the first to have been written as a result of the participant-observation method. Very soon after, and unbeknown to me, two American professors, Professor Lloyd Fallers of the University of Chicago and Professor Peter Benedict, of the university of Nevada, arrived in Turkey and settled, respectively in Edremit and Ula, two small towns in the Western Region of Turkey. These two studies are now in the process of being prepared for publication. Also, a survey of village and town life in Turkey is shortly to appear under the title of "A Reader on Turkish Society".

This information means that some material will soon become available and a beginning can be made in the comparative study of small towns in Turkey, while the Reader will present an opportunity to situate the small towns in a much wider context. The great drawback will be the fact that there have not been, at the moment of writing, studies on small towns situated in other regions, such as Central Anatolia or the East of Turkey. There are cogent reasons for this, although this is not the place to go into them. At any rate, a beginning has now been made, at least for the Western Region.

The foregoing will help to explain why I decided to work on a small town. There were other more personal or accidental factors. I had come to Bodrum unexpectedly and after a few days became intrigued by the setting and the inhabitants. I had also just finished reading Laurence Wylie's "Village in the Vaucluse". Bodrum seemed a suitable town for my projected study and I decided to investigate the validity and the feasibility of such a project. Two further stays, one lasting six weeks in the summer of 1966 and the other one month in the following winter convinced me that the study would be both valid and feasible.

First was the fact that Bodrum was the centre of a *kaza*—or district—and therefore that I would have at my disposal official records about the town and could appeal to the representatives of the government departments for help and information. Further enquiries showed that while Bodrum was poor in relation to the rest of the Western Region, it was richer than many similar districts in other parts of Turkey. While there were no large landowners, there were very few people with no property at all. Politically and religiously, the town seemed to do no more or no less than conform without evidence of extremism in either field.

The size of the town was a most important consideration. The national census of 1965 had shown the population of Bodrum to be just above 5000, a figure which had not changed appreciably for the last ten years, despite the fact that the decade had proved one where the birth rate soared. It became clear that Bodrum was losing its inhabitants to other places, and thus shared the fate of a multitude of other small towns in Turkey, the result of the rapid urbanisation which took place in the country after the fifties. A study of Bodrum would, I hoped, help to show the reasons for the exodus.

Although Bodrum is defined legally as a town and possesses a municipality, it is in fact permeated by rural characteristics, that is, a cluster of features indentified with populations which earn a living from the land. The people of Bodrum continue to be influenced by these traits of character when they leave to go elsewhere in search of education and work. Since the same phenomenon of migration happens in all the small towns of Turkey which have not experienced the arrival of industry and which still perform a

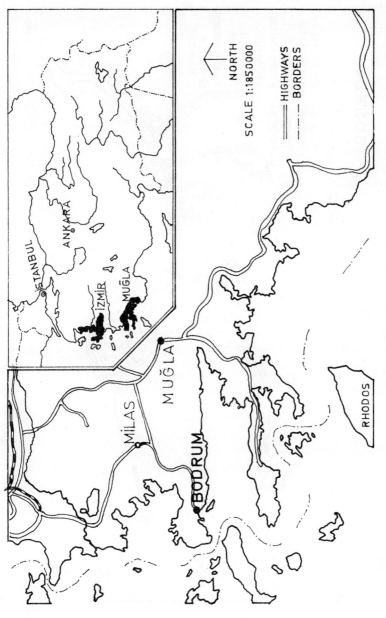

Map 1 – Location of Bodrum

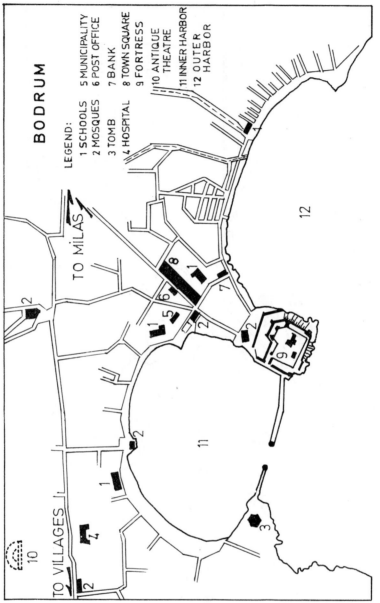

Map 2 – Plan of Bodrum

linking function between the rural hinterland and large urban centres, these same rural characteristics permeate a large portion of the population of even the biggest urban centres in the country, a fact which has meaningful consequences in the conduct of many aspects of national life.

Some figures compiled from the writings of Professor E. Tümertekin of the University of Istanbul will serve to illustrate the above: while there are 443 towns in the same population group as Bodrum—below 10,000—town-planners, geographers and sociologists in Turkey consider that from the functional and social point of view, the overwhelming majority of towns with a population of 20,000 and less share the same functional and social characteristics. The total population of these two groups of towns amounts to just over a quarter of the total urban population of Turkey. And this in a country which is urbanized at the rate of 30% only. Furthermore, the three largest cities in Turkey—Istanbul, Ankara and Izmir—with a total population of three and a half million people, receive 40% of the immigrant population, that is one million and a half.

Hence, a study of Bodrum, once the purely local aspects have been discounted, may be useful in indicating characteristics and trends which belong actually to a much wider area. Fundamental social attitudes, such as the relations between children and parents, young and old, men and women, citizens and government officials, politicians and administrators, could be safely said to be very similar in the nation as a whole, since such a large portion of the population is still very close to its small town origins. This should not cause surprise, since the fact is common to all countries which either are entering the industrial age or have experienced social upheavals or both.

Bodrum, however, possessed an additional attraction from the point of view of the study. It contains a differentiated social group, referred to as the "Cretans", which are the children and grand-children of the Turkish refugees from Crete. This, coupled with the fact that until 1935, access to the islands of the Southern Dodecanese was free, introduces into the town a flavour which is peculiar to it, and which saves it from utter provincialism. Communities which live by the sea are perceptibly more sophisticated than those which are land-locked. Here, coupled to that of the sea was also the historical fact of relations with an alien community, relations which are almost immemorial. In this light, such activities as smuggling, for instance, take on a slightly different complexion, become, to so speak, an exchange of goods and services among communities which maintain their perennial economic inter-dependency claims over national ones.

Last, but not least, I realized that as a woman working alone, I would be able to come and go unhampered to be given the coope-ration of all concerned. This requires some elucidation.

Turkish society is still sexually segregated, even though women enjoy the same economic and political rights as men. Anywhere but in the upper social and economic strata of Istanbul and Ankara, the sexes conduct their social lives separately and any kind of social study must therefore be conducted by a man and a woman together, since one of them will find that the other half of the community is closed to him or her. I discovered that I could, in Bodrum, pene-trate in both worlds without the slightest difficulty. The world of men was almost as open to me as that of the women and thus infor-mation acquired through men could be checked with the women, and *vice versa*. I might have been able to do a similar study in the Black Sea region, but I doubt very much that I could have done so in the East or in Central Anatolia. I must add that the fact that I was a teacher—a profession still widely respected in small places—facilitated the proceedings.

There were also things I had to guard against. Being Turkish was an immense advantage but carried the risk of a loss of objectivity in time. Having lived all my life in very large cities, some of my habits could shock the local population; being a woman, I ran the danger of having interviews degenerate into gossip sessions; and being a university teacher, I ran the risk of being identified in the people's minds as "one of them", the government, and thus having many things kept from me. However, my fears proved to be unfound-ed for the most part and the book has, I hope, the necessary objectivity.

Having ascertained the foregoing, I came to Bodrum and settled in a hotel for a period of six months, from September 1967 to Febru-ary 1968. The hotel was empty, and so was the town, since the tourist season was over.

From the very beginning I was given unstinted help by all, granted free access to the files of all the government departments and the Bank. Thus I was able to obtain figures from the primary sources represented by such offices as the Registry Office, which records births and deaths, and causes thereof; the Municipality which keeps a record of population, marriages and divorces, in addition to various services; the Post Office for figures concerning communications; the Education Officer and the headmasters of the schools, the Agricultural Office which keeps records of land holdings, agricultural machinery and other agricultural information; the Agricultural Bank, for agricultural and other credits, savings and the form of these; the Tax Office; the Court with its records of cases and election returns, the police for lists of offences and their classification.

It may well be asked why I did not use the figures available at the State Institute of Statistics. The reason is very simple: national statistics are tabulated by administrative districts, that is provinces—*vilayets*—and districts—*kaza*. Bodrum being a *kaza*, the centre of a district, is lumped together with all the villages in the district for all statistical purposes, from population to income, from the amount of arable land to the number of votes cast. In other words, it was impossible to extract figures for the town itself. These had to be compiled personally from the local records of the government offices.

While these figures are accurate, they do not go far enough. Records kept previous to 1955 proved chaotic, incomplete, badly written out by a variety of hands. Some were kept in the old Arabic script, superseded by the Latin script in 1928. These were transliterated for me by an elderly clerk. Some figures, like those of the Tax Office, were so unrealistic as to be absolutely useless and I listened to the advice of the officials and discounted them. I ended up by taking the ten-year period preceding the study and checked earlier figures as far as possible with other sources, such as interviews and some provincial records.

Interviews were conducted with one fifth of all the shop-owners and craftsmen, while all of the boat-builders, oil-press owners and such like were interviewed since there are very few of them.

The information about everyday life, such as family budgets, the use of appliances, etc., was compiled by drawing up a questionnaire for one hundred families representing a pre-selected sample in each of the eight quarters of the town. I visited each family and filled out the questionnaires myself. Here a point must be made. Interviews, except those with the government officials, the professional men and some of the more educated people very often took place in the presence of third and sometimes fourth and fifth parties! My arrival in a café or a house would be the signal to congregate, out of pure curiousity. It was extremely difficult to keep persons other than the man or woman concerned from answering. Very often, in some house I would be given a baby to hold while writing down the answers. Some interviews had to be scrapped, since hospitality and courtesy prevented either my hosts or myself isolating ourselves.

I also kept a diary and a set of cards upon which I recorded sayings and proverbs which seemed to recur often in conversation.

From the start I made my purpose clear. While the inhabitants of the town understood that someone would want to write a book about the place, they did not understand why I wanted to go into such detail about their lives. To them, a book about Bodrum could only be a book that would extol the town's touristic attractions and thus bring more tourists. Some wealthy people were reluctant to talk about their business and some were vaguely suspicious, thinking that I might be "from the government". But in a very short time reticences were cast off and the people of Bodrum came to accept my explanation that the story of a town and its inhabitants was worthy of a book, and I was given every assistance. They considered that the book would help "the government" and "other Turks" to learn about their troubles, about the lack of water and electricity, the lack of work and their daily struggles. Very often, when I pointed out a seemingly strange occurrence, they would discuss the point and genuinely try to find an explanation. I can say, with the utmost truthfulness, that this study is as much their work as mine.

In some instances I have changed the names of my informants or of others who appear in the book. In others, I have kept the names at the express wish of the persons concerned. Among those whom I want to thank here under their own names are Mr. Turgut Nalbantoğlu, my first mentor and now my good neighbour and friend; Mr Macit Iskenderoğlu, the District Officer, and his staff. Mr. Alim Ekinci, the doctor; Mr. Osman Bilgin, the Education Officer; Mr. Mehmet Ergene, the Judge; the Orals, my host and hostess in the Artemis Pansiyon, whose lounge was turned into a study and meeting room during that winter; "Djange", Mr. Süleyman Cahit Uysal, who knows everything and everybody and helped me in a thousand small things; Foto Barut, who gave me some photographs, and Ismail Kasa, who kept a restaurant in those days and provided me with bread, wine and reflections about life in Bodrum. Last but not least, I want to thank Mme. France Loriaux, who took all the photographs, unless otherwise indicated. The maps were drawn by Mr. Mehmet Asatekin of the Middle East Technical University, Ankara.

I also owe a debt of gratitude to Mr. Orhan Özgüner, Dean of the Faculty of Architecture at the Middle East Technical University, who granted me leave of absence.

I must likewise express my appreciation to Professor and Mrs. Lloyds Fallers, of the University of Chicago, who read the manuscript and provided many a helpful suggestion, and Professor Nieuwehuijze, from Guelph University (Canada), who also read the manuscript and suggested changes. Finally, my gratitude goes to Mrs. Joyce Stotesbury Haskal who edited and typed the manuscript in its present form.

F. M.

GUIDE TO TURKISH PRONUNCIATION

Turkish is spelled phonetically. Additional vowels and consonants have been devised to fit conversion to the Latin alphabet, and are pronounced as follows:

i   as in *it* or *in*
ı   something between the *i* in f*i*g and the *u* in f*u*g
o   as in *o*range
ö   same as the German *ö*
u   as in J*u*ne
ü   same as the French *u*
c   like a *j* as in *J*ohn
ç   like *ch* as in *ch*atter
ş   like *sh* as in *sh*e
ğ   the "soft *g*", elongating the vowel sound between two conso-
    nants following a vowel, i.e. Muğla—Moo-la and pronounced
    almost like a *y* between two vowels.

One U.S. dollar is worth 14 Turkish liras. *
One pound sterling is worth 36 Turkish liras. *

One *dönüm* of land represent 1000 square metres or one quarter of an acre

---

* rate of exchange prevailing at time of publication.

PART ONE

THE ENVIRONMENT

CHAPTER ONE

HISTORY

Bodrum is over thirty-five centuries old. Halicarnassus, as it was called then, was the main port of the Kingdom of Caria and lay between the Thalassocracy of the Achaeans and the Kingdom of Mira, itself a subject state of the Hittites. It became a part of the Lydian Empire and fell to Cyrus II when Croesus lost the battle of Sardis. The capital of Caria was then Milasa, the present-day Milas, and Halicarnassus itself was invaded by the Dorians who made it a part of the Dorian Hexagony.

In 480 B.C. Artemisia, Queen of Halicarnassus and a loyal ally of Xerxes, mustered five boats and joined the Persian fleet at Salamis; there she distinguished herself by an act of double treachery which was made to look like one of the few victories of the Persians.

She had tried to dissuade Xerxes, who thought highly of her advice, from giving battle at Salamis on the grounds that the Greeks were better at naval battles and that Xerxes' allies were a poor crew: "...these Egyptians, Cyprians, Cilicians, Pamphylians, what a miserable lot they are!" The difference between the enemies could not be "greater than that between men and women". Be it as it may, she entered the war. Pursued by an Athenian trireme, and having no room to turn, she promptly sank the boat in front of her, commanded by a friend, and thus persuaded her attacker that she was an ally. His turning away was interpreted as a rout and Xerxes, to whom the incident was related and for whom things were going badly, exclaimed: "My men have turned into women and my women into men!" Needless to say, no one survived to tell the true story. This is how Herodotus relates the incident, but then he was a Carian who had no reason to wish the Carians well since he had been exiled from his birth-place, Halicarnassus. In defence of Artemisia, it may be said that she knew her pursuer had orders to bring her back alive against a reward of 10,000 drachmaes, so much did the Athenians resent the fact "that a woman should appear in arms against them."

Halicarnassus was a prosperous and beautiful town and in the following century King Mausolus transferred his capital from Milas to Halicarnassus and built himself a palace on the spot where the municipality stands today. The walls came down to the sea and there was a secret harbour, the remains of which can still be seen. When he died his wife and sister, Queen Artemisia II, built him a magnificent tomb and thus gave Halicarnassus its most famous monument and the world a new word. She then began a reign no less brilliant than that of her ancestress. Vitrivius, an engineer with Caesar's armies, relates her most famous exploit:

> "... the Rhodians, regarding as an outrage that a woman should be ruler of the states of all Caria, fitted out a fleet and sallied forth to seize upon the kingdom. When news of this reached Artemisia, she gave orders that her fleet should be hidden away in that harbour with oarsmen and marines mustered and concealed, but that the rest of the citizens should take their places on the city wall. After the Rhodians had landed at the larger harbour... she ordered the people on the wall to cheer them and to promise that they would deliver up the town. Then, when they had passed inside the wall, leaving their fleet empty, Artemisia suddenly made a canal which led to the sea, brought her fleet out... and towed the empty fleet of the Rhodians out to sea. So the Rhodians... were slain in the very forum.
>
>   So Artemisia embarked her own soldiers and oarsmen in the ships of the Rhodians and set forth for Rhodes. The Rhodians, beholding their own ships approaching wreathed with laurel, supposed that their fellow-citizens were returning victorious and admitted the enemy. Then Artemisia, after taking Rhodes and killing its leading men, put up in the city of Rhodes a trophy of her victory."

Queens and Kings succeeded themselves until Alexander came. After a long siege and because he could not subdue the citadel, he laid the city and the surrounding countryside waste. The city, according to Cicero, was almost deserted. Halicarnassus continued as a small port, falling under the domination of Rome and later of Byzance. As far as is known, no event of universal importance took place after that until 1261, when a group of Turkmen led by their *Bey*, Menteşe, arrived in Muğla from the Cilician shores and established themselves in Caria.

The territory of the Menteşe eventually stretched as far north as the Menderes (Meander) River and as far east as Fethiye and Denizli. The *Beys* "traded" with the islanders from the Dodecanese and used Halicarnassus as one of their main ports. Their rise took place at a time when the Seljukide Empire was declining and when the Ottomans had not yet consolidated their position in Anatolia; they established themselves as the unquestioned masters of the region, building forts of their own and policing the main roads. Indeed, just as they resisted the generals sent by the Byzantine Emperors against them, they also resisted the Seljukide sultans and later the Ottoman sultans. At the outset of their power, they did not hesitate to ally themselves with Tamerlane against Bajazet, and when Bajazet died, they took sides in the quarrels which opposed Bajazet's sons to each other. When one of them, Mehmet I, eventually succeeded in establishing himself as sole ruler, he decreed the destruction of all the forts in the country. It is at this time that one of the Masters of the Order of St John was granted land in Bodrum to build a fortress in exchange for the Izmir Castle which had been destroyed by the Mongols. When the Master of the Order, Philibert de Naillac, protested to Mehmet I claiming that he wanted Ottoman land, Mehmet replied: "The place I gave you is mine, Menteşe is my vassal". This is how the Knights came to build Bodrum Castle destroying, in order to get stone, the Mausoleum which had fairly successfully withstood earthquakes and invasions for the last seventeen centuries.

With power came wealth and culture. One of the Menteşe became a follower of Mevlana and was able to send his spiritual father a present of "five young men and girls, ten good horses, ten pieces of scarlet cloth, thirty squares of silk and gold and silver money." To this day, the Bektaşi and Mevlevi influences are felt in the region and the traditional domestic copper ware still bore, until a generation or two ago, the five-pointed symbol of that mystical sect.

Eventually, like the other *Beys* of Anatolia, the Menteşe had to give way to the Ottoman state-makers. The *Beylik* of Menteşe became a division of the Empire and later a *Vilayet*, or prefecture, of the Turkish Republic, with Bodrum as a sub-prefecture. "Bodrum" was a mis-pronunciation of the name of Petronium, given to the township which grew around the Castle of St Peter, from which the Knights had been expelled by Soliman the Magnificent at the end of the 16th century.

Bodrum never relived the splendour of its antiquity. From the time of the Roman conquest on, it became and remained a backwater. The roads fell slowly into disrepair. The town was not rebuilt until the nineteenth century. Bands of highwaymen, the soldiery of the Mongols or the Menteşe, Algerian and other pirates made constant forays inland and along the coasts. The population took refuge in the Castle, coming out at daybreak to work their fields, returning at nightfall. It is thought that the population numbered about two hundred families. In 1671, Evliya Çelebi, the Turkish Marco Polo, records while on his way to Mecca that Bodrum is a small place "with poor houses, without a mosque, inn, baths or market, surrounded by vineyards and olive groves which make up the livelihood of the inhabitants". Some of the people who were better off built themselves small forts outside the walls of the Castle. These are called *kule*—towers—and a very few of them are still inhabited by the descendants of the original builders. These are rectangular structures, with slitted windows and a door placed very high. Some have dungeons. A ladder used to be lowered in the morning and taken up at night. Staircases have since been built leading up to the doors, windows opened and the slits filled in with cement "to stop the cats from coming in". Little Mehmet Külcü, of Külcü Kule, is terrified that his parents will tear down the tower in order to have a "modern" house built with the stones— many of them Mausoleum pieces. He is aided and abetted in his pleadings with his father by the town's brace of intellectuals, the Director of the Museum and the Director of Education.

By 1847, the Castle stood empty. Captain Spratt of the Royal Navy made a map of Bodrum at that time and it is seen that there are only about two hundred small houses built in the middle of the fields. Spratt also inked in a small area in the outer harbour which he labelled the "Greek Quarter", for in the early eighteenth century, a naval boatyard was started by Mustafa Pasha, an Otto-man admiral, the surrounding hills stripped of their great pines, and Greek shipbuilders were attracted from the islands. They stayed and prospered, built themselves a large church and many small chapels, and this situation continued until 1914. When the First World War broke out, the Greeks continued to live fairly peacefully in Bodrum, while each boat coming from the islands brought refugees from Crete and Cos. It is only when the French bombed the town in 1915 that the relationship between Turks and Greeks—which had been based since the eighteenth century on a division of labour and a mutual tolerance for customs—broke down. The able-bodied Greek males were sent to Central Anatolia, there to await the end of the hostilities.

However, the War of Independence, following right after the armistice, delayed their return. At the end of the War of Independence, they were sent straight to Greece where their families joined them, after having sold their goods and chattels in Bodrum. In 1923, under the exchange of population provision of the Treaty of Lausanne, the Cretan Turks began to arrive in large numbers and were installed by the Government in the houses which had belonged to the Greeks. Cretans who had been living in other quarters of the town moved into the "Greek quarter" to be nearer relatives and friends.

Turkey meanwhile had become a Republic, Bodrum became a sub-prefecture or district in the new administrative structure and its leading citizens joined the People's Republican Party (PRP), the sole party at the time. In 1950 the multi-party system was instituted and Bodrum voted overwhelmingly for the strongest challenger, the Democratic Party (DP), which came into power then. The 1960 *coup d'état* resulted in the disappearance of the Democratic Party from the political map, but again, just like the majority in the country, Bodrum returned to the polls to vote the successor of the Democratic Party, the Justice Party (JP) into power.

Today the town contains two communities, calling each other "local" and "Cretan", and although half a century has elapsed since the refugees came to settle here, the differences are still to be felt in many aspects of life. The group which settled in Bodrum are the families of Turks who fled the Cretan massacres of 1897 and those who came after 1923. The townspeople differentiate between them by calling the former refugees and the latter "the exchanged". The wealthier and more respected members of the Cretan community are those who came as refugees between 1897 and the end of the First World War.

To hear the locals speak one would imagine that the Cretans— those "half-infidels"—have nothing in common with the Turks. However, they are in fact the descendants of the Turkish Janissaries and civil servants which ruled Crete from the time it was taken by the Ottoman fleet in 1669 until 1898, when it was abandoned to allied armies as a result of the agitation of Greek patriotic groups. During the two hundred and twenty-nine years that the occupation lasted, the island was ruled fairly lackadaisically and the soldiers and civil servants settled permanently. Many Cretans converted to Islam, many Janissaries married Cretan women and, like in other Ottoman possessions, the ruling minority acquired the local dialect and spoke it at home, in all but the most exalted or educated

families. The Moslem religion became the focal point of life, moslem
festival days the occasion for a sense of identity and communal
protection in a basically hostile environment. Now and then there
were explosions of violence and ethnic hatred, but normally speaking
life was lived side by side, each community borrowing words from
the other and recipes for food. It is one of these explosions, however, which led to the first exodus of the Turks, first to Cos and then
to Bodrum.

The story of the 1897 massacre is still vivid in the minds of the
eldery "Cretans" and was told to me by the town's oldest builder,
Derviş Usta. Derviş Usta—*usta* means master craftsman—is hale
and merry, with a white stubble, pink cheeks and blue eyes. His
wife died some time ago and he has not been the same since, say
the neighbours, for she was a large happy woman who used to make
people roar with laughter at her stories, told half in Turkish and
half in Cretan. His eldest son is also a builder and Derviş Usta still
supervises the masons and carpenters working for his son's customers. Ibrahim has three daughters and no sons and Derviş
Usta is sorry about this, since the family tradition of having an
unbroken line of alternate Dervişes and Ibrahims seems broken,
but he is hopeful since his daughter-in-law is still young. He has
one son working in Germany and another son and daughter living
in other towns. This latter son married a Turkish girl—that is a
non-Cretan—"although" says Derviş Usta, "he could have married
fifty girls here". The girl was not too happy in Bodrum "away
from her parents" but, said he, "my wife taught her to cook our
kind of food and my son is happy". Now and again he goes off on the
bus to visit them and his grand-children. When he comes back,
his Bodrum grand-daughters meet him at the bus and take him
home slowly through the long main street of the Cretan quarter.
They go home to the large house he rented and then bought when
the Greeks left. Another house was built for his son when the latter
married and the two houses communicate through an inner courtyard. In the summer, the whole family piles up into two rooms
and all the other rooms are let to tourists.

Derviş Usta has a sense of history and politics. He reads a lot
because he is "curious" and is very accurate in such matters as dat-
ing events. He is interested in the family history and the history of
the Turks in Crete. One afternoon, in Fazıl Kaptan's café he told
me his version of the Cretan massacres of 1897:

One night in 1897, the Greeks attacked the Turks living in the villages of the Istiya district and it is said that three thousand Turks died that night. It is at that time that old Devlet Hanım had the lobes of her ears cut off because her attackers wanted her earrings. They thought that the little girl lying prone by the bodies of her parents was dead. Today, she is very old and can be seen in the streets of Bodrum, with her *futa*—the white and black cotton shawl worn by the Bodrum women—covering her mutilated ears.

This was not the first time that such massacres had occurred. All through the years, small bands of Greeks attacked Turks and *vice-versa*. But in 1897, the Greek resistance had been better organized by the Greek independence movement from the mainland, the *Ethikae Hetaireia*, and the Ottoman commander was unable to control events. The survivors of the massacre left the villages and poured into the nearest towns, especially Kandya. There was another massacre. The Turks, terrified, having lost homes and cattle and with nowhere to go, attacked the Greeks, supported by the Turkish population of the town. Derviş Usta said that the Turks killed as many Greeks, if not more.

At this stage, the European powers stepped in. The French occupied Ispirlonga, the British Kandya and the Italians Hanya. Derviş's father was a café-owner and the café was next door to the prison. From that day on, there were two flags flying on the prison roof, and two sentinels by the prison gate, one Ottoman and one French. The French ordered the surrender of all weapons, but some of the Turks who were fishermen and seamen told Derviş's father and others that they should give their arms to them and that they would carry the arms into Anatolia, the motherland. At night, the Armoury was broken into by the Ottoman officers and all the arms and ammunition were given to the seamen. When the French came in the morning, the Armoury stood open, its doors broken and its stores empty. Derviş's father and his brothers together with the other men were informed against and a search party of French soldiers came to the café to enquire. Not finding their men there, they came to his home and Derviş Usta remembers his mother opening the door and telling the French that she had not seen her husband for two days and nights. Derviş's father and his friends had fled to Bodrum in the night in the sailboat of another refugee. The journey was a hazard in those days, said Derviş Usta, because there were no engines in the boats and people's lives depended upon the winds.

The French then declared that all the Turks who wanted to leave Crete could do so. Derviş Usta's family all left in a boat which was sailing that very day.

There were sixty-five families in the boat. After they started, the wind fell and they had to drop anchor in Cos harbour. They did that "since Cos was Ottoman soil, just like Anatolia". The leader of the Turkish community there prevailed upon them to stay in Cos, since he was intent upon increasing the size of his community. The families decided to stay and the man wrote to the Porte in Istanbul for credits to build them houses. When I asked Derviş Usta how many families settled in Cos during that period he said, "Well now, let me see, three hundred houses were built and in those days there were six and eight people in one family". This is how it happened that most of the Cretans who eventually settled in Bodrum arrived here *via* Cos.

In 1912, when the Italians took Cos along with other islands in the Dodecanese, the Cretan refugees came to Bodrum and began to make a new life for themselves. There were Greeks then still living in the quarter of Kumbahçc, grouped around a largish church. "Djange" Süleyman—so called because he changes money for tourists—has a father who still remembers the arrival of the Cretans. They all came, "one boatful", about four hundred people, and began to look for houses to live in. In those days the Cretans lived all over town, wherever they could find a house for rent. Süleyman's father, who is a "local" married a "Cretan" girl, which was quite remarkable in those days, and is thus better disposed towards Cretans than the rest of the local inhabitants. According to him, the Cretans taught the locals to eat various things which they did not eat before, either because they did not know them or because they had religious superstitions about them. "Teoman's uncle brought a sack of dried beans once and he 'nearly burst his navel' before he managed to sell them", he said, adding that the locals did not eat ripe tomatoes because they gave one a fever, or sea-food since the religious leaders declared it was "sinful food, having no blood in it".

Teoman's family, one of the two wealthiest and most respected families in the town, also came at that time and his father and two uncles, penniless but active, immediately began to organize the buying and selling of the local agricultural produce, tobacco, figs and olive oil. They became quite wealthy and acquired land and houses. The other Cretan refugees began to build boats and work in fishing trawls and sponge boats and opened shops. The Cretans, like the Greeks, were sea-oriented and had a talent for commerce and organization. With their arrival, Bodrum began to lose its character of a purely land-based economy and acquired new trades and crafts, such as stone-cutting, lime burning and carpentry, which had been traditionally exercised by Greeks.

Middle-aged and elderly Cretans speak the Cretan dialect among themselves, using many Turkish words as well. Adolescents understand when they are addressed in Cretan by their parents, but do not speak the dialect and they answer in Turkish. No child of school-going age can either speak or understand the dialect. One of the things which displeases the locals is the fact that the Cretans "refuse" to speak Turkish!

Ever since Alexander decided to make a détour through Halicarnassus on his way East, the town had always received the last echo of distant world events, such as refugees from the Crimean War, bombing by the French warship *Dupleix* in World War I, political prisoners who had displeased the Sultan in far-off Constantinople. Nature provided the indigenous catastrophes: a plague of locusts in 1851 where, it is recorded, over forty tons of dead locusts had been gathered, and a few earthquakes the last of which took place in 1933 and brought down the minaret of the New Mosque.

Even today, Bodrum is far from the centre of things. It is too well protected by its mountains and too far from the capital. It took modern administration, modern political organization and some economic development to integrate it to some extent into the rest of the country. But the process is far from complete. As for the Menteşe, they gave the nation a few civil servants and a mayor or two.

CHAPTER TWO

THE PHYSICAL BACKGROUND

One hears about Bodrum very early in life, although it is not called that; at school, the Seven Wonders of the World are mentioned, among them the Hanging Gardens of Babylon and the Mausoleum of Halicarnassus. But then one may never hear of the place again unless a chance trip along the Aegean coast brings one back to the place where the Mausoleum was built, and it is a little surprising to realize that one of the Wonders was not suspended in a void but solidly established in the midst of a township.

However, if Bodrum is approached from the land, then it means that one has heard about it and is going there especially to see it. For it is out of the way to anywhere, the last stop of two buses which leave Izmir every day in the morning, arriving here around tea-time.

The road out of Izmir leads the traveller straight down to the Menderes (Meander) Valley, the Meander "who flows in looping curves" and on both sides of which, as far as the eye can see, cotton is grown, harvested, flooded by the swelling river and grown again year after year. Then the road follows the shore of Bafa Lake, as large, as blue and as full of fish as an inland sea, and finally starts on its climb through the Five Fingers Range, the ancient Latmus where Endymion, it is believed, was put to rest eternally. The mountains are covered with sparse red pine forests and in the lower reaches with millions of olive trees. The pines have little pots attached to their trunks, and the resin slowly trickles into them, that resin which, according to Ovid, "hardened into amber by the sun... to be an ornament one day for Roman brides".

Now and then one catches a glimpse of a village with stone houses or a water cistern shaped like a breast and whitewashed, for in this country there is no running water and all water has to be dug for or collected from rainfall. The earth is reddish, the Mediterranean *terra rossa*, or pale brown with shining grains of sand in it. The topsoil is thin, the underlying rock always showing. From now on there will be no flat expanses. Hill and mountain, creek and bay, stony paths running for miles between tiny fields where wheat is grown, or little bowls sheltered from the everlasting winds where angerines flourish, rather than oranges. At this point, the silvery silence of the olive groves is broken; the cricket zone has begun, a part of that long area all around the Mediterranean where the chirping of the crickets can be heard for months on end, from sunrise to sunset.

A bus or two, a train of sturdy brown camels carrying wood, cement or manure, a few trucks is all that one encounters. In the winter, the trucks carry the tangerine crop to Izmir and Istanbul or as far east as Ankara. In the summer, dusty tourists' cars go up and down, to and from Izmir, to and from all points in the Aegean and the Mediterranean. Little boys wave from the side of the road, clamouring for newspapers which are first read and then put to a thousand uses. Or children are seen, at school time, walking back home at leisure, with bags of all descriptions in their hands. Girls walk along, spinning wool on their cross-shaped spindles, taking home two cows or a few sheep. Men plough fields, with oxen as in Central Anatolia, but sometimes with a sturdy horse. And when a man and wife travel, it is the woman who sits on the donkey and not the man, as in other parts of the country.

Suddenly, around a bend, you come upon a beautiful sight: down below, set upon a shining sea, Bodrum Castle waits between two cresent-shaped bays. People who come by car always stop here to take a picture; not so the bus. After climbing the bad road leading out of Milas, the last important township before Bodrum, it picks up speed and careens down, like a horse smelling the stable at last. Indeed, only a few minutes later, the bus stops dead right in the middle of a large dusty square.

You have arrived in Bodrum.

GEOGRAPHY

The town is situated on the southern side of a largish peninsula surrounded in the north by the Gulf of Mandalya, the west by the Aegean sea, and the south by the Gulf of Kerme, the ancient Ceramos. Opposite Bodrum, and beyond the two islands of Karaa-da—known of old as Arkonnisos—and Cos, the long peninsula of Datcha stretches to Tekir Point, the ancient Cnidos, where Aphrodite had her temple. At this point the Mediterranean begins, the Cycladic Sea ends. Bodrum is roughly on the same latitude as Syracuse and Granada, on the 37th parallel.

To the east of the peninsula rises the Menteşe Range which comes

right down south to the Gulf of Kerme. The Range divides into
two smaller ranges. The Belen Mountains and the Tirman Mountains, both over two thousand feet high, encircle Bodrum and come
down to the sea with only a little land around the two bays and in
the folds. Around the town they are not higher than one thousand
feet. Through the corridor made by the two ranges the north wind
sweeps down upon the city and its gardens. The tops and sides
of the mountains are bare of trees, the result of the search for timber
and for farming land, and then of erosion. In November, after
the first rain, they become covered with green grass and flowers,
anemones, narcissus, wild orchids; in August, they are parched.
The thyme, sage and other fragrant bushes are all that can be
seen. Only the tangerine trees, the cypresses and olive trees keep
their varied greens.

This is dry country. The average annual rain-fall is 882.4 mm
and comes down during the last two months of the year and in
January. There are no rivers or streams. The rain is collected in
ditches and channelled into the cisterns and stored for future use
to water the animals or the fields. The wells, of which there is one
in every field and courtyard, fill up. In the years where it has
not rained enough, the water in these wells gets salty from the sea.
The water has a high content of lime, ranging from a low of 17%
to a high of 60%. In the hills, little stone walls are built around
each olive tree, to retain the moisture.

Bodrum is cooler than other places in the Aegean. Its average
temperature in the summer is 29°C and in the winter 12°C. But
it can get as hot as 37°C and as cold as −3°C. When this happens,
the large puddle in front of the church freezes and so does the water
in the taps and fountains. Sawdust and wood stoves are hurriedly
installed and the town's streets are deserted. The north wind, the
ayaz, blows through the narrow streets and penetrates every crack
and hole.

At the place where the twin bays meet and upon which the Castle
stands was a tiny island, called Zephiria in antiquity. Zephiria was
well named, for all year round the winds blow in Bodrum. They
blow from all directions except the east, where the mountains
stop them. They blow mostly from the southeast and from the north-
west. The latter cools the summers while the former deposits a thin
layer of salt on the pastures, which is good, and on the tangerine
groves, which is bad. The winds have their local names: the *ayaz*

and *poyraz* are the north winds, the *lodos* is the southeast wind, the *batı* the southwest wind. The sailors and the fishermen and indeed everyone in Bodrum know their ways and can tell for how many days each wind will blow; thus, the *batı* blows for 28 days, the *poyraz* for 75, the *lodos* for 123 days. The fishermen know the number of days which each separate storm will last. On 28 January, for instance, the dreaded *ayandon*—a corruption of St. Anthony—will blow for three days. If it does not, it means that "it must have blown behind the mountains in the north". In March, there is the "March nines", in April three small squalls, in May the last storm, "the carob-dropper". On these days, no one goes out fishing and the men sit in the cafés, with an ear cocked to detect the changes in the direction of the winds.

The peasants, for their part, have other ways of observing the weather. Thus, when the world enters the sign of the Fish, on the 21st of February, they say that "embers are falling on the air", which means that the weather is beginning to get warm. A week later, "they will fall on the earth", meaning that the period of germination has started, and still a week later that "they have fallen on the sea". On the 21st of March, under the sign of the Ram, the plants begin to show; on the 21st of May, the sign of the Twins, the period know as *ülker* begins: it gets very hot, the sheep are taken is so that *ülker* may not "hit" them and all harmful insects die and are varried away to sea. *Ülker* means the Pleiades, the Seven Sisters.

Today, even though each boat has an engine as well as sails, windlore is as alive as ever and everybody, women as well as men, wake up in the morning and tell each other that the direction of the wind is this or that and what the sea is likely to be doing behind the islands.

It is then decided whether or not the tangerines can be picked, or whether the boats will have to be back at nightfall. In this country of bays and creeks, the winds always played frightful tricks upon the people. They sank Ulysses not far from here, and hundreds of triremes and other vessels, carrying oil, wine and tiles from Ceramos to Europe were lost, to be recovered today by teams of diving archeologists. The work of the volcanic sub-strata, which caused the earth to heave and double up from below, was completed by the winds which carved and polished the mountains from above.

Administratively speaking, Bodrum is the chief town of a sub-prefecture (or district) and part of the *Vilayet* or prefecture of Muğla, which lies 144 kilometres to the northeast. The town itself is divided into eight quarters—each run by a locally elected *muhtar* or clerk. All of Bodrum's official business with the capital is conducted through Muğla. To get to Muğla, people have to go through Milas another sub-prefecture, as indeed they must to go anywhere. But in any real sense, Bodrum has no links either with Milas or Muğla. Its life-line is to Izmir, 283 kilometres north. In the summer, a passenger and freight boat of the state-owned Maritime Lines comes to Bodrum every week on its way to Iskenderun, at the furthermost southeast corner of the Mediterranean, and stops again on its way back. In the winter, when there are no tourists, the same boat comes once a month. It picks up a passenger or two and a few cases of dried figs in transit to Istanbul to be despatched from there to the ports of the Black Sea. But every day two buses leave Bodrum early in the morning and arrive in Izmir around lunch-time. Until a few months ago there was only one bus, belonging to a Milas company. Now a second bus company has been put into operation by some local people and, although the tickets are twice the price of the Milas bus, the towns-people prefer to take it: "Why should our money go to the Milas people? Let it stay in Bodrum", they say.

The buses carry the people of Bodrum to Izmir to buy and sell, go to the dentist or to the hospital, and trucks go back and forth carrying canned goods and fresh fruit, meat and fish in the tourist season, a few refrigerators and washing-machines, spare parts, the supplies needed by the chemist, the rolls of material and the shoes needed by the drapery stores. Young girls and boys go to Izmir to sit for entrance examinations to the *lycée* or college and travel back and forth on school holidays. Although there is a government hospital in Milas, people who need a delicate operation are taken to Izmir in the only taxi of the town. Young men, returning sponge-divers and shop assistants run off to Izmir to sow their wild oats in the bars and cabarets and respectable women go to visit a married child and do some shopping. The bus journey, six hours there and six hours back, has become a part of daily life, whereas in the old days it took three or four days to cover the same distance. Many people make the return journey in one day when a spare part is urgently needed for a jeep or a boat.

In the summer the bus is overcrowded and hot, full of tourists from abroad and other parts of the country. But in other seasons it carries only the people of Bodrum and their friends and relatives. As soon as they spot each other at the bus stop, conversations start which will cease six hours later. The bus stops many times on the way, to pick up the mail, a letter or a parcel, a commuting school-teacher from a nearby village, or to allow people to drink some water or a glass of tea and, in the summer a glass of *ayran*, the cooling mixture of yoghourt and water. The six hours pass very quickly and a trip to Izmir is very often a combination of business and pleasure.

The walls of Halicarnassus enclosed an area much larger than that enclosed by the city limits today. The city then stretched inland to the north for about two kilometres and the walls came down to the sea. Two main gates led out of the city, which are still the main points of entry into Bodrum, the Milasa Gate to the east and the Myndus Gate to the west. They were linked by a road which is called today the Turgut Reis Road, after a famous admiral of the Ottoman fleet. The Myndus Gate leads out of Bodrum to the villages in the west of the peninsula and the Milasa Gate leads out to Milas and to Izmir.

Captain Spratt's 1847 map of Bodrum and its port is still fairly accurate. Then, as now, the houses were arranged along two main lines: one, the shore road on both sides of the Castle and then the Milasa-Myndus Road. The squarish fields, planted with either figs or olives in those days, are shown clearly, each with the owner's house on it. Only the old Greek quarter, now known as the Cretan quarter, is solidly built -up, with little alleys leading down to the sea. In the inner harbour area, there are fewer roads and they all link up with the Myndus-Milasa road. The local population was land-oriented, while the Greeks were sea-oriented, as were the Cretan refugees who came later to replace them. Looking at more recent maps, one can see that development took place mostly behind the Castle, which is the shopping and market quarter, and to the east, beyond what was the eastern limit of the ancient walls. Looked at from the sea, the areas around the inner and outer harbours appear quite different and the impression is confirmed when one walks through the streets of both areas. In the "local" area, the original inhabitants' area, or as some like to say, the "Carian" area, there are a few large houses on the sea shore surrounded by deep gardens and, further north up the hills the houses become smaller and poorer. These houses are covered with red-tiled roofs and the poorest ones are not even whitewashed, but show their weathered stone. In the old Greek quarter, the houses are pressed close together, communicating by inner courts, lined up along narrow alleys leading to the sea. The shape of the houses is Aegean, square white cubes placed side by side or on top of each other. The wooden shutters and the doors are painted blue, the same blue which in some Mediterranean countries is reputed to ward off the mosquitoes, in others the evil eye. Red tile roofs are increasingly popular, even though the older people think that the old way of covering roofs with a special purplish, clayish earth called *geren* is better. It keeps the rain out, cool in the summer and warm in the winter. But such roofs have to be re-covered every winter and red tile is considered more practical and richer-looking.

In the rest of the town, the roads meander around houses and fields, following old property and inheritance patterns. They are lined with stone walls and are unpaved. In fact, only the road along the shore on both bays is covered with concrete. Further up, in the poorer quarters, the roads are the beds of ancient streams called *irme* and are inaccessible to any but people and camels. Even the donkeys find them unmanageable.

Nowadays bricks and concrete blocks are used to build houses. But until quite recently the walls were built in the same way as described by Vitrivius: a wall was made of two thicknesses of stone with rubble filling in between. As a result, the older houses have walls two to three feet thick. Glass windows are a recent addition and most of them were added later on the outside. The majority of the houses have wooden shutters opening inwards. The houses of the poor have wooden shutters only.

In the Cretan quarter, the houses have an inner court and in some instances these courts communicate, permitting the women to circulate without going out into the streets. Each court has a well, a grape-vine and a few pots of flowers, But in the "local" part, there are flower and vegetable gardens growing luxuriously around the houses. "These Cretans", say the locals, "they only know the sea; how can you expect them to grow flowers"!

Walking through the town, the noises and smells are also different. The Cretan quarter is noisy, with women talking loudly and children playing on the streets. In the early fall, the smell of drying sponges fills the little alleys. But in the local quarters it is very quiet. There is the smell of tangerine or lemon blossom, of honeysuckle and jasmine, the throbbing noise of the engine watering garden and field, the braying of a donkey or the mooing of a cow tethered to a tree in the yard. There are few people on the streets, the men are at work or in the cafés, the women indoors with the children. There are no fishing nets hanging on the walls or stretched on the road, but a truck or a jeep thunders by, taking tangerines to town, bringing peasants to the market, taking flour, pretol and passengers to the villages beyond the Myndus and the Milasa gates. A train of camels may swing sedately along, carrying bricks or wood or the trousseau of a local bride.

In the centre of town, behind and to the left of the Castle lies the shopping centre consisting of three streets not over a hundred yards long, the market place where buses arrive and where the PTT, the District Officer's office, the military service station and the petrol station are grouped. Other government buildings, such as the Tax Office, the Customs Office, the Land Registry Office, the Education Office and the Courthouse are scattered in the Cretan quarter, where more houses are available for rent. Every Friday, the streets surrounding the market place come alive with the peasants coming in from neighbouring villages bringing fruit and vegetables to the town and buying groceries and yard goods. In the tourist season, the two shopping streets are full of foreigners and Turks looking at shop windows, eating and drinking in the restaurants and cafés. But in the autumn and winter the streets are quiet; except for Fridays, most of the shops are deserted by their owners away in the countryside looking after their tangerine groves. At night, the cafés and restaurants are taken over by the local inhabitants, returning fishermen and spongedivers, spending the pay they received that very day, or unmarried government officials, eating supper before going to play bezique or poker in the Town Club.

In this area, most of the buildings are one-storied, except for the Bank and one or two others. The Customs, the police station, the quarantine office, the Harbourmaster and the Tourism Office are all here. So are the three large yard-goods and general stores, the only shipchandler, the offices of the municipal and sub-prefecture doctors, the two pharmacies, the five butchers, and most of the town's tailors, barbers and grocers.

The streets are barely wide enough to let a truck go though, or a large American car. Dogs frolic all along it, shopkeepers visit each

other endlessly and the cafés are sending *ayran,* coffee or tea out to
the shops. It is here that people can be found, messages given and
received, the postman met, and everybody greeted. These two
shopping streets form the information centre of Bodrum. There are
only one hundred and forty telephones in Bodrum; of these only
thirty-nine are in homes, the others are in government offices, shops
and hotels.

POPULATION

The population of Bodrum has remained fairly stable since the
nineteenth century. Records in Muğla show that there were 5540
people in 1891, that is just before the Cretans began to arrive in
appreciable numbers. The first national census, taken in 1927,
shows a figure of 4290 and that of 1941 a figure of 5874.

Today Bodrum is one of a great number of small towns—71.34%
of all urban centres in Turkey where only 18% of all the urban
population lives.

The national census of 1965 put the population at 5137, almost
equally divided between men and women. In the age groups 7-14
and 15-64 there is a larger number of men—844 for both groups.
This proportion holds for the town of Bodrum as well. However,
upon investigation another figure appeared. The second figure was
6532 and was compiled by the municipality as the result of a door-
to-door survey taken in the last two months of 1966. The discrepancy
between the two figures was accounted for in this way by the officials
of the municipality and the school teachers who had acted as census-
takers: they said that when they started on their rounds on the
morning of the census day, they found as many as almost one-third
of the houses empty. This was due to the fact that in the months of
October, when the census was taken, a considerable number of
people were away: the sponge-divers, fishermen and sailors were
at sea, the owners of tangerine groves out of town looking after the
crop and a great number of children already away at school in
other towns. As for the inhabitants themselves, many of them claimed that they had been included in the census in other places, in
other ports, but many were at sea or in remote fields and groves
and were not interviewed at all. This view was confirmed by some
of the government officials stationed in the town.

There was also, as was to be expected, a discrepancy in the
number of households: the 1965 census showed 1422 households

while the municipality showed 1734. The average size of households was given as 3.6 in the 1965 census and 3.1 for the municipality census. This is well below the official Western region average of 5.5.

The writer consequently selected the municipality figure of a population of 6532 divided into 1734 households living in the eight quarters of the town. One tenth of the population is of Cretan origin and lives in the quarter of Kumbahçe, the old "Greek" quarter.

Table 1
Distribution of population according to quarters

Quarter	Nos.	Households	Persons per household
Türkkuyusu	564	176	3.2
Eskiçeşme	662	250	2.6
Yokuşbaşı	355	114	2.5
Yeniköy	681	206	3.3
Tepecik	555	186	3.0
Kumbahçe	1505	404	3.7
Çarşi	588	203	2.8
Umurca	721	195	3.7
Total	6532	1734	3.1

Table 2
Size of Households: Distribution by Quarter

No. of Persons in one H'hold	Eski-çeşme	Türk-kuyu	Yokuş başi	Tepe-cik	Yeni-köy	Umarca	Çarşı	Kum-bahçe	Total
1	37	25	26	15	27	31	29	49	239
2	48	49	25	45	39	44	48	74	372
3	45	30	15	30	44	41	38	80	323
4	65	32	26	36	43	80	42	90	417
5	33	17	15	18	25	22	23	67	220
6	19	11	3	9	15	28	7	22	114
7	4	6	2	4	4	4	6	14	44
8	4	2	1	—	—	—	—	2	9
9	—	—	—	1	—	—	—	2	3
10	—	—	—	—	—	—	—	1	1
	256	172	113	158	197	250	193	401	1742

Bodrum cannot easily be identified by income-group, as can larger cities. The income groups are disposed like tiers in this town shaped like a theatre. The wealthier people live near the water, and as one goes inland and up the people get progressively poorer. In the last decade or so, however, there has been a noticeable concentration of the poorest families on the upmost tier and on the outside of the most eastern and western points. Thus, Yeniköy, Eskiçeşme and Umurca can be considered as the poor quarters and the eastern part of Kumbahçe as the poorest of that quarter. These two tables show that it is the richest and poorest quarters which have the smallest families. The poorest because people have to go away to earn a living elsewhere and the richest because the children were able to receive a good education and have settled in larger cities. Kumbahçe is the exception, since the Cretans seem to like larger families.[1]

What is striking is the large number—611—of families[2] with only one or two persons. This confirms the pattern in Bodrum. These are old people whose children live away from town or who have children living elsewhere in Bodrum after marriage. The Bodrum custom is that when a son marries, a house is built for him, even if it is only a one-room structure called a *dam* (a roof). The *dam* is often built on the land surrounding the main house and has one door giving on to the family courtyard and another leading out into the street. This last acquires a number and counts as a separate household. When a girl marries, she goes to live in the house built by her husband's parents. Only the very poorest have an old mother or father living with them. Everyone in Bodrum thinks that Enis does not marry because he is too fond of flirting with tourists; actually "how can I marry", he says, "without a house to call my own?" Although his father is one of the richest men in the community, he refuses to build a house for his son. On the othe hand, Fazil Kaptan, who owns one of the most prosperous souvenir-shops in town and is part owner of several sponge and fishing boats, is extremely nervous about not being able to find a plot of land near his house so that a house can be built and his son married.

It is not that there is a dearth of plots for house-building. The built-up part of the town covers a small area, but families like to be near each other and in the course of years, houses have been

---

[1] This may be due in some measure to the employment factor: most of the Cretans are sponge-divers and fishermen and away from home for long periods.

[2] In this study the terms "household" and "family" are interchangeable since the type of family is the nuclear family comprising father, mother and children only.

built side by side all along a street to accomodate the children as
they married one after the other. It is very usual to find a street
in which many families have the same surname, and this does not
include married daughters who often also live near the house of
their parents, especially in the Cretan quarter. Table 3 serves to

Table 3
Family Distribution by Quarter

Quarter	In the same street	In neighbouring streets
Eskiçeşme	4 families each of Aydoğan, Baseğmez, Dansikci, Danaci and Bircan 5 families each of Yenilmez and Durmaz 6 families of Filiz	13 families of Sinop
Tepecik	8 families of Uslu 4 families of Cingöz	7 families of Karakaya
Türkkuyusu	4 families each of Toker, Değirmencioğlu and Çanakçi 5 families of Öncel	4 families of Mutlu
Yeniköy	4 families of Kandemir 5 families of Zorlu 6 of Çakir	7 families of Öziçer
Yokuşbaşı	4 families of Dalga, of Kader and Turan	6 families of Çotra
Umurca	4 families of Çimen 5 families of Özakman and Kocair 6 families of Acaröz 10 families of Bardak	9 families of Çirakoğlu
Çarşı	4 families of Çirakoğlu of Uyar and of Tercan 5 families of Karakaş	4 families of Serçe
Kumbahçe		5 families of Cengiz, of Nalbantoğlu, of Pilgir, of Ağan and of Tabak

give an idea of this type of family distribution. The families who
have only two or three members living in the same street have not
been included, because they are too numerous, neither have the
families which have members in more than one neighbourhood,
since they are too few.

In the past three years, since tourism began in Bodrum, people
from other parts of the country, especially Izmir, Istanbul and An-

kara, have started to acquire land along the sea coast at constantly rising prices. This has prevented the local inhabitants who live near the water from buying land for their children and they have to go further into the quarters and higher up to find suitable places. It is to be expected that distances will increase as time passes between the parents' houses and those of the children and that the day may come when they will have to live in different neighbourhoods.

CHAPTER THREE

ECONOMICS

Bodrum and its surroundings have always been poor, by Aegean standards, though not as poor as districts to the south such as the Reşadiye peninsula. The peasants scraped a living from the small and stony fields; the townsmen, originally peasants themselves, worked at a few trades but relied mainly on revenue they received from their fields in the villages. The agricultural produce,wheat and dried beans, barley, acorns for the tanning industry and carob-beans for the film industry, was loaded on to sailing boats and sold in Izmir or in the Dodecanese Islands. More often than not, it was the sellers themselves who took the produce in their own boats and travelled across the Aegean. The islands were also a good market for cattle and poultry, olive oil and manure. The boats brought back coffee and tea, sugar and rice and petrol for the lamps.[1] The peasants wove their own wool and their own silk. The surplus was sold to the townspeople. Every adult in Bodrum remembers the noise made by the silkworms while feeding and the click-clack of the weaving shuttle.

In Bodrum most of the shops were owned by Greeks. The Turks were tailors, cooks and pastry-cooks and worked as seamen aboard the sailing boats. Carpentry and building were done by the Greeks, for there was a popular belief that Muslims should not make lime or break stone. Teoman's uncle remembers that when he convinced Deli Selim—now a prosperous builder—to build him a wall, the latter took on the job but ducked behind the wall every time some-one went by! Baking was also done by the Greeks since the Turks baked their own bread at home. "Djange"'s father said to the writer that it is only when the Cretans came that they began to eat shop-made bread "baked by a Moslem". Since the Turks did not eat meat and kept the precious cattle for wool and milk, it is also the Greeks who owned the butcher shops. But both Greeks and Turks worked at boat-building, a trade which had been estab-lished in Bodrum in the eighteenth century. There were one or two

---

[1] Until 1935 trade with the Islands was free. The closing of the Islands to the mainland trade and the subsequent depression made the region one of the poorest in the country.

cafés. one in the Castle, and the drinking *tavernas* were owned and run by the Greeks. When a Turk wanted *raki*, he used to send for it in the "Greek quarter". It took a Cretan to manufacture contraband *raki*, and so it can be said that it is thanks to the Cretans that Turks finally tasted Moslem-made bread and drink.

In fact, the Cretan massacre of 1897 opened a new era in the economic life of Bodrum. The Cretans who arrived in Bodrum had a flair for commerce and were free from taboos about various trades and crafts. Most of them arrived without money or goods and, not possessing land, began to look around for a way to earn a living.

One of them, Teoman's grandfather, can be said to have been the pioneer of commerce and trade in Bodrum. Old A was illiterate and possessed of strong religious principles. He was learned in the holy books but equally learned in business. He arrived here with his three sons and their young families and very soon realized that trade could be organized in Bodrum and its produce exported to foreign lands. Soon, old A and his sons had organized the tobacco trade, buying tobacco from the peasants, curing it and packing it in Bodrum before sending it to Izmir and Istanbul and even to Europe. Soon the family was prosperous enough to lend money to the peasants in advance of the crop, thus making it possible to plant more tobacco. In the same way they gathered the fig and olive harvest and sold these to wholesale distributors in Izmir and Istanbul.

A and his sons soon acquired land of their own which they planted with olive and fig trees and A's grandsons were sent to college in Istanbul, but returned and continued to trade. In the meantime, the example was followed. P, a bright and ruthless man from one of the surrounding villages, arrived in Bodrum and set up a trading-house. He soon put the smaller traders out of business until he came up against A. There was only one thing to do: the two "giants" joined forces and divided the specialities. A kept the tobacco and P took the rest. At the end of each year they shared the profits. P had had the land from his father and grandfather and P's sons began to plant that land with tangerines of a new species which had been brought in by a relative from Rhodes. P's sons went to college in Istanbul, came back, married well and increased the family's wealth.

During the inter-war period, the A's and P's ran the commercial life of Bodrum and its surrounding region. They acted as bankers, giving credit to peasants and loans to shopkeepers, thus doing what the Agricultural Bank is doing today. They all joined the PRP, the single party of the era, and wore its insignia, keeping in touch with political personalities, sitting at "*raki* tables" with the higher civil servants. Today the two families are the prestige families of Bodrum, even though some of the A's have declined. There has only been one marriage between the two families, both preferring to keep their wealth among their own relatives. And when the multi-party era came, the A's joined the new opposition party— today called the Justice Party—while the P's remained PRP. Thus, in matters of marriage and politics, the A's and P's maintained the Cretan-local dividing line. Characteristically, the P's have had politically active members and one of them is the most serious opposing candidate for mayor, while the A's carefully refrained from active political involvement.

The 1914-1918 war and the period following saw the emergence of lesser traders. The Cretans who came as the result of the Exchange of Population Agreement also looked to commerce for a living and some locals tried to follow the P's example. Today the town's gossip recognizes fifteen families as "rich" and of these, only four, including the P's, are local. All the others are Cretans who made money out of shops, trade, sponge and the fish business. Each group enriched itself by buying tangerine groves or converting family land into tangerine-growing land. Lately both groups have invested in the new economic opportunity, tourism, the Cretans more than the locals.

PROPERTY AND INCOME

It is impossible to find out what people's income is in Bodrum, except for civil servants and labourers. One of the reasons in fear of taxes, the other the reluctance to let anyone know how much money one has. A third reason is that few people in Bodrum have a single source of income. Two sources are the rule but three or four are very often encountered. Aunt Zubeyde's husband owns land, buildings and fishing-boats and he also acts as a sponge broker. The K's have shops, land and are distributors of agricultural machinery. The B's own tangerine groves, export tangerines—their own and other people's—and are petrol and fuel oil agents. The P's own tangerine groves and sell fertilizers and insecticides.

All the same, there are no great fortunes in Bodrum. Two or three men are reputed to be "millionaires", which means that they have something between one or two million liras;[1] only three people have land in excess of one thousand *dönüms*.[2] But most of this land is in the form of scattered holdings and much of it is maquis-covered hillside. The land-holdings are for the most part in the surrounding countryside, usually in the village from where the family originated. As for real estate, the overwhelming majority of the people of Bodrum live in their own house, and a smallish group owns other property such as plots, stables, warehouses and shops in town. The following tables give an idea of the distribution of this property:

Table 4
People owning only one piece of property

Yeniköy	125
Yokuşbaşı	91
Eskiçeşme	168
Çarşı	131
Kumbahçe	327
Tepecik	80
Türkkuyusu	107
Umurca	166
Total	1195

Table 5
People owning more than one piece of property

No. of Persons Owning more than 1 piece of prop.	House	Plot	Stable	Ware-house	Oil-Press	Café	Shop	Res-taurant	Total
Eskiçeşme									
25	2								50
5	1	1							10
2	1						1		4
3	1			1					6
4	1		1						8
3	1				1				6
1	3								3
1	3	1							4
2	2							1	6
Total: 46	77	6	4	3	3			4	97

---

[1] in 1967, T.L.9 to US$ 1
[2] one *dönüm* is 1 thousand square metres

No. of Persons	House	Plot	Stable	Warehouse	Oil-Press	Café	Shop	Restaurant	Total
Yokuşbaşi									
15	2								30
3						1	1		6
4				1	1		1		12
1						1	1		2
3	2		1						9
2	1	1							4
1	3			1					4
1	3		1						4
1	2	2							4
1	3						1		4
Total: 30	49	4	4	5	4	4	9		79
Yeniköy									
35	2								70
7	1		1						14
5	1	1							10
2	1					1			4
3	1						1		6
1	1						1		2
12	3								36
2	2			1					6
1	3		1						4
1	3		1						4
1	3	1							4
8	5								40
2	3	2							10
1	4		1						5
Total: 81	187	10	10	2		2	4		215
Tepecik									
14	2								28
2	1					1			4
4	1						1		8
1	1		1						2
4	1	1							8
1	1							1	2
5	1			1					10
4	3								12
1	2			1					3
2	1	1		1					6
1	4								4
1							2		2
1		1		6					7
Total: 41	65	7	1	14		2	6	1	96

No. of Persons	House	Plot	Stable	Ware-house	Oil-press	Café	Shop	Res-taurant	Total
Türkkuyusu									
29	2								58
3	1		1						6
1	1			1					2
4	1	1							8
5	3								15
1	2		1						3
3	2			1					9
1	4								4
1	3		1						4
Total: 48	96	4	5	4					109
Kumbahçe									
29	2								58
5	1						1		10
2	1		1						4
9	1	1							18
2	1			1					4
2	1				1				4
1						1	1		2
4	3								12
1	2		1						3
2	2	1							6
1	2			1					3
1	1			1			1		3
1	4								4
1	2						1	1	4
1	2	1						1	4
1	1						3		4
2	5								10
1	4			1					5
1	2		1				3		6
1	1	1		5			2		9
1	4			6			1		11
1	18	1	1	2					22
Total: 70	147	14	5	18	2	1	15	2	206
Çarşı									
25	2								50
4	1			1					8
6	1						1		12
1	1					1			2
1						2			2
1							2		2
1				1			1		2
1	1						1	1	3
2	1			1				1	6

No. of Persons	House	Plot	Slable	Ware-house	Oil-press	Café	Shop	Res-taurant	Total
3	1						2		9
1	2					1			3
1	3								3
2	2	1							6
2	1	1					1		6
2	2						1		6
1	4								4
1	3						1		4
1	3	1							4
1	1	1					2		4
1	1						3		4
1	1			1			1	1	4
1	5								5
1	4		1						5
1	3	1		1					5
1	1					1	2	1	5
1	3	3		1			1		8
1							5	1	6
1	2						4		6
1	4	1					2		7
Total: 67	117	11	1	10		5	41	6	191
Umurca									
18	2								36
4	1		1						8
1	1					1			2
1	2					1			3
1	1	2							3
1	3								3
1	2	1							3
1	3		1	1	1			1	7
Total: 28	52	3	5	1	1	2		1	72
Grand Total 413	790	All other forms of property							1065

These tables show that when we add to these figures the people who own only one piece of property—see Table 4—a total of 1608 people own 1987 houses and 273 pieces of assorted real estate units. At today's prices, a house will cost T.L. 20,000 on the average and the average for other pieces of property has been estimated at the same rate. The total value of all this real estate comes to something like forty-five million liras. The average real estate wealth of each of the 1608 people is therefore T.L. 27,900. It must be remembered that only about 125 people do not own any property at all in town and have to rent their house.

To give an idea of the ownership of land inside the town, the following table was compiled; although it does not reflect the situation in land holdings outside Bodrum, the distribution points to the fact that most property is small property. In both tables, the largest land and property holdings belong to some of the fifteen "rich" families, such as the A's, the P's and the K's.

Table 6
Distribution of Land inside the Town

No. of people		No. of dönöm
17	own	1
24	,,	2
16	,,	3
18	,,	4
29	,,	5
5	,,	6
6	,,	7
2	,,	8
1	,,	9
1	,,	10
2	,,	12
1	,,	20
122 people	own	481 dönüm

This is land on which tangeries are grown and does not include the gardens and plots which surround each house. The value of one *dönüm* of tangerine land today varies between T.L. 10,000 and 12,000. Except for land along the shore, the value of a tangerine plot is twice as high as that of a building plot.[1]

A small survey conducted in order to find out people's income yielded, after correction, the following results: 41.5% of the people consulted have an income of T.L. 300-500 per month, 5% have an income of between T.L. 500-700. Incomes above these figure are earned by groups which cover less than 1%. It must be added

---

[1] The Ministry of Village Affairs Village Inventory (p.69) mentions that 1485 families living in town own 28,465 dönüms distributed over 30 villages in the district. We may assume that most of these people live in Bodrum; this, however, is only a supposition.

that the correction of declared incomes was made by consulting competitors, neighbours, shopkeepers and sundry people who made it their business to find out about these things. The files of the Tax Office presented such an unrealistic picture that they had to be ignored. The total picture which emerges is of a community where there are many poor but few destitute and few rich. It may be added that incomes are more fairly distributed in the local community than in the Cretan.

Bodrum is a town without industry. Its workshops and shop-keepers cater to the needs of the man who derives a living from the land and from the sea. Physically, as well as economically, the town presents the characteristics of a large village with urban features, a market town which may remain so, since it does not have either the manpower or the material and natural resources necessary to industry. With the development of tourism it has begun to acquire the features of all resorts: pensions and hotels and a fleet of small boats which take the tourists diving and fishing. Very few people, as yet, earn their living entirely from tourism, as we shall see later. Under these circumstances, the land and the sea are the two basic sources of income, and the crafts and trades are their natural com-plements. It is when land is considered that Bodrum, as a town, cannot be studied separately from its hinterland—the district of the same name, with its thirty villages.

The land

Only 30% of the district's land can be cultivated, and is. The remaining area is either covered with pine woods or with maquis. There are no rivers or running water, and all the water needed for cultivation is collected from rainfall, in wells and cisterns. The cultivated area covers 4,000 acres divided as follows: 40% olives, 40% wheat and barley and some tobacco, 15% fruit, mostly tange-rines, and the remaining 5% market vegetables.

This land is cultivated by the district's six thousand or so families who own anything from a little below four *dönüm* to something like sixteen *dönüm*. These plots, small as they are, yield enough wheat, olives and tangerines to allow the owners a standard of living which is much above that of the peasantry in the many areas in the centre and east of Antolia. The fields are small and scattered and full of stones. The earth is either clayish or sandy, with underlying chalk rock which provides the building stone. The district people thus find two important materials on their doorstep: stone to build their houses and wood for warmth and cooking. A certain amount of cattle raising is done, to provide the town and Izmir with meat. The government leases the small and deserted islands which dot the coastline for pasture and even the poorest field can bring in some income, used that way; for the Bodrum cattle are tough: the cows clamber up and down the hills and feed on thistless when there is nothing else. With the first rains, in November and until the end of March, there is grass on the hills and then the cattle are fattened.

The average peasant family owns something like four or five *dönüm* by which are met their needs in wheat, olives and oil, and vegetables. The family owns a cow and a sheep or two and a few chickens. This will meet their needs in milk and cheese and yoghourt, wool and eggs. With this régime, the children have to leave the parental home: the girls get married and the boys go to Bodrum or elsewhere to find work.

The tangerine crop is the most valuable, but it requires an investment which is usually beyond the means of the peasant. The trees have to be watered throughout the summer and if the family cannot afford a motor pump, then all they can manage is two or three *dönüm*. At harvest time, the tangerine traders of Bodrum buy up the groves and send the produce to the large cities. Olives are another source of income, but figs are slowly being replaced by other crops because they do not yield much money.

The people of Bodrum work their land by hand. There are only four tractors in the whole district. With the advent of tangerines, however, over a thousand water pumps with engines and over two thousand spraying pumps have been bought. The latter are often lent among the neighbours, but not the water pumps, as they use fuel oil, which is expensive by peasant standards.

The people of Bodrum carry their loads on their backs, on donkeys and on camels. The roads and lanes of the district are such that even if people could afford trucks, these would not be able to get through. In recent years, Jeeps have been doing a good deal of carrying between Bodrum and the villages, whereas trucks are used to transport tangerines on main highways. Peasants bring their produce there, by camel or donkey, where they are picked up by the trucks and transported to Bodrum. In many villages, horses but more often donkeys and mules, are used to draw water from the wells.

The small fields are ploughed with oxen and wooden ploughs. The other tools used are made of wood with iron ends. All these implements are manufactured locally in Bodrum by the ironsmiths and in the larger villages by the village smith. The small size of the fields and the quality of the soil yield too little to enable the peasant to mechanize, and the nature of the land would prelude such mechanization anyway. Because of this, a certain amount of man-power is still used on the land.

Land workers in Bodrum work for people who have largish holdings but especially for those who live in town and cannot take care of their fields in the villages. These owners all have what is called an "*ortak*", a sharecropper who cultivates their land for them, and shares the produce of the crop. When there is no partner, then a "gardener" is engaged at a yearly wage. Tangerine groves are cared for by gardeners.[1]

Around the Bodrum area and in Bodrum itself, long-standing conventions govern the relations between owner and partner, partner and labourer, owner and gardener. These conventions change according to the nature of the crop and varies according to whether or not tangerines or wheat, olives or figs are grown, The usual arrangement in the case of a partner is that the owner provide the land, the seed, the fuel oil and insecticides, while the partner provides the labour—his own and whatever labour he hires. The produce is then divided by three, the partner taking a third. In the case of gardeners, the annual wage of the gardener is paid by the owner, all expenses are paid by the owner as well and the gardener gets nothing else, if he happens to work for a tangerine owner. But if he plants vegetables, olives or fruit, then he has a right to a third of the harvest. Gardeners earn an extra income out of two activities which traditionally are paid for by the owner, over and above the annual wage: one is the ploughing of the grove and the other is the daily wage which he and his family earn as pickers and packers in the tangerine groves, or pickers in the olive groves.

In Bodrum they dislike employing people, believing that a stranger will never work hard enough and will automatically rob

---

[1] The sharecropper is called a "partner" locally.

them. "Work done by a stranger", they say, "is never as well done as by yourself", adding that a partner or a gardener must be changed every two years, as only new brooms sweep clean. Consequently, they will only employ labour when they have to. With the coming of tangerine cultivation, two specialities have developed: the tangerine grower and the pruner. Apart from these two specialities, there is no qualified agricultural labour, except for the old speciality of "olive-shaking".

Olive trees need little care and less water and the crop is one of the most valuable in the region. There are no olive groves inside the town, only isolated clumps in the gardens which provide their owners with the year's needs. The groves are outside the town and it is estimated that the district contains one and a half million trees, yielding something like five million liras per year from olive oil only. A small proportion of the crop is kept for curing and eating at home, and the remainder is pressed in the oil presses of the district and Bodrum, for sale to the oil brokers who will re-sell the crude oil to factories in Milas and Izmir.

This very ancient crop has ancient conventions attached to it. In the course of the years fields have changed hands but in many cases the ownership of the trees has not. As a result of this, many of the village quarrels and lawsuits are caused by claims of people for the crop. The grafting of a cultivated olive branch onto a wild olive tree anywhere automatically gives the grafter the right to the crop; as the years go by, the heirs begin to contest the crop, no one remembering clearly who grafted what tree. This is further complicated by the fact that the government has been promising the ownership of the crop for trees growing on public land, provided the trees are grafted. In the course of time some of the public land has been sold and the original grafter's heirs have claimed rights to the crop. One day, while I sat in an oil pressing establishment, watching the olives arrive and being crushed, a particularly good-looking lot came in ,brought by Deli Selim the mason. While people commented on the quality of the olives, the camel-driver who had carried the load to town said to me: "my grandfather grafted those trees, you know", whereupon Deli Selim became furious and said: "do you mean you now want the olives?" The camel-driver said he had no such intention, he was just stating a fact. It took a few friends to calm down the mason, known for his quick temper, while the camel-driver looked on with the satisfied half-smile of a man who knows what is right. In Bodrum itself such conflicts do not exist because land has changed hands many time and deeds are available. To the east of town the original ownership was Greek and no one remembers what hapened then.

The picking of olives is governed by custom also. A grove owner will leave the picking and gathering of olives to his "partner". The man will employ an "olive shaker" who will go early in the morning and shake the trees with a long pole, making the fruit fall on the ground. This is delicate work, for the olives which are not yet ripe must not fall and the ripe olives must not be bruised, also the branches must not be broken. Work of this nature is considered a craft and the "shakers" get a higher wage than usual for it, T.L. 20 a day. After the olives have fallen, the women move in to gather the crop. Their wages vary between T.L. 7.50 and 10 per day and are paid by the "partner". At the beginning of the season the women will prefer to receive oil instead of money and, once they have estimated that their needs for the year have been met, will then begin to take money. Olive-picking is an additional source of income for many families in the poorest quarters of Bodrum and some of the women will travel as far north as the Menderes Valley in the olive-picking season.

The "partner" will, in turn, receive one-third of the crop for his pains. In Karaova to the northeast, the "partner" receives one-half and these rates have not changed for years; no one expects them to change either. Two further customs are followed in Bodrum: the olives which fall down on their own, before the shaking takes place, belong half to the "partner" and half to the owner. After the shaking is over, the olives which remain on the ground belong, in their entirety, to whoever happens to gather them. These are not gathered by the "partner" but left to the poor women, who wait for the occasion. These are called "gleaner's rights" and the same custom prevails for all crops in this region.

It is reckoned that five kilograms of olives will yield one kilogram and, in good years, one and a half kilograms, of pure oil. This will depend on the rainful of that year and on whether or not some care has been given to the trees, such as hoeing and fertilizing. The Bodrum olive is preferred to the Milas olive because, although it is smaller, its oil content is higher. The taste is patriotically preferred. In Bodrum, all the cooking is done with olive oil, butter being too scarce and the alternate uses of milk being preferred.

Meat and dried vegetables are all cooked in olive oil. When the oil is good, one gets used to it in time.

Every family gets its supply of olives and its two or three petrol tins of olive oil by working for it or from relatives and friends. The fresh olives are dipped in water for days on end, the water changed every day until they get "sweet" and are then stacked in earthenware or glass jars. They are served with olive oil and lemon juice added. It is the staple breakfast food and the substitute for a proper meal in many poorer families. "Bread and olives" in these parts is the equivalent of the bread-and-cheese diet of other regions of Turkey.

Nine-tenths of the olive crop is sent to the presses for the manufacture of oil. Sold in Bodrum, the oil is worth five liras a kilogram, but after it has been bought by middlemen and gone through refining processes in factories, it is sold for eight liras a can in the cities. By then it has lost much of this acidity, but also its colour and its flavour. In Bodrum few people buy canned oil. Some of the higher civil servants do and a few of the wealthiest locals.

The olives are brought to the presses in baskets or sacks by hand, by camel or by donkey, the carrier being paid in oil. Only a very large load will come by camel. The sacks are emptied into masonry stalls built outside the press, one stall per owner, and the olives await their turn there for pressing. They range in colour from a dull green to purple to black. The press is a large dark room divided into two. There are no windows, only a wide door and it is pervaded by the fragrant odour of freshly pressed olive-pulp. Everything in the room has been burnished by oil, the wooden parts of the presses gleam darkly and the floor is soaked by years of waste-dumping.

In one room the olives are dumped beside a large stone vat into which two huge stone wheels grind the olives into a pulp. The wheels are driven by a motor, but in the old days it was operated by a horse and in older days still by men who used to stand on a stone slab and press down with their feet. Out of the vat and into a masonry trough the "hot oil" or "first pressing" pours through. This is most prized and reserved for the owner and his relatives and friends. The thick brownish pulp is then put into jute sacks and stacked into the press in the other room. The press is operated by men pushing a large beam around an axle. The beam makes a large block of forged iron bear down on the sacks. At first the oil pours freely;

then, as it begins to ooze out, pails of hot water are thrown on the sacks and the last drops of greenish -yellow liquid are coaxed out. This oil pours into another trough through a thick pipe which loses itself in the mounds of waste covering the floor. After this, the oil will be scooped out and the petrol tins filled and sealed by pressing down a fat cactus leaf onto the opening. The oil is ready for the buyers.

The men work bare-chested and barefoot, and run like dancers after the burnished beam. The remains of their breakfast, olives bathed in oil, or figs dipped in oil can be seen in a plate or two with chunks of bread next to them. The owner stands or sits, smoking a cigarette, appraising his revenue, chatting to the camel driver or to a buyer. The owner of the press does not get paid in money. He gets 10% of the oil and all the waste. He sells the oil to the buyers and the waste to soap and fodder factories.

Hasan, the owner of the only mechanical press in town, is a big man, still young and who has got a really enterprising mind. His press is mechanical because the sacks are being pressed by a motor, like the wheels. But in his press also water has to be heated in cauldrons over wooden fires and carried by hand, the sacks have to be filled and emptied by hand and the oil separated from the water by hand. His ambition is to have the whole operation mechanized so that "the press will look like a barber shop and the men will be able to work in suits". He designed all the pieces himself and had them forged in Izmir. In order not to leave the press idle, he also rigged up a flour mill and, according to the season, his press is either all white or all brown. In the winter he works in his metal turning shop.

Hasan did it all by himself. He boasts of the fact that he did not get any help from the government "since I do not have an uncle' in high places" and he intends to go on this way. The reason why he wants to mechanize and produce oil in a more hygienic manner is because he thinks that sooner or later the government will start regulating these presses and he wants to be ready for the day. With this mechanical press he can get as much as a ton and a half of oil a day during the season, working day and night, while his less mechanized neighbours can only get three or at most four hundred kilograms of oil. He also gets one lira for grinding ten kilograms of flour and reckons that for three months in the year he makes an income of around T.L. 20,000; this does not include his income from the metal shop.

Olive trees are very productive every other year. This year the crop was poor. Hasan worked full-time but only one of the three other presses of Bodrum opened. The owners of these small presses made their living from other sources.

Figs, like olives, are a perennial crop in Bodrum and its surrounding countryside. Although the Bodrum figs are not as large and as good as the ones grown further north, they have been a source of income and a staple food for centuries. Dried, they are taken to the fields and eaten with some olive oil and a chunk of bread at the midday meal. Stuffed with almonds and roasted in the oven, they are a delicacy eaten in the evenings by the fireside. But the largest part of the crop is still sold by the Bodrum merchants to other merchants in Istanbul and Europe.

Before the road was built, figs used to be sent to Izmir by boat and then on to Istanbul for distribution to the Black Sea ports. From there they would be sent to the rest of Anatolia and the Bodrum boatowners and the State Maritime Lines used to make a regular income out of this traffic. Nowadays the figs go by truck, like the tangerines, as the last step of a process which begins with picking.

The figs are not picked when they are ripe ,but a little later, in August, when they turn yellow on the tree. Since there are no more large groves, it is usually the owner and his family who pick the fruit. After the figs have been picked, they are left to dry on a piece of clean ground and become hard. They are then put in sacks, loaded on to donkeys and brought to town, where they are sold to the two or three trading-houses which still deal in dried figs. The sacks are emptied in the warehouses belonging to the traders and dumped in sea-water to soften them and prevent rot. At this stage, the women and girls who specialize in stringing figs are hired and begin coming to work every day.

Long tables with benches alongside them are set up and the sacks and baskets are emptied on to them. Each woman is given a wooden handle with a long iron "needle" stuck on the end and balls of white cotton. The figs are swiftly impaled on the needle, the thread pulled through and a ring is made by tying the ends of the thread. Now and again the women dip their hands in a pail of sea water, which is standing on each table. Their hands get red and sticky; a smell of fermenting figs spreads in the street around the warehouse; droves of bees arrive and buzz all day in and out of the storehouses. After a few days, the women's hands split and the sweet juice of the figs, mixed with the salt water, angers the wounds.

As the rings of figs are made, they are sent to a room next door. In this room, a few men or young boys pack them in a white muslin bag, stamp the bag with the merchants' name and keep a log. The muslin bags are then placed in cardboard cases and the process is completed. All these operations take a good part of the price, but for many families which do not have the means to transfer their land into tangerine-growing land, or who cannot because the soil is not suitable, figs are a small but regular source of income. Contrary to olives and tangerines, fig trees produce fruit every year.

Nowadays, there are only 200,000 trees left in the district, with an average family holding of anything between one hundred to two hundred trees. Each tree yields about thirty kilograms of fruit and the peasant family, after having picked it, will sell it to the trading houses for half a lira a kilogram, after having kept the two hundred or so kilograms it needs for its own consumption. A family with an average earning will earn something like T.L. 3,000 a year from its fig trees.

The women who string the figs do not receive a daily fixed wage, but are paid by the kilogram and a woman who is a fast worker will earn as much as T.L. 20 per day. The men who pack and stamp the bags, however, get the same wage for work for which is much cleaner and easier. The difference lies in the fact that the latter work requires literacy, and most of the women of the poorest quarters of Bodrum do not know how to read and white.

The trading houses re-sell the figs at double the price, and the figs sell for a little more in the retail shops. The traders do not get a large income from the dried figs but continue to deal in this commodity because there are few other outlets. The firm which processes the largest quantity of figs, more than half the annual production, actually earns money by selling building materials and distributing bottled gas. Figs, anyway, are doomed except in those areas where water is absolutely unobtainable; in others, sooner or later other crops will replace them and fig processing, like tobacco-processing, will cease in Bodrum.

The Bodrum tangerine is known all over Turkey. It is not very large and it is not seedless, but its flavour is incomparable. The crop is relatively new, having been introduced to Bodrum some forty years ago by a landowner who had seen the fruit in the course of a trip to Rhodes. However, the culture of citrus fruit has been known for much longer. Çelebi, our chief source of information about the history of Bodrum mentions that "lemons and bitter oranges are cultivated here and confectioners living in the country are specially charged with making sweets for the Palace". Even today, the preserves made with the skin of bitter oranges and bergamots are highly prized by the visitors to the town and the Bodrum pastry-cook makes a side income by selling his home-made preserves to the tourists.

Tangerines have become appreciated as a winter fruit and a change from oranges in the markets of Istanbul, Izmir and Ankara and commanded a good price from the beginning. From 1950 on, the Agricultural Bank began to give "production credits" to citrus growers and made it possible for many a small land owner to grow tangerines. It is this fact which led the people of Bodrum to transform fig groves and even olive groves into tangerine land. The care and expense involved in growing the fruit is high and the Istanbul and Ankara wholesale distributors govern the prices. Even so, the people of Bodrum are well satisfied, although a bad year makes them curse middle-men and the Tangerine Cooperative roundly. But when a Bodrum shopkeeper or craftsman has some money to spend, he will acquire a *dönüm* of tangerine land inside the town or in its surrounding countryside. When one takes a walk in town in the summer, the whirr of the water pump can be heard all the time, bringing water to the trees planted in the yards around the houses.

Bodrum produces something like 16,000 tons of tangerines each winter and the price of a ton varies between T.L. 4.50 and 6.00. But the expense involved in growing, picking and packing the fruit constitutes half the price. Most of the fruit is picked and packed by the owners and then loaded on to trucks operated by the trading houses. The trader thus transports his own fruit free and charges the growers for the trip. The fruit is despatched to the wholesale markets in Istanbul and Ankara and, in time, the wholesalers send back the invoices and the money. The growers have no control whatsoever over any of the operations to which the crop is submitted once it leaves the town, and have to get what prices they can. Neither can they afford to make the fruit wait for better prices, since tangerines will spoil quickly.

Another way of selling the crop is to sell it while the fruit is still on the tree. Well known assessors walk through the groves and are able to estimate the yield almost to a case or two. The crop is then sold and the money obtained as soon as the fruit is cut. If the prices are good, the owner loses, if they are bad, the assessor loses. In this way, many people prefer to take a small loss rather than have the bother and expense of doing their own picking and transporting.

The picking of tangerines is always done by women, who receive T.L. 10 per day for the work. Picking tangerines is a delicate operation because the slightest scratch on one tangerine is likely to damage a whole case. Women also pack the tangerines by size in wooden cases; after a while they can tell the different sizes at a glance and select the tangerines as they go along. But the making of the cases is a man's job, for which the going labourer's rate is given, T.L. 15 per day. Women's work is always less well paid in Bodrum since theirs is casual labour and of a kind that men will not touch. Also there is constant under-employment. These wages will be paid by the owner of the garden who will usually employ the partner and his family as pickers and packers, the partner working as a case-maker and carrier.

Bodrum, with its 8000 *dönüm* of tangerine groves which provide employment for something like 2,000 families has not, however, managed to organize itself for the marketing of the fruit. The job of seeing that the growers get a fair price falls on the Tangerine Cooperative, but this latter has not been able to do it properly. The Tangerine Cooperative was established in 1956 and was very popular at the beginning because it gave its members packing cases and paper—the costliest item bar transportation in the selling operation—on credit. However, the attitude of mind which pervades all financial and commercial transactions in Bodrum, made up of individualism and short-sightedness, prevented a healthy development of the Cooperative. Although political opinions played no part in the running of the Cooperative, the members lost interest in it soon as they got money. The people who accepted positions—unpaid—on the Board began to act on their own, and use the Cooperative to make contracts abroad and sell their own crop. Once they achieved their purpose, they stepped down. Today the same attitude prevails. Of the two thousand odd producers, only three hundred and seventy are members, and passive members at that. Some of the members have continued to sell their own crop in the usual way but are determined to seek ways of exporting the fruit, since this type of marketing does away with the middle-men.

These are the main agricultural crops in Bodrum. Others, such as almonds and vegetables, cereals and carob-beans, provide some income for their owners but do not represent important contributions compared to olives and tangerines. Wheat does not grow in large enough quantities to answer the needs of the population and flour has to be imported from other towns, as well as such staples as dried beans and fodder for cattle and poultry. The people of Bodrum know that the land will not be able to yield a higher income and feed all the children in the family and they hope that a factory will be built one day so that their produce can be processed *in situ* and freed from the graft of middlemen. But this hope is not yet fulfilled and will not be for a long time to come for, as they say, "the government knows we shall vote for them, why should it court us with factories?" On the other hand, the rich men of Bodrum are too conservative and too distrustful to band together and build their own factory. And so, they work and wait, hoping that prices will be good and that the rains will come in time. If it does not, there are still enough people who are willing to hold a rain-prayer meeting, although it has been many years since one was held.

The rain-prayer meeting takes place by the edge of the sea and it is a solemn occasion. When I asked people to tell me how it was conducted, nobody could recall exactly the various steps in the ceremony, which involves the gathering of seventythousand small stones, each one of which is prayed over and then cast into the sea. After that is done, the normal prayers of the day are read and the rain-prayer closes the ceremony.

Here is a free translation of the prayer.

THE RAIN PRAYER

Merciful God, there is no God
but You

Only You can grant our wishes
You are the wealthy and the only One
We are the poor

Send us rain and grant us strength
and generosity.

Oh God, send us quickly the rain which is
full of goodness
which has no harm,

Oh God, water your servants and your animals
Spread your bounty
Revive your dead land.

Oh God, give us rain, do not prove our hopes empty.

Oh God, your servants and your lands
and your other creatures are so hungry, so thirsty
and so poor that they can only appeal to You.
We can only complain to You.

Oh God, complete our labour and give milk to our
beasts.
Water us with the bounty of the skies and make the
bounty of the earth ripen our plants.

Oh God, take away our worry, our hunger and the curse
which is upon us.

Oh God, we ask You for the gift of rain
For only You can grant it to us
Send us much rain.

THE SEA

If it were not for the sea, life for the "Bodrumese" would be much duller. The peasants inland have not come to the point where they can boast about the size of a turnip, but the boastings about the size of fish, whether finally caught or not, are tremendous and unabashed.

The sea brings expected and unexpected gifts; news, in the first place; wood for burning; tar; little shells which can be sold to the souvenir-makers; the octopus or squid which will enrich the evening meal; lengths of piping and even sometimes, the capital of an antique column. Until a couple of decades ago, according to the ancient tradition of piracy in these parts, the sea brought a rich and dangerous booty: contraband tobacco and cigarette paper, coffee and tea; sugar and flour; while cattle and all kinds of food were going in the opposite direction, to the islands. Ahmet's wife, who is very religious and never misses any kind of religious meeting, tells with pride of the days when she, a bride of sixteen, carried a gun, and helped her husband brew fig-alcohol to be sent to the islands. The Greeks unloaded their contraband "right here in front of the house", and not as now, when people have to go "the devil knows where in some far-off bay". Smuggling was not only lucrative, but easy. There were a couple of policemen in the town and the usual brace of customs people but everyone knew "what was what" and a sweet freedom reigned.

The "Bodrumese", especially the Cretans, often go to prison for smuggling. No one considers this as shameful and the victims— or heroes—talk about it freely, as do the families. Usually, they go as the result of a "mistake" and when they come out, they make a bee-line for the creek or bay where the "mistake" has been waiting for them, down below in the sea. And a few days later, they take the early bus for Izmir and come back with money to spend on drink or on clothes for the family.

Smuggling is more a tradition than a profession and a very ancient tradition at that, mentioned by as respectable a source as Thucydides:

> "... for in early times the Hellenes and the barbarians of the coast and islands, as communication by sea became more common, were tempted to turn pirate, under the conduct of their more powerful men; the motives being to serve their own cupidity and to support the needy. They would fall upon a town unprotected by walls, and consisting of a mere collection of villages, and would plunder it; indeed, this came to be the main source of their livelihood, no disgrace being yet attached to such an achievement, but even some glory. An illustration of this is furnished by the honour with which some of the inhabitants of the continent still regard a successful marauder and by the question we find the old poets everywhere representing the people as asking of voyagers—"Are they pirates?"—as if these who are asked the question would have no idea of disclaiming the imputation, or their interrogators of reproaching them for it."

Today, when the smuggling of antiquities has become an international trade, aided and abetted by museum abroad, one can hear the people of Bodrum ask, when they see a tourist arrive and enquire about archeological sites, "Is he a smuggler?" with very much the same results as those mentioned by Thucydides!

It is not only the fact that the Aegean coastline is particularly suitable for smuggling which has created this tradition. The cause must also be traced, at least in modern times, to the political and economic régimes. During the last century, those who presided over the financial destinies of the country saw fit to establish monopolies, the profits of which mostly went to those European powers who held the Ottomans in financial bondage. Monopolies were instituted for everything: fish and silk, tobacco and oil, in fact on many of the main sources of income of the people in these regions. Smuggling was the only way in which the people could save some of their production from the Monopolies' administration and make some money. In the same way, the "new style" of smuggling, which prevailed through the First World War until the Second, flourished because manufactured goods were scarce or unobtainable and because the islands of the Dodecanese were poor in foodstuffs but rich in manufactured products freely imported by the Greek government. And so smuggling took the form of an island-mainland barter and at least two of the Bodrum fortunes were made that way. Last, but not least, there is the fact that the islands and mainland are economically complementary and that trade between them had been free until 1935.

The sea today is governed by a multitude of regulations more complicated than a tangled-up fish-net. Goods are available for the asking in any shop and seamen can no longer enter and leave the islands freely. There is nothing to smuggle nowadays, as old Ahmet said to me, "nothing worth the risk, anyway" he added. Brandy? Arms? No one would pronounce these words openly and yet smuggling goes on, more and more discreet, and one suspects, of things which get more and more dangerous.

Smuggling is a way of earning money, not a living. Those who have to earn a living are the fishermen and the sponge-divers. Fish has become one of the largest revenue-bringers of Bodrum, and sponges a source of foreign currency. Both are precious commodities and a total of five hundred families, a third of the population, depend an these trades for their subsistence. This was not always so, because there was no way in which the fish could have been sent out. It is only in the late forties and especially since 1950 that fishing began to acquire its present importance. The Agricultural Bank played an important role here, as it did in the case of tangerines, because it provided credits with which people could acquire boats and fishing and diving equipment. In 1953 a cold storage plant was built.

The Bodrum fishermen do not go far on their fishing trips. They fish the Kerme and Mandalya Gulfs, where they can find all the fish they want. It is the Greek fishermen who come closer to the coast in search of fish and it is said that deals are made in the middle of the sea, since by selling fish to the Greeks, the Bodrum men can avoid being fleeced by the wholesalers and middlemen of Bodrum and Izmir. However, this does not happen too often, for the coast patrols are on the look-out and unpleasant incidents may ensue.

While there were only four of five small boats in 1950, now, eighteen years later there are six trawlers, thirty-five smaller boats called *piyade* and something like ninety small boats which are used for fishing, carrying tourists on trips or loads to places on the coast which cannot be reached by land.

The fish is loaded on to trucks at night and is sent to Izmir, packed in blocks of ice. There, the wholesale distributors sell it and send back the money to the fishermen here, after a good many deductions. Just as in the case of tangerines, the Bodrum fishermen cannot control the prices and has to take what comes to him.

There are about a dozen fishing techniques used in Bodrum, according to the season and to the type of boats. The trawlers begin to fish in September and stop in May, but all the other boats fish all the year round, using various types of nets, according to whether it is depth or surface fish they are after. Fishing with dynamite, though expressly forbidden, is quite often resorted to, even though the method is extremely dangerous to the fisherman. The divers report that all around the coast there are deep crevices caused by the dynamite. The fishermen have tried to organize themselves into an association for the protection of their rights and survival of the fish but, like everything else, individualism and mutual distrust prevent the fishermen from really working together. Since the price of fish has been going up steadily in the last three or four years, the fishermen content themselves with what they earn. The Fishermen's Association has not been able, any more than the Tangerine or, as will be seen later, the Sponge Cooperative, in interesting the Government in their plight.

Working conditions in fishing boats are governed by tradition, a tradition which has been handed down by the Greek fishermen. In the trawlers, after the cost of food and fuel has been met, the value of the catch is divided thus: 40% is shared among the team of six fishermen and the owner takes the remaining 60%. Everything which the nets bring up— seafood and shells—belong to the crew in their entirety and each man takes as much fish as his family can eat each time they come into port, which is every other night. When sponges are found among the catch, the crew and owner share the profit in the same proportions as above. In the smaller fishing boats another usage prevails. The catch is divided into as many shares as there are men on board—usually three—plus a share each for the boat, the engine and the equipment. If one man owns all three, he will get four shares, the last one representing the value of his work.

It is not easy to determine the income of the small fisherman because he is subjected to weather conditions and his catch varies in quantity and kind from day to day. He cannot go out for most of the months of January and February and for a good many days in December and March because of the strong gales which blow inland from the south. But a man working in one of the trawlers can count on an income of T.L. 500 a month, from the 15th September till the 15th May.

Diving for sponges is not an old occupation in Bodrum and began only in the 1930's, when a Cretan "entrepreneur" brought a diver from Kalymnos to teach young men the difficult and dangerous art of diving for sponges. The Cretan equipped a few boats with a machine called a *kangava*, which is a kind of underwater rake, and sponge diving became one of the principal occupations of Bodrum. Divers used helmets and heavy suits to work in, while in the *kangavas* the work was not dangerous since the men did not leave boardship and worked at operating the machine. Soon this last method became more popular and by 1950 there were fifty boats equipped with the rake.

The sponge-boats go out in April and come back in late October, after having worked their way up and down the neighbouring coasts, but they rarely go beyond the Marmara Sea or Antalya on the Mediterranean coast. The boats are stacked with fuel and food and the men stay away as long as the weather permits. The sponges are washed and dried on board and at the end of the season, or when the boat is full, are brought back to Bodrum to be stored in depots, yards or houses waiting for the sales.

There were at one time a few men who dived without any kind of equipment at all, using a block of stone to sink into the sea and working below as long as their breath lasted. This method disappeared in time, after claiming many victims. Five years ago, an important development took place. Two young men from Istanbul who were ardent underwater fishermen, came to Bodrum and when the local divers saw with what ease they moved under water in their rubber suits suggested that they should try sponge diving. The young men not only tried it but earned a lot of money and trained many other divers to dive with respirators and rubber suits. So much so that today, while the number of *kangava* has gone down to forty, the number of boats using rubber-suited divers, or "fish-men", as the local term is, has gone up to thirty-five.

Sponge diving, like fishing, is submitted, to many regulations designed to protect the product, but, as in the case of fishing, the need to earn money as quickly as possible and in the easiest way is such that most regulations are ignored. The result for sponges has been that the beds are getting rarer and that divers must go down deeper and deeper each year. Last year, in the waters of Bodrum, divers had to go down as far as 60 to 70 metres. When they do this, they risk getting the "bends" and every year a "fish-man" or two die in this way, while the number of partial disablements is higher.

Sponge diving is a more lucrative occupation than fishing, and except for the danger, an easier one. But the sponge divers are men for whom danger holds a fascination and a glamour which other work does not offer. As years pass, those who find that they are not cut out for the job abandon it and become fishermen or look for other work; but there is always a supply of new young men to go diving. Ismet, who was one of the first to learn diving with a rubber suit, dives with the same ease as others walk. For many years he did not find the type of work on land that would satisfy him, and then he discovered skin-diving. Now, whenever he feels out of sorts, or has a cold, he goes diving, whatever the season, and feels better. Ismet is a typical sponge diver, only more so. The under-water kingdom is his playground, and he plays with large fish as others play with cats and dogs, with the difference that for the sake of play, he often puts his life in jeopardy. Like all divers, he is a great boaster and better. The divers dare each other to dive deeper and deeper, and many a time he has been hauled back on board half conscious. Tourists who come to Bodrum and want to learn to skin-dive have a special friend in Ismet, who teaches them with love and patience. Boat owners know of his skills, and whenever something has to be rescued from the bottom of the sea, whether an anchor or a whole boat, they appeal to Ismet to do the work. He never refuses, for each new job is a challenge which he cannot resist. "There is nothing that I cannot do down below", he says, "nothing at all". One of his greatest pleasures—apart from teaching diving to girls—is to go after some large fish, his spear in hand, and follow the beast through the underwater growths of weed and rock. He is fascinated by the beauty of the underwater world, by the strange shapes and colours. "Believe me", he said once, "although I dive for a living, I often forget everything and look for hours at all the beautiful things."

Not all divers have Ismet's sense of beauty but all feel the "otherness" of the sea-world. Their recklessness does not only apply to the conduct of their work but to money. Although a skin-diver can earn as much as T.L. 600 and sometimes much more a month, few are ever out of debt. After months of privation at sea—where diving demands abstention from smoking and drinking and eating too much—they return to land ready to blow themselves up and spend wildly. At the beginning of the season, they get some money in advance, to leave to their families, but at the end of the season they get into debt again.

Just as in the fishing-boats, the sponge divers earn their living by getting a share of the catch. In the *kangava* they get one eight of the catch, four-eights going to the boat; and in boats which employ skindivers, they get 35% of their individual catch. Skin-divers are jealous of their catch, not because of the money, but because of the prestige attached to a man who gets many sponges each time he dives; once they have discovered a bed, they will pick the sponges and then surface as far away from the bed as possible. But since they all do it, no great harm is done. Each roams the bottom, according to his idea, and emerges half an hour or so later with his white cotton net bulging with black and glistening sponges, mixed with sea-shells and a fish or two.

The forty *kangava* and thirty-five boats employing skin-divers collect something like seventeen to eigtheen tons of sponges each year, with a force of three hundred and fifty men. One kilogram of sponges is sold for T.L. 250 to 300 according to the kind. The sponges are bought up by the Sponge Cooperative, the five sponge trading-houses and by individual buyers.

Contrary to other products, sponges are goods which are exported in their entirety. Industry in Turkey does not use them and thus this could be a most valuable source of foreign exchange, were the government to regulate the trade properly. As it is, the whole operating of selling and exporting sponges has, to all intents and purposes, become the monopoly of the Greek dealers from the island of Kalymnos. In October, the dealers arrive in Bodrum on a tourist's visa and begin the bargaining and the buying. They are

entertained by the trading-houses and by all those who make a
living from getting and giving information. The Kalymnos dealers
are informed about each sponge-diver, and learn all about the man's
situation, his family, his debts, his needs, and those in greatest need
become the first target of the dealers. The price given here will
govern all future transactions. The divers, hounded by the fear of
not being able to repay the bank loan and losing the boat, having
no other way of disposing of their catch, willy-nilly take, in the
end, the price offered by the Kalymnos dealer. Added to this, there
is a further difficulty. Kalymnos is a world trading centre for sponges
and each dealer has his contacts—usually a relative—in New York,
London or some other European city. In these circumstances it is
impossible for the Bodrum sponge diver to break into the world
market.

It could be expected that the Sponge-Divers' Cooperative would
be able to help the sponge divers and free them from the pressure
of the Kalymnos dealers. But the Sponge-Divers' Cooperative is no
better than the Tangerine Cooperative. It cannot offer the members
better terms than those of the bank and does not dispose of funds
large enough to enable it to buy up the whole catch. Also, the Cooperative has lost a lot of money because it cannot use the same weapons
of pressure that the bank can. The sponge divers are friends and
relatives and are reluctant to seize the boats and equipment of a
fellow sponge-diver, whereas the bank does not have the same
scruples. It is thus that of the one hundred and fifty sponge-divers
of Bodrum, only thirty-nine are members of the Cooperative and
that the profit continues to be shared by the trading-houses, the
Kalymnos dealers and their Bodrum informers.

THE SHOPS AND THE CRAFTS

What strikes the observer in Bodrum is the great number of certain kinds of shop in the town, such as grocers, barbers, tailors and
shoe-makers. It is only after a while that one notices other facts: the
fact that none of these shops works full-time, the fact that almost
none employs more than two people, the fact that none of the owners
relies on the shop for his living. The shop is usually owned by the
man who works in it and the goods are obtained on credit from
firms in Izmir. In this way, the expenses of running it are not large
and the day's takings are an additional part of the income. The

exceptions are the carpenters, boat-builders, tool-repair shops. These work at the trade for a living, and get it.

Still, almost all these shops were opened in the last three decades. The old description of Bodrum, "two grocers and one bakery". held good for a long time after the Republic was established. It is really since the late forties that the people of Bodrum began to earn enough money to buy shop-made goods, and since the early fifties that the number of shops and workshops has known its greatest increase.

There are thirty-three grocers in Bodrum, an average of one for every fifty families. Each neighbourhood has two or three grocer shops, usually very tiny places which do not carry more than a dozen or a dozen and a half commodities. It is only in Kumbahçe, the Cretan quarter, Tepecik, the old "rich" quarter and the market district that one finds the largest grocers. The most salient feature about all the grocers is that not one deals exclusively in foodstuffs. They each carry a certain amount of hardware and the kind of household goods which are prized as wedding gifts or as part of a trousseau. All the shops also carry the cheap hand-towels and small cakes of soap which are used in these parts as wedding invitations.

In this sea-going community, there are no chandlers. One of the largest grocers, situated between the market and the harbour, carries and sells rope and nets, chains and buckets, nylon and cork and also lengths of rubber and plastic hoses which are used by the gardeners. The owner, who has many other lucrative occupations— such as lending money—also sells heating-stoves, sewing machines, radios, and has lately acquired the distribution of a brand of washing-machines.

The food sold in the grocers is usually of poor quality. Spaghetti and dried beans are fast-moving commodities and come in large sacks. Fishing and sponge-boat owners buy large quantites of these items to feed their crews at sea. The packaged brands of spaghetti, dried vegetables or rice do not sell well and are bought mainly by the strangers who have settled here and the civil servants. The same goes for olive oil and cooking fats. Luxury or semi-luxury goods, such as biscuits, sweets, canned vegetables or fruit, toilet soap and toothpaste are practically non-existent. Lately they have come on to the market in the summer, to satisfy the needs of the tourists and those among the inhabitants who can afford them, are beginning to buy them.

My friend laughed when I remarked on the fact that so few things were sold and the Cretan grocer-cum-chandler said: "Oh, you should have seen this place before we came. There were one or two grocers and all they sold were a few potatoes and some henna for the brides. These people lived like peasants, they did not even have chairs." Another of my friends recalls, "I was the first to have a 'modern' shop with a refrigerator, canned goods and glass to put sugar and flour in. The townspeople liked it, although few bought these fancy things, but the peasants who went by on market days thought that I had opened a pharmacy!" Y.E., who has one of the largest grocery stores in the rich neighbourhood of Yeniköy has a large refrigerator and goes to Izmir personally to make sure he gets "the best". But his line of fancy sweets has not sold. "A mistake". he says philosophically.

The grocers do a brisk trade on market days, Fridays and Mondays. Mondays are the days of the "little market". On these days, the villagers who come from the surrounding villages go into all the shops of Bodrum and especially into the grocery stores. They buy needles and thread, soap and salt, tea and coffee, sugar and whatever else they may need. Many of the grocers display their goods on the pavement, the better to attract custom.

But the other days are not so busy and there are some months, "the onion and garlic" months, when no one has any money, when the stock is not renewed and where practically no trade is done. These are the months which see the "flies come and go", June to September. The tangerines are nothing but little green balls on the trees, the sponge-divers are far away on the Mediterranean and so are the fishermen.

Trade becomes brisker in the autumn and reaches a climax in December, January and February. The harvests are in, and these past years this period has coincided with the fast and feast of *Ramazan*. Spending is the thing and weddings follow each other fast.

All the grocers try to have another source of income. S. was the first to open a tourist agency, and is married to a girl whose father has a large tangerine grove. Our grocer-cum-chandler is one of the richest men in the district because he was the man who introduced credit in town, "thereby", said an old captain to me, "encouraging laziness and sin, drink and cards" ... "Is this true", I asked the grocer, "did you do these things?"and he answered with a smile, half-shy and half-sly. The rich grocer in Yeniköy has two *dönüm* of tangerine land. So has another, who shuts his grocery store in the summer for a month or six weeks in order to look after his grove. The grocer who has one of the largest shops facing the market place and who practically monopolises trade with the villagers, also has a tangerine grove and deals in spare parts for automobiles and jeeps. But one of the poorer grocers, in the poorest neighbourhood of Yokuşbaşi, said that he only had half a *dönüm* of tangerine-growing land and that he barely made a living.

The Bodrum grocers do not buy their stock from the nearest town, Milas, or from the provincial headquarters, Muğla. They all buy their goods in Izmir. The larger ones go there themselves, about once a month, the smaller ones give a list to one of the two bus-drivers or telephone their men in Izmir. The goods are loaded on to the bus the next day and, for a small consideration, reach the shops in this way. In fact, all the shop-owners in Bodrum do likewise.

These goods are seldom bought cash down. In the case of the largest grocers, as much as 50% of the stock is bought on credit, while the poorer grocers have to pay cash or get a little credit if they happen to know the supplier personally. On the other hand, the credit system reputedly introduced by our chandler has spread like wildfire. Somtimes 30%, but more often 50% of the customers buy their groceries on credit, and all agree that this results in a loss of 10% or thereabouts. Only S. admitted that he charged a "small premium" when he gave credit. The others denied it vigorously. "How could we do such a thing to friends and relatives", they asked indignantly.

Who were the people who bought on credit? Here everyone agreed: the two groups who used the institution most were the government officials, especially towards the end of the month, and the fishermen and sponge-divers, who bought on credit from season to season and sometimes did not repay for two or three years. The store owner facing the market place was more explicit: the village grocers who bought from him were the worst offenders. Then came the government officials, then the sponge-divers who wanted credit for three months, and then the tangerine growers and farmers who wanted credit for periods of six to twelve months. The grocers, although they complained about this state of affairs, did not close shop and did not contemplate such a measure. The "small premium" did the job apparently.

However, all the grocers agreed that they did not particularly want their sons to carry on with the business. The boy should study and go as far as possible in his schooling, "Things are changing", said the poor grocer from Yokuşbaşi, who had no son, "the fathers may be farm labourers, but the sons become shop-keepers".

This "change" was further shown by the fact that few grocers thought of using any capital they may get to enlarge the shops, or fit them out better. They wanted to acquire souvenir shops, or deal in spare parts, or invest "according to the circumstances". Further acquisition of land was not something that they insisted upon. They were quick to see the changes coming to the country and to Bodrum, the new opportunities offered by tourism, by the increase in cars, by the growing needs of the surrounding countryside. Land, even precious tangerine groves, was no longer the path to wealth.

The butchers of Bodrum are a merry half-dozen, all working in the same place, the eighteenth-century famed *han* or inn, in the middle of the main shopping street. A balustraded gallery runs all around the square building, overlooking the courtyard. In the old days, the stables were underneath this gallery and nowadays it is in the stables that the butchers have their shops. The animals are not slaughtered here, but in the municipal slaughterhouse. Here they are skinned and the skins salted and rolled away to be taken to the dealers in Izmir, while the carcasses are cut up for the family men to come and choose from and send home.

But in actual fact very little meat is sold, about 5 to 6 tons a month. By noon-time, the shops are empty and cleared and the butchers free to do other things. When I went to see them, a couple of tables were dragged from the coffee-house next door, we all sat around it, coffee and tea was ordered and we began to talk.

A few years ago there were two more butchers. One went to prison; one became the partner of another. All except one are the sons of butchers and two are the grandsons of butchers. Two are related. And they did not seem to think that their sons should do something else. Furthermore, they would all like to have more money so as to enlarge the shop, buy refrigerators and engage in cattle-raising.

The butchers all complained good-humouredly that the trade did not pay. They had to pay a municipal tax for slaughtering, storage and transport and they could only charge T.L. 10 for a kilo of meat. They did not even want to quote the enormous prices charged by the cattle-breeders. Their profit was a bare 15%. All the heads nodded around the table and I was looked straight in the eye. "Why not get together", I suggested, "and form a cooperative, and thus become stronger?" Oh, but they did try, in 1944. But some of the older people were difficult, no one trusted anyone else, and besides each hoped to get some of their neighbour's customers. Of course they recognized that a cooperative would be better from the credit point of view. One could control credit, and refuse credit to people who are incapable of paying. Because the story here was the same. People were poor, only a few months in the year and *Ramazan* were satisfactory times, over 50% of the trade was trade on credit and the government officials and the sponge-divers and fishermen were poor customers.

The most popular—and cheapest—meat was kid, "it is easy to digest". Young beef came second, and lamb third, because lamb was more expensive, T.L. 12 per kilo. As a matter of fact, the meat consumption of the inhabitants of Bodrum is below the national average—one kilogram per person per month. To some extent, this is supplemented with fish, although the local population does not eat as much fish as the Cretans.

This community has no less than 24 tailor shops. All their owners are proud of their work and boast that Istanbul had to wait for a son of Bodrum before it acquired a truly great gentlemen's tailor, which is largely true.

No tailor is so young that he cannot remember the day when most of the work consisted of sewing the hand-woven cloth which the villagers, as well as the townsfolk, wore. One half of the peninsula wore the blue cotton *gökdon* ,a type of jodhpur and the other half, who had to clamber incessantly up and down the hills among the maquis growth, wore the *menevrek* made of goathair, which did not catch in the spiky vegetation. Nowadays, only an old man or two still wear these. All the others wear ready-made cheap jackets, their wives make their shirts, the collarless *mintan*, and they come to town to have trousers made.

Most of the older tailors of Bodrum were apprenticed to one or other of the five tailors who worked in the town forty years ago. They all spent some time working for relatives in the same trade in Izmir and Istanbul and then came back to open a shop here. They are usually alone, with an apprentice or two when things get busy, but usually they take work home in the evenings and their wives help them with the finer needle-work. It is difficult to get apprentices, younger men preferring to learn one of the mechanical trades.

The customers prefer to bring in their own cloth, since they can save on that part of the suit. The average price for a suit is T.L. 100-150. The people who can afford these prices are the shop-keepers, the merchants, the boat-builders and the richer grove-owners. I.O., who is also a member of the Municipal Council, prides himself on the fact that he has customers as far as Milas and is also a ladie's tailor. While the others did not seem to mind contract work for shops in Izmir and Istanbul, if and when this became available, he spurned it saying that "tailoring was an art".

The tailors are no exception to the other merchants. They also are forced, especially in the case of the govenment official, to sell on credit. And again, about 50% of their trade is on credit. In spite of this, they did not seem to complain too much. They all had a few *dönüm* of tangerines and the tourist trade was helping them, since tourists found that their prices were lower than those in the big centres. But they did not particularly want their sons to continue the line. They wanted them to study and, in the case of the status-conscious I.O., to go on to university.

When I remarked on the large number of tailors for such a small community, they said that it was a result of unemployment, that boys who could not find work were apprenticed to them and that they ended up by becoming tailors, "of sorts", added I.O. With their income from tangerines, and the fact that the Bodrum people are fond of clothes, the tailors did not seem too unhappy. I.O. could even contemplate the day when he would build a mosque and enter the hotel business.

There are seven drapery stores in Bodrum, all situated in the market and around Government Square, where the weekly market is held. There is no great difference between the kind and quality of the goods, which are mostly bought by visiting peasants or the low and middle-income groups of the town. The better-off people buy their materials and shoes in Izmir and only go to these shops for their simpler needs. All the drapers keep a large supply of knitting wool and all sell buttons, needles and pins and sewing and embroidery thread. The largest stock in materials is made up of cotton velveteen printed with bright colours, in the winter, and of cotton prints in the summer. A few lengths, three or four, of men's suiting material are also available. The drapers have begun to bring in ready-made clothes, such as children's suits, raincoats and some ladies' coats in the last two years and I even saw, for the first time, a mauve nylon nightgown, hung by the neck, amid fishermen's raincoats in one of the shops. The drapers also keep a stack of plastic shoes, very popular, because extremely cheap, with the peasants and poorer people, but they do not sell shoes, as these are made and sold by the fifteen odd shoe-makers of Bodrum.

K, who has one of the two largest shops in town, started it with the help of his father, a rich and influential tangerine-grower, twenty years ago. He sits in his shop all day and receives his friends there and when he gets bored, he goes into the café next door, where his customers will come to see him. On Fridays, however, he stays in the shop because his one assistant cannot cope with the rush. On that day, dozens of peasant women, draped in their *futas*, will come in to buy thread or velveteen, or even all the materials needed for a trousseau.

K makes a large income from the shop, but he also earns money by renting his house as a *pension* in the summer and also by selling his tangerines. If it were not for these two other sources of income, he would not be a member of the top "fifteen", as he is, and would not be able to hold his political position. Like all other shop-owners in Bodrum, he has to give some credit and it takes a long time to get the money back. "If only all my customers were Cretans", he says, "I would earn a lot of money, but they are a minority". Although it is difficult to sell something to a Cretan woman, because she is difficult and has "whims", K reckons that she is his best customer. The peasants and local women are not difficult, but they do not spend much on their clothes. This impression is confirmed by the other drapers in town; they all complain about the fact that they have to give credit and wish that all their customers were Cretans.

The fifteen barbers of Bodrum are all men who give the impression that barbering is something they do for fun and when the spirit moves them. All have other occupations and sources of income— tangerine groves, cafés, souvenir-making shops, even shares in the fishing-boats. The barber shop, however, is kept on with a boy helping the barber, to cater to the needs of some old customers who would be lost without their favourite barber to shave them. The men of Bodrum rarely shave, and some look as though they never did. But on market-days, or when the sponge boats return, or when a wedding is in process, then the barbers do a brisk trade for a few days. After that, the shops go to sleep again, shut most of the day with their owners in pursuit of other gains.

The most prosperous barber makes T.L. 300 a month, and the most modest a bare 100. For a shave costs less than one lira and there are many days in the month when nobody comes in. Under these circumstances, it is surprising to find that every barber-shop has an apprentice, who does make a few tips and a small amount of money each week. When asked about this, the barbers said that the boys were the children of poorer relatives or neighbours and were taken on to give them something to do, and please the parents. No one expected the apprentices to really become barbers and to open a shop of their own.

The fifteen shoe-makers of Bodrum are all men who, at the same time, are shoe-repairers. There is only one exception, old Uncle Hüseyin, who has his table and chair set out in front of his house in the Cretan quarter and who only does work for the poorer people of the neighbourhood. On the other hand, there is clever Plati, who makes shoes on contract for one of the best shops is Istanbul and whose work-shop fills with elegant women in the summer. Plati is an artist and makes shoes when he pleases and for whom he pleases, but people speak of the "line" of his shoes with the same enthusiasm as they speak of the lines of a boat. Most of the other shoe-makers would like to follow his example and also work on contract, but they lack the knack of "getting to know people" and so must be content with serving the needs of the community. Most of the women in Bodrum have one pair of shoes "for visits", and wear rubber tongs or slippers at home and to go to the neighbours, and the men own only one pair of good shoes. In the winter most of them wear rubber boots because the streets of the town become a chain of puddles. As for the children, most wear plastic or rubber boots or shoes.

The shoe-makers also have other sources of income, such as a field or a grove from which they get some money. Plati, the son of a poor Cretan load-carrier—"he could carry one hundred and

fifty kilos on his back", said someone, "and died of it"—was moved
to make his trade pay, and succeeded. But the same motivation
does not animate the other shoe-makers, who work in their shops,
receive their friends and give the work back whenever the spirit
moves them.

In Bodrum itself, the soil is chalky and sandy, but in the vicinity
of the town, there are wide stretches of clay. The municipality owns
these clay fields and allows the potters to use them in return for a
small fee levied on each pot.

Although the area around the Kerme Gulf was known in ancient
times for its ceramics and tiles, the Bodrum potters do not make anything except the crudest pots and jars, which they sell to the peasants
on market days and to the townspeople for a small sum. A large jar
will cost T.L. 2.50 and a large water urn T.L. 5. The inhabitants
of Bodrum use earthenware jars to store almost anything, from pick-
led vegetables to olives, from dried beans to cracked wheat. Earthenware vessels are often used as bowls in which to mix the bread
dough, or dishes for eating. The potters also make miniature ampho-
ras for the tourist trade, which are later covered by small sea-shells
by the barbers' mothers and sisters—for some reason, it is the
barbers who seem to sell all these little vases to tourists.

The three potters of Bodrum have worked at the same trade for
generations. They work at it from father to son, with no change
in the technique. They use a foot-operated wheel and only a small
piece of wood to smooth the side of the jars. The clay is piled up in the
court-yard and sieved through a rough sieve made of wire and
left to sort itself out in pails of water. After the object is finished, it
is baked in an oven build of stone and fed with wood brought
down from the hills. Very few of the pots are glazed.

When I went to see Bardakçi, whose surname means Potter, he
was dyed red from head to foot, and his nephew was also smeared
with red clay. Because Bardakçi has no son, he passes on his craft
to his nephew. But the nephew does not want his son to become a
potter: "I want him to have a clean trade, where he can wear
clean clothes, and I want him to be able to sleep at nights and not
get up to feed the fires", he said. All the while the wheel was turning, making a soft burr, and the lump of shapeless clay, which had
been put on the bench, suddenly gained in height, rounded itself
and sat there, finished and perfect, as if no hands had ever touched it.

In the old days, potters' money, like blacksmith's money, was considered honestly earned and free of sin, and people who wanted to go on a pilgrimage to Mecca used to come and exchange their own money for that of the potters. Today, potters are proud of their craft but have begun to feel unhappy about their working conditions. "Very soon", they say, "we shall not find anyone to continue the craft".

The six ironsmiths and sixteen carpenters of Bodrum are men, who have benefitted from the boom in tangerine growing and in building, which began four years ago and is still continuing. They are the only shops— with those of the boat-builders—which use power, fuel or electricity to operate their machines. Since the Bodrum electricity supply is rather eccentric, most of them use fuel oil to work their equipment. Most of the engines use 10 HP and operate wood lathes, planes and metal-turning machines. All other work, such as hauling, finishing and joining, is done by hand.

Each *usta*—master craftsman—is helped by three or four apprentices, which are the best paid and most regularly employed apprentices in Bodrum. The ironsmiths do repair work on engines, on sponge-rakes, and on boat parts and jeep parts. They also make agricultural tools by hand, heating the iron on wood-fed fires. The most original piece of work that one of them had to do of late was to construct the top cone of the Old Mosque minaret, which had been blown down by a gale. Since the shop was too small to contain the ten-foot skeleton of iron, the work went on in the street, with every passer-by stopping and commenting on it. The cone has held up well and the iron-smith is as proud of this as of anything he has made in the last ten years. The ironsmiths also make all kinds of smaller parts, used by the tin-smiths and boat-builders and they are among the minority of craftsmen in Bodrum who make a reasonable living. Like other craftsmen, they want their sons to study and become doctors or engineers, and many have sent their sons to technical schools or colleges in Izmir or Istanbul.

The carpenters of Bodrum do not make furniture, for the community does not use much of it. Only one of them specializes in household furniture and makes the double bed and couple of armchairs which have become required items in a girl's trousseau. Some of them have made tables and chairs of a simple style for the new restaurants, but the people who have opened hotels and restaurants prefer to buy their requirements in Izmir. The carpenters work most of them for the builder, making floor-boards and ceiling beams, windows and door frames. They buy huge trunks, whole trees from the Forestry Department and pile them up in the street in front of the shop. More often then not, the trunks are split in two with a large hand-saw, operated by three men, and then brought in to the workshop to be cut into beams or planks. The *ustas* charge rates which are fairly high, as high as those in Istanbul and Ankara, and have thus become members of the high-income group in Bodrum. Gone for good are the days when carpentry was considered an "infidel's trade", and locals and Cretan carpenters alike earn money and buy themselves a few *dönüm* of tangerine land.

In the eighteenth century, when an Ottoman admiral established a naval shipyard in Bodrum and deprived the hills of Bodrum of their pine trees, a tradition of boat building was established and which survived, even though only a few men built only a few boats. It is only when the fishing and sponge-diving began to flourish, after 1950, that boat-building received and impetus and in the past ten years, five boat-building yards have come into existence.

The yards were all opened by apprentices who learned their trade from Ziya Usta, a Cretan refugee who started boat-building in the late thirties. He had learned the craft in Crete as a boy, and thought he could do well here, as had done the Greek boat-builders before the War of Independence. Until three years ago, boat-builders built boats for the fisher men and the sponge-divers, but since then visitors from Istanbul and abroad have come to appreciate the graceful lines of the Bodrum boats and, finding the prices cheaper than elsewhere, have begun to have pleasure boats built. Nowadays, the prices have soared so high that many people are thinking of having their boats built elsewhere, further south on the coast, where the prices are still reasonable.

The Bodrum boats—the *tirandil*, the *piyade*, the *gulet*—are all sailing boats which are fitted with engines as well as sails. The *tirandil* and the *gulet* are broad-bottomed and hold well in any kind of weather, while the *piyade* is fast and easy to manoeuvre, the ideal "sea-bird" as the people of Bodrum call it. Most of the *kangava* are *gulet*, most of the skin-diving sponge-boats are *tirandil*, because they can turn round in a very small space, an invaluable characteristic when the divers are below, fed with an air-line from the ship's compressor. Most of the fishermen use the *piyade*, the "sea-bird" which can go out in all weathers. Although the port does not have barges, many boats are built to carry loads to different points of the coast and all these boats carry tourists in the summer and thus make an extra income. Four of the big fishing trawlers, or *trattas*, are converted into cruise-boats in the summer, sleeping anywhere from ten to twenty people and are thus put to use in the season when fishing stops.   The boats are all made by hand. Only the boards and beams are cut by machine, and the rest of the work is done slowly, each part by the *usta* or the apprentice who is best at it. The sails are sewn by three old sailors who do not go to sea anymore. From the day a largish boat is "put on the bench" until the day it is lowered into the sea, with the usual sacrifice of a lamb, the people around the market and the harbour drop in and examine the work, offering suggestions and praise. On the day when it is finished and when the boats goes out on its maiden voyage, the old captains watch it from the harbour café and criticize its lines, much as a woman would criticize the lines of a suit. Nowadays, all eyes are on the work of a young craftman, who is thought to be the best "line-builder" of all the craftsmen, Ibrahim, who is the apprentice of one of Ziya Usta's apprentices.

Like carpenters and ironsmiths, boat-builders earn a very good living and pay their apprentices well. But like them, they can only employ three or four young men and the competition is hard. Again, like carpenters and ironsmiths, preference is always given to someone from the family and it often happens that a talented apprentice sooner or later sets up as a rival to his *usta* and relative. At the moment this is not resented because there is enough work to go round; even the rising prices will probably not make a difference, since Bodrum prices will continue to be lower than those of Europe or Istanbul. The builders do not keep books and do not make cost estimates. They charge what they think the customer is willing to pay, and have no means of finding out about prices in other areas. Until the strangers came in, they never signed a contract or drew up a specifications' list, but built in the traditional way, after a casual chat with the fishermen or sponge-diver concerned. Since they did not earn enough to pay income tax, they did not keep books and now find, like carpenters and iron-smiths, that all the paper work is beyond them.

Tourism

The newest, and to the inhabitants, the most exciting occupation
in Bodrum is the tourist business, the business of sleeping and feeding the thirty thousand odd tourists who come to Bodrum from May
until October, and who land on these shores after having exhausted
the possibilities of other places nearer home. The prices in Bodrum
are still low enough and the inhabitants still innocent enough to
have become a real attraction. Since the road-building activity of
the government has made access to Bodrum relatively easier,
the Turks have also begun to travel through the country for
their holidays, an unheard-of thing ten years ago, and make up a
group of tourists which tries to compete with the foreigners for
cheap pensions and hotels.

When the first tourists began to arrive, they stayed at the one
hotel available, a modest building in the market area which had
served the needs of travelling salesman and farmers from other
places. The *han* or inn which is now used as a butcher-shop and
sponge depot, was used by the poorer peasants and visiting sponge-
divers. A few of the town's citizens organized themselves into a
Tourism Association in 1959 and began to campaign in the town
asking the restaurants to spruce up and the inhabitants to take
in paying guests. The idea of taking money from a guest was met
with bewilderment and even horror and many of the earlier tourists
stayed in some of the best homes of Bodrum without paying. In
1960, the Tourism Association devised a way to save the hosts from
embarrassment: they would get the money from the tourists and
give it to the hosts afterwards. This usage slowly established itself,
some tourists leaving the money under the pillow before leaving
and people began to earn some money in this way. "Now", says the
Association's general secretary, "the people who were ashamed
to take money five years ago hang around the bus station to grab
tourists before the neighbour has a change to do it!" Now, six
years after the Association began work in earnest, there are thirty-
five houses which take guests and fifteen hotels and *pensions*, the
pension being, in fact, a modest hotel.

The tourist business looks so hopeful—in spite of crises such as
Cyprus—that many of the better-off merchants in town are now
investing in hotel-building. Many of the old and charming houses
in the Cretan quarter have been pulled down, and small hotels

of a nondescript style have gone up instead. Needless to say, it is the Cretans who are most enterprising, but more and more of the locals are following in their footsteps.

The Tourism Association is the only professional association which works well and which has got results in record time. This may be due to the fact that the risk in taking in tourists was almost non-exsistent, and that the loans given by the Association were interest-free. Because of the loans, many people improved their homes, putting in proper bathrooms, arranging the courtyards and even getting a refrigerator and a telephone. Just as in the Tangerine and Sponge Cooperatives, party considerations do not play a role in the Tourism Association, even though—human nature being what it is—some small advantages accrue to one or two of the Association's members. By and large, it is the only Association which does not recieve criticism and whose work is truly appreciated.

The Tourism Association is run by men who appreciate their city and are aware of its economic potentialities. The members of the Board are on the look-out for visiting artists and photographers, for lovers of ancient sites and constantly ask for advice to improve things. They were able to draw financial help from the Ministry in Ankara and have used the money to print brochures and hold exhibitions in Istanbul and Ankara. They have dined and wined journalists, both foreign and Turkish, and have finally put Bodrum on the map.

THE BANK

The most prosperous activities of Bodrum have been made possible by the Agricultural Bank, the only bank in Bodrum, and as its members are wont to say, "a state within a state" in the country. Indeed, the Bank is a public corporation, responsible to the Ministry of Commerce and the only giver of credit to people who deal in agriculture or fishing. The Bank is one hundred years old, but in the days when the Empire was bankrupt and in the first decade of the Republic, it had not been able to extend credit to producers. On the eve of the Second World War and in the years immediately following it, the conservative financial mentality of the PRP had prevented the extension of credit to peasants whose productivity was low. After 1950, the Democratic Party gave very large amounts of credits to the peasants, without taking national solvency into account. But as a by-product of this reckless national policy, peasants everywhere benefitted to such an extent that the prohibitive rates of interest—as high as 9%— and the constant rise in prices do not seem to them too high a price to pay. In the meantime, the Bank keeps the mortgages of practically all the cultivated land in Turkey.

The bank has its duties defined in Law No. 3202. It is to assist, through the credit mechanism, the "small farmer". And immediately one encounters difficulties; for the kind of small farmer described in the law does not exist in Turkey, least of all in Bodrum. The "small farmer" is a man who farms his plot unaided by anyone, not even his family, and who has no other means of support. But the inheritance law leading to the increasing division of the land, the growing needs of the people make a small farm practically useless. So everyone is trying to work part-time in the town, while the wife and children look after the plot of land. This is certainly the case with the vast majority in Bodrum.

When a farmer needs money, he can borrow on his land or on his crops. The amount of credit is reviewed every five years by the bank and has to be approved by the Head Office in Ankara. In order to borrow, the farmer has to bring his title of ownership. However, many in the hinterland do not have such a document. The land is theirs by common knowledge, and in these cases they find a couple of witnesses who act as guarantors. If the farmer fails to repay, the guarantor usually pays up and appropriates the land. There are a few men in Bodrum who are reputed to have made a "fortune" that way. Because the peasant is afraid of taxation, he usually estimates his land below the real price. He thus gets a smaller sum from the Bank, but makes do with it. As for the guarantor, the deal is profitable since the sum he eventually pays the Bank with is far below the real value of the land.

Another way to borrow is to mortgage the crop. Each crop has a scale, which is also changed every five years. The loan is repaid at harvest time, and in all cases the interest is high, about 9.5%.

The original idea for the crop credit was that at various periods of the year, credit could be obtained for the work which needed to be done then: such as fertilizer credit in March, irrigation credit in the summer, and so on. For the tangerine crop, the credit is to be given in two parts, 40% in early spring and the remaining 60% in the summer.

The largest amount of credit is given for purposes known as

"working credits", given for the purposess of operating farms, buying seed, irrigation, buying agricultural implements, buying oil-
presses and the like.

However, the country is poor and the people need money, so
that they tend to come to the Bank and ask for all the credit they are
entitled to in a lump sum, and this sum is almost always used for
various other purposes: to marry a son, build a house, repay a
debt contracted to a money-lender in town or in the village. The
Bank manager then does his best to reason with the applicant and
uses his authority to refuse the loan. Most of the time he has no
means of checking, except when it is too late: at harvest time,
and then the harvest is so poor that it is obvious the man had used
the money for something else.

When a man cannot pay up and neither can his guarantor, the
Bank can, legally, seize his land and his equipment. But this is rarely
done, things are made to wait, which results in an increase in
expenses. One of the main reasons for not seizing the land is that
the sale of a small plot will hardly bring in the equivalent of the
original loan and the operation is not worth the trouble.

In the villages around Bodrum, the Bank has established Credit
Cooperatives which it controls every month and whose chairmen it
has to approve. Most people are members of these cooperatives,
where they go for short-term, i.e., harvest-time loans. However, if
a man happens to be a member of the Tangerine Cooperative, he
cannot become a member of the Credit Cooperative. Neither can a
member get short-term credit from the Bank in such cases, but
only medium to long-term credits, i.e., 5 to 10 years. These loans
are used to open up unused tracts of land, do major irrigation work,
plant an olive or a tangerine-grove.

The Bank also acts as a normal deposit, savings, and commercial
bank. In the first place, it is the deposit bank for the government
agencies in the area. And then it is used by businessmen for commercial purposes. But the total amount, in the Bodrum area, of commercial credit given is about one fifth of the agricultural credit, and
this is given, obviously, to the townspeople. The Bank has never
been able to recuperate all the loans it has given when they are due.
Usually one half is recuperated, the rest is carried forward.

The Bank manager, with whom I was talking at the edge of
the water, looked melancholy: "There is a lot of money tucked away
in the villages. The peasants keep it in their mattresses. I remember

once, on a tour of inspection, I had to change a large note. "Wait a minute", said an old man, and he went over to his bed, opened up a corner of his mattress, and changed a thousand-lire note."

Those who use the bank most for their savings are women and old men who want, among other things, to make sure of their "shroud money". There is a reluctance on the part of older people to put money in the Bank because it brings in interest and interest is considered sinful. About fifteen people in the town have left their money in the Bank with the proviso that this money should not earn interest. In order to stimulate savings, the Bank manager asked the *Müftü* of Bodrum to talk to the peasants about this, but the *müftü* refuses, insisting that interest is sinful. At one time, even, the *müftü* of Turkey gave a talk on the radio to the effect that bank interest was not sinful, but useful.

Be that as it may, there is not much money to be saved, anyway, in this area. In the last few years, five or six people in the town have drawn all their money from the Bank and are known to lend it out to people for as much as 30% interest. Our friend, the rich grocer A., is known to have lent money thus to "half the countryside", and there is an old lady in the town who does the same. During the "onion and garlic months", people need money and mortgage their little plots to these usurers and very soon they are landless. The people who are considered rich in town are so considered because they own a lot of land. The ownership of houses is not very important—it is normal for a man to have his own house— and to have a house or two built for his sons. But land is another matter, and that can be turned into tangerine groves and the income from that put into jeeps, cattle, or in the new touristic ventures.

People are reluctant to act as guarantors in banking transactions. Since they cannot refuse a relative or a friend when he comes to ask for this favour, they have to find ways of getting out of their promise as best they can. Often, as they come into the manager's room, they manage to hang behind the man who is applying for a loan and signal to the bank manager not to accept the guarantee, which puts the manager in a difficult position, or sometimes they come to see the manager before the appointed day and ask him not to accept him as guarantor when the time comes. The manager, for his part, has to refuse to become part of the game, which may be unpleasant for him in the long run if the man who comes with a request such as this is weathly or important.

The Bank has the right to put up for sale a piece of land the mortgage of which has not been paid up. But it rarely does so, since the price it can ask for it is unrealistic and often does not cover the mortgage. Also, people are reluctant to buy what they call "cursed land", they consider this unlucky. So the Bank warns, threatents and waits, and people eventually pay up by getting deeper into debt.

All the same, there is no doubt that the Bank is the most important institution in the town and that without it, all agricultural or sea-going activities would come to a standstill. The Bank in Bodrum has come to replace the family or the cooperatives as a source of credit. It is only when the cooperatives are able to play their part properly that the Bank's usefulness will diminish.

Table 7

Occupational Table of Bodrum

Trade	No.	People employed
Fishing	46 boats	150
Sponges	75 boats	350
Grocers	33 shops	40
Butchers	5 ,,	10
Bakers	7 ,,	12
Barbers	15 ,,	20
Potters	3 ,,	6
Tailors	24 ,,	30
Drapers	7 ,,	9
Quilt-makers	1 ,,	2
Drug-stores	1 ,,	2
Radio repairs	2 ,,	2
Household equipment	3 ,,	3
Building materials	2 ,,	5
Pastry-shops	2 ,,	3
Stationers	2 ,,	2
Shoe-makers	15 ,,	21
Photographers	4 ,,	4
Carpenters	16 ,,	40
Ironsmiths	6 ,,	15
Tinsmiths	2 ,,	2
Boat-builders	5 yards	24
		752[1]

---

[1] The remaining population is made up of civil servants, professionals which together number about a hundred families and people who earn an income through casual labour and the land. Most of the people listed above earn additional incomes from tangerines and other occupations. It is estimated that there are 50 men who work as load carriers and 200 as unskilled labourers.

CHAPTER FOUR

POLITICS

The background

There is one public holiday in Turkey which carries a special importance. That is Republic Day, on the 29th of October. It is observed with great pomp and ceremony in all the larger cities of the country with military parades and speeches by politicians. But in Bodrum the main feature and attraction of the 29th of October is the parade of the school-children. This year, for two or three days before the holiday, children assembled in the school yards and began to rehearse on the drums. There was no other musical instrument, and they were going to play the small drums during the parade. Some of the children had been selected to appear in local costumes and their mothers were busy sewing the trousers and blouses, the little jackets and veils. Old trunks were opened and searched for a bit of lace or embroidery. During this time, the programme went overboard. The din in each neighbourhood where there was a school was terrific, but the children enjoyed making this, for once, lawful noise.

On the morning of the 29th, they began to assemble in the school yards as early as 7 a.m., although the ceremonies were not due to start until 10 o'clock. Then, at about 9, they proceeded down to the square, the Republic Square, and took up their positions on three sides of it. The man in charge of operations was the Director of Education, Osman bey. The Bodrum jeeps, decorated with paper flowers and carrying a banner saying "We bring far places nearer", lined the fourth side. Then the local bus came along, loaded with children, and stood by.

In the town, all the shops except restaurants and cafés, were closed. The townspeople lined the four sides of the square, mostly standing, a few sitting on chairs borrowed from shops or cafés. The women had taken up a position on the terrace of the B School and were waiting for their children to pass. Because the square is not very large, the first and second grade children were not part of the parade, to the great indignation of the parents, and they watched wistfully as their elders were taking up their positions.

The town was decorated with flags, and some of the government offices had their doors ornamented with palms or laurel branches, there was even a small arch built of wood, laurel and palms and with a banner saying, "Atatürk founded the Republic we shall make it live."

There was no particular excitement in the air, but the sight of well-dressed, excited children made everyone feel good. "What is a *bayram* without children?" said people to one another.[1]

While the children were assembled by flustered teachers, the town's notables, the government employees, some shopkeepers, went to pay their respects to the *Kaymakam*, the District Officer, congratulating the representative of the State on the 45th anniversary of the Republic. They all wore jackets and ties, even if some took their ties off as they were coming downstairs again. In front of the heavily decorated Military Service Office, where there is a bust of Atatürk, wreaths were deposited. The Museum had contributed an amphora made of green leaves full of flowers, the Municipality its perennial wooden laurel wreath ("Here it is again" said the people laughingly, "they want to save money"). The two main parties had plaques with their symbols, the "White Horse" for the JP and the Seven Arrows for the PRP, and there were other wreaths from the schools, the Youth Club, the Hunter's Club, the Bank, the Women's Union and the main government offices.

After the official visiting was over, the *kaymakam*, the commander of the Military Service Office and the mayor went round the square congratulating the people, shaking a hand or two, and then sat down in the tribune of honour, in front of the B school, between the jeeps and the Youth Club boys. In the middle of the square, a small platform had been built and draped with the flag and now, after the national anthem, the *doyen* of Bodrum's schoolteachers went up and delivered himself of the Speech.

The speech was delivered in the usual oratorical style and reminded the people of the occasion, of how Atatürk, our Father, had delivered the Turks from the "sultans who sucked our blood" and from the "foreign enemies who had sworn to destroy us". Then he asked for and received the homage of one minute's silence in memory of the glorious victims of the War of Independence. After that, representatives from all the schools came up one by one onto

---

[1] *Bayram* is a feast day or holiday.

the platform and recited poems in the same declamatory style. We were all getting gloomier and gloomier, there were murmurs around me, among the Bodrum "intelligentia" about "is this the way to be happy about the occasion, why can't these schoolteachers cook up something more lively, why can't we have recorded music and have the children sing rather than recite this awful poetry", etc., etc. But at last it came to an end and the parade began.

The schoolchildren went by, playing their drums, the older ones smiling in response to parents' and relatives' greeting and compliments, the smaller ones turning their head away in self-important detachment. The mothers had tears in their eyes, the fathers proudly pointed out their offspring. Each school had its little groups of children in local costume and one school scored a huge success by having a group go by representing the crafts: little boys and girls dressed as pastry cooks, shoemakers, blacksmiths, bakers, nomad shepherds and camel drivers. The Youth Club went by, egged on by shouts and warnings about the afternoon football match where they were going to play against a team from Izmir, but the real joy came with the Hunter's Club, who went by with their rifles and their inseparable dogs; they halted in front of the tribune and shot in the air, and the people cheered and the dogs rushed madly around, looking for the prey. Then the jeeps went by, honking away, followed by the brand-new Bodrum bus. So everyone went away with a smile and feeling quite exhilarated. This, they felt, was a proper way to celebrate.

The High School was carrying a banner saying "We are the guardians of the Motherland and the Republic", and the Red Cresent Society had a banner saying "To become a member is a debt paid to the Motherland". The Boy Scouts marched past, in their only activity of the year, carrying a banner saying "To live is to act".

In the evening, two of the Castle towers were illuminated, and the Bodrum musicians sheltered on the pier under the awning of the customs house, played Bodrum songs. But there was little dancing and watching because it was raining hard. The town settled down to two days' holiday, the Town Club filled with properly dressed government employees, the cafés filled with the usual crowd, the streets filled with children and the women went about their everyday tasks, as usual.

The speeches and the poems heard on that day sound familiar

by now. Most of the poems are printed in the reading books of the primary schools and the speech is invariably the same, whoever delivers it. The reason why no one really listens is because everyone knows them by heart, ever since they were at school and were first acquainted with the history of the Republic and its founder, and the successful repulsion by the patriotic forces of the invading enemies. The Republic, now forty-five years old, is not questioned even if it is critized for its godless premises by the religious right wing. The motherland, *anavatan*, is fiercely loved. Mothers, with tears in their eyes for their sons departing to the army, will say to you: "of course he must pay his debt to the motherland, but it is hard for mothers", and over the Cyprus crisis men said to me again and again, in the cafés and eslewhere, that while they were prepared to give every drop of their blood to defend the motherland, they did not see why they should do so because Makarios stirs up trouble in some island or because of politicians who only know how to create problems where there were none before!

The patriotic feelings of the Aegean are now a matter of legend. The Aegean *efes*, mountain braves who did, or did not behave like Robin Hoods from time immemorial in this region, put their bands at the disposal of the patriotic forces in the first days of the War of Independence, when the Greek armies disembarked on Turkish soil. Unruly and fiercely independent they did not do so for the love of the Sultan or the Empire, or even for the love of the young commander that Atatürk was in those days. The motherland was attacked and they were going to put their pistols and daggers at her disposal. The text-books contain some of these stories and recall these days, with the emphasis on the duty to love and defend the motherland and the Republic.

When it comes to the state and politics, however, the textbooks are silent. They enumerate the attributes and duties of the National Assembly and the Administration but there are no comments on either. Family discussions and, later, experience will enlighten the citizen on these subjects.

And so they do. With the result that the older members of the community see their grandchildren complain about things that they were complaining about in their youth. The imperial tradition of authoritarianism and centralisation, served by one of the classic examples of bureaucracy—the Ottoman bureaucracy—still permeates political and administrative life. Authoritarianism made itself felt through the gendarmes in the era of the one-party system, and centralisation and bureaucracy continue to sap initiative and slow down the normal business of life. For Turks in general and the people of Bodrum in particular, those who are to blame for this state of affairs are "the government" and the politicians.

Politics, say the Bodrum people, are a necessary evil, "necessary" here taking the meaning of perennial. There is always a government, it is in the order of things. It does not matter if the party is run by the party of your choice, the evil is there. The Prime Minister is a man who is admired and approved without reserve by his followers, and denigrated and made fun of by the people of the opposition. Apart from him, politicians are corrupt, selfish, indifferent to the plight of the citizens, and only interested in holding on to their seat or ministerial armchair, the source of unlimited power and wealth.

In the same way, bureaucrats are not thought of as public servants, but as little men invested with the authority of an all-powerful government. They themselves, needless to say, do not think of themselves as public servants, but as the executors of the law, interpreted as narrowly as possible so as to avoid dangerous consequences. Fear of initiative and responsibility discourage initiative and responsibility in the public. The people curse the bureaucrats for incompetent fools and the bureaucrats curse the public for being ignorant and bothersome.

These attitudes are transmitted from father to son, and people hate to have to go to a government office and transact business. They will look for people in positions of importance to help and so hope to cut the red tape to a minimum; they will employ lawyers who know more about the regulations than the civil servants themselves. If the worst comes to the worst, they will go themselves and knock on the doors of power. If, however, they happen to be poor and unknown, they will give up, sometimes abandoning their rights for the sake of a quiet life. In all cases, the attitude is one of guarded watchfulness, of keeping oneself to oneself, a public version of the defensive attitude which is observed in private life. The government is the most dangerous "stranger" of all, and must be treated accordingly.

The Bodrum people do not differ from the rest of their countrymen in this respect. They have seen the Castle used both by the Empire and the Republican régime as a prison for political rebels. Always far removed from the centres of decision, they see that the situation has not changed. Their business is transacted through Muğla, 144 kilometres away, and some of it has to be transacted through regional offices, like Izmir, 290 km. away, or Aydin, 210 km. away. During the one-party régime, which lasted twenty seven years, the same mayor ruled the town and screened them effectively from whatever political personality happened to visit the town. And in the multi-party era, which has lasted now since 1950, they are not visited by important men because the party in power is sure of their votes and they do not have to be courted. Furthermore, ever since the proclamation of the Republic, Bodrum has only had one deputy in Parliament. He soon became a Minister and national problems took up all his time. Earlier on, during the one-party régime, there had been another deputy who "did nothing".

The party in power from 1923 to 1950 was the People's Republican Party, founded by Atatürk. Based on a Rousseauean philosophy, the "one people, one party" theory behind the PRP carried with it the hope of knitting together the hinterland and the capital of the newly formed Turkish state, and the desire to mobilize all the progressive forces of the nation in order to turn the country into a modern political and economic unit. The fact that deep into the countryside religious, Ottoman and other dissident forces were still alive led the PRP to resort to force, from the early Revolutionary Courts to the later methods of the authoritarian state. Among these were, for instance, the collection of taxes from the people by gendarmerie and the pressure put on all notables to come out openly in favour of the PRP, by joining in rallies and wearing the party insignia. However, the PRP did not have economic favours with which to reward its supporters, in smaller parts of the country such as Bodrum. Besides, the étatist policy did not leave room for the development of entrepreneurship which was to be witnessed in the last two decades. The country was poor and what small fortunes had been made, here and there, were stored in the form of gold coins in earthenware jars, buried in far-off fields. The banks which were established for the development of industry functioned in the largest centres and the Agricultural Bank, which ante-dated the Republic, had no credits to distribute to farmers and peasants.

Bodrum, small and remote, of near-impossible access, was ruled by a mayor who seemed to have been a kind of Jekyll and Hyde character. Endowed with the authority of the PRP, of which he was, for a time, the local party chairman, and with a domineering personality, he was a good mayor but an insufferable tyrant. Imbued with the superiority complex of the educated—he was a doctor—and the Istanbul man, he badgered and humiliated the local population, believing that the strong medicine he gave them was good for them. Given his personality and the political atmosphere of the time, it is not difficult to imagine the different results: the well-to-do and respectable families joined the PRP and wore its insignia, women included, with an enthusiasm which was not always feigned. But the poor acquired a horror for the new authoritarianism. The mayor represented a party which found itself obliged to extract taxes from peasants by force; coupled with the extreme poverty of the peasants at that time, this antagonized the countryside for good. What was more serious is that the new era had held hopes for the poor peasant and that the Republic had been presented to him as the ideal régime, where the state is the arbiter and wielder of justice. In reality, the PRP did not succeed. In Bodrum, the man of means continued to hold the destitute in his power ,apparently supported by the party in power. The government was blamed and the general situation did nothing to alter people's conceptions about the state, politics and the administration. The very considerable achievements of the PRP in the rest of the country, and especially in the largest centres, did not affect the people of Bodrum, who did not even hear about them, communications being practically non-existent in the pre-war era.

The Second World War brought more poverty and more hardships. Bodrum witnessed the battles in the Aegean and heard echoes of the larger conflict and appreciated the fact that the PRP kept the country out of the war. Nevertheless, the poor felt the pinch and ceased to use certain commodities such as sugar and tea because the prices rocketed. They also had to declare the amount of flour they milled—a staple—to the authorities. By the end of the war, Turkey was ready for a change and in 1950 new elections heralded the advent of the multi-party system. The victor of the election was the Democratic Party, which had come about as a splinter group of the PRP. The victory was total and unquestioned. For the reasons mentioned above, Bodrum, like the rest of Turkey, produced a DP majority.

The new party brought with it a new brand of populism. The

personnel of the DP was closer to the grass-roots, more intimately connected with the countryside, and therefore, better known to the local electors. While the Bodrum people as a whole voted DP, the well-to-do families voted PRP, but did not henceforward advertise their political affiliation. As the years went by, they found it embarrassing to turn about and, while they ceased to be active PRP supporters, they did not become DP followers. In some cases, a member of a family would become a DP man, occasionally as the result of other causes, such as a clash of interests or a family quarrel. Such cases, however, were rare and the majority of the families remained PRP. In the meantime, Bodrum acquired a deputy of its own, and a DP mayor, the first a local, the second a Cretan.

The structures for economic development had been laid down by the PRP and the DP built on these. The Agricultural Bank began to lend money for every kind of agricultural activity, from bee-keeping to sponge-diving. Marshall and later technical assistance aid was used for a large programme of road-building. Tangerine growing became a growing proposition and all the people who had a field or who, hitherto planted with fig trees or rented out for pasture, began to grow tangerines. These could now be sent out of Bodrum to the big cities, Istanbul and Ankara. Fish could be sent on the day it was caught and catch the early housewife in Izmir the following morning. The fact that the bank credits were not controlled and and that the money borrowed for agricultural purposes went to other things did not worry the people. Their standard of living was getting higher. In 1957, the Bodrum deputy had the harbour built. Prices were rising too, but only economists in the universities and the PRP, now the opposition, worried about the indiscriminate spending by the government and the inflation which, in the late fifties, increased at a gallop.

When the little man began to breathe, and the peasant did not have to pay his taxes regularly any longer, the business community of Bodrum cashed in on the new régime. Trading-houses now had greater quantities of produce to collect and sell, and could also bring in consumer goods. The state of the market was such that they did not have to court the good will of the DP. They were discreetly PRP and conducted their business. It is only when the DP began to get into trouble politically and financially that some of them joined the DP as a result of pressure. The major, being a Cretan, took with him into the DP camp, a number of the better-off

Cretan families.[1] The important thing to note is this: had the Bodrum traders been modern-minded capitalists, they would have wanted to embark on financial and industrial ventures which would auto-motically have led them to join the DP officially, But they were not. They were making money in the good old-fashioned way—as they still do—on a small scale compared to national standards, but on a scale sufficient for them. Conservative by nature, peasant by origin they lacked—and still do— the entrepreneur mentality which needs the party in power to get on. To give an example: they never required credit from the Bank in an amount for which approval from the head office in Ankara had to be received. They were their own banks and not a few of them lent money to people in return for interest. With the development of tourism, they invested modest sums in small guest-houses and did not think of banding together to build a large modern hotel, for which credits would have had to be obtained in Ankara. As a result, the big strength of the DP lies with the little men, with craftsmen and shop-keepers, peasants and fishermen.

The 1960 coup d'état—always referred to as The Revolution— which toppled the DP government to re-establish a proper working of the constitution and the democratic machinery, did not change the loyalty of the DP followers. A new constitution received a bare majority vote, the DP electorate returning a "no" vote, but was put into operation nevertheless by the military government. The PRP had to form a coalition government with the heir to the DP, the Justice Party, the JP. During the 1965 elections, the JP scored the majority of votes again. The Bodrum mayor elected in 1950 was re-elected in 1963. It does not seem to matter that prices have gone up, that the government has put taxes on practically everything, that the town is practically not run at all. The JP supporters vote out of gratitude to the DP and out of antagonism towards the PRP and rather than have a good mayor, who might be a PRP man or an independent, they still vote for the JP candidate, the present mayor. The interests of the party are always considered to be above those of the town.

The following table shows the election results in 1965. It will be seen that many of the contending parties did not receive any votes at all, but that unexpectedly, the Labour Party, which was entering

---

[1] Today only five of the "rich" families, all Cretan, are partisans of the JP, successor to the DP.

elections for the first time since the establishment of the Republic, received a few. The townspeople estimate that these came from PRP voters who had lost hope in the PRP. Most of the Labour Party votes came from the poor quarter of Eskiçeşme and the poorer parts of the Cretan quarter, which are inhabited by locals.

Table 8
Election results of 1965 by quarter

Quarter	No. of voters	Votes cast	PRP	JP	CKMP	MP	TIP	YTP[1]
Kumbahçe	809	531	90	415	5	—	12	—
Umurca	380	286	19	254	1	—	2	—
Yokuşbaşi	237	153	13	135	—	—	—	—
Çarşi	385	221	40	161	—	—	4	—
Türkkuyusu	354	251	57	177	1	—	4	—
Tepecik	325	182	56	118	4	—	2	—
Eşkiceşme	521	323	46	257	5	—	10	—
Yeniköy	413	291	11	260	4	—	2	—
Totals	3424	2238	332	1677	20	—	36	—

173 votes were invalidated. The low—for Turkey—participation, 65%, is due to the fact that the elections took place early in October when many voters were away. Some of the sponge-divers came back from near-by seas especially to vote, however. Even so, the results were overwhelmingly in favour of the JP and confirmed earlier results. The JP hopes to better their 1965 75% while the PRP hopes to better their 14%.

It will be noticed that the poorest quarters, Yeniköy, almost totally inhabited by causal labourers and sponge-divers, Umurca and Yokuşbaşi, were the places with the lowest PRP vote.

Two instances, which took place in Bodrum, one in 1963 in connection with the election of the mayor and the other in 1967, in connection with the building of a new road between Bodrum and Milas, go to illustrate this attitude. In spite of public frustration and anger, in both cases, the party in power survived, even though it did not emerge unscathed.

Bodrum has had the same mayor for 18 years and it looks as though this will continue indefinitely. Ever since the two-party system was established in the country, municipal elections have

[1] CKMP = Republican Peasants' National Party; MP = National Party; TIP = Turkish Labour Party; YTP = New Turkey Party

become extremely politicized and the municipal elections are an exact replica of the national ones. The mayor here is a political personality, a prominent local trader who has always been a politician first and a mayor last. He is not popular in the town, but the party machinery sees to it that he is regularly elected every four years and that a majority of JP partisans are elected to the municipal council. He is one of the three men who run the local party organization behind the scenes. He holds no official position in the organization, because his office of mayor forbids it. But few decisions are made, and no man is elected to an office of importance without the mayor and his two friends taking the lead in the operation.

While the people accept the political personality of the mayor as something natural and right in its way, they do not approve of him as a mayor. They all feel that they are unable to change the course of events and that they will have to put up with him as long as he is willing to put up with them. However, on one occasion, a few years ago, he was nearly defeated by a new candidate, a man who did not belong to any party but who is a member of one of the wealthiest and most prominent if not the most prominent family in town, a family which, although allied to some JP members, has been traditionally PRP.

THE INDEPENDENT CANDIDATE

It happened before the elections of 1963. The mayor had put up his candidature again, but even in his own party there were some who thought it was time for a change. They could not, however, allow a man from the opposition to win and no JP man could put up a rival candidature. So people began to look around for a good man, who would be politically uncommitted and the choice fell on H, who was approached by people from both parties and promised support. He was very doubtful about the outcome and did not want to be beaten; he could not imagine that partisan feeling would disappear so completely as to allow an independent to win and he put his name down on the eve of the last day, because people had repeatedly promised their support. He began to go around the neighbourhoods, making speeches. The first speech was made in the Cretan quarter and that very day the trouble started; the PRP candidate came to listen and applauded H. noisily, thereby damning him in the eyes of the audience which was largely JP.

This was pure party spite, since the man had no chance to get a majority of the votes anyway. The PRP candidate did not appear at any of the subsequent meetings but the damage had been done. The mayor, for his part, delineated the strategy for the JP: H was to be accused of being a PRP man in disguise, committed to PRP policies in secret; no other attack was to be made against him. When H. stressed the importance of tourism and said that the municipality ought to work for the development of tourism, and lead the touristic effort by building restaurants and cinemas, he was reported as saying that the restaurants and cafés would be closed by him when he became mayor and that the municipality would operate these. As a result of this whispering campaign, he lost heavily to the JP candidate. About 7% of the JP votes went to him, and the JP people who had promised him their support, such as the local party chairman, turned round and made their peace with the party old guard. The day the results were announced the mayor and the local party chairman went round the market arm in arm, to show that there had been no breach in the party.

The results were as follows: the JP candidate for mayor received 1591 votes, the independent candidate 576. Out of a total of 3320 votes, 2167 cast their votes for the mayoral candidate, 2002 for the Council.

The partisan feeling is intense. At the time when a PRP mayor had the main shore street in the Cretan quarter cemented—it had been a stretch of pebbly beach until then—the inhabitants sent their children out at night to destroy the work that had been done in the day-time. Their feelings for the PRP was such that they were willing to forego one of the most vital facilities, a proper street to walk on.

The PRP was disliked, and still is. It lost three quarters of the votes to the opposition party, in 1950, when multi-party politics became established. But there were serious reasons for it. The party had emerged, after twenty years of unchallenged rule and a war, riddled with vested interests, old men, antiquated structures, and a tremendous economic problem on its hands. A road tax was collected, for roads which were never built; revenue and agricultural taxes were levied from peasants who had barely survived the economic crisis created first by the depression and then by the Second World War. And these taxes were often extracted with the help of gendarmes; it is said that once the gendarmes waited for the people to go to the mosque, and then tackled them when they were coming out after prayers. The PRP mayor—the man who had paved the streets of Bodrum and brought it electricitly—behaved like some movie dictator, forcing people to stand to attention when he went by, having people beaten up, and such arbitrary and offensive behaviour did nothing to make the people fonder of the party. Once the PRP was ousted, in a great surge of revolt and relief nothing was going to help it come back again. Today the PRP vote is a bare 14% of the total vote in Bodrum and the influence of its leaders is entirely negligible. The one or two rich businessmen who belong to the party here put their business interests first, the party second, and this suits their JP business friends.

This was pointed out many times during discussions in the cafés and elswhere. The municipal police had never been known to administer a fine and the town's by-laws are broken with impunity. The shop-keepers, the traders, the craftsmen have their personal arrangements, are careful not to hurt each other's interests, and this is one of the reasons why there are no serious rifts within the party itself. While the leaders behind the scene are "gentlemen", they see to it that simpler men are elected to the party offices, "men without ties", who are closer to the people and more accessible. For the latter, the honour thus gained more than compensates for the lack of real power and everyone is more or less happy with the state of affairs. After all, as long as you keep the PRP out...

THE ROAD CRISIS

The second event and its consequences illustrate the position of the Bodrum JP in relation to the national JP; it was brought to a head following the visit of the Minister of Communications, who has since left his post, but not for reasons that have anything to do with Bodrum.

For years now, Bodrum has been promised a new road to Milas by the government. An asphalt road, free from the multitude of dangerous curves, and which would cut down the uncomfortable two-hour journey to Milas. Visiting politicians, the party chairman of Muğla, a minister or two all came and went and made the same promise, but the road is still long and hazardous, trucks with the tangerine crop overturn and lives are lost; and a trip to and from Milas takes practically all day.

When it was announced that the Minister of Communications was on a tour of the region and had been persuaded to appear in Bodrum, people became very excited and promised each other that they would once more make an effort to get the road.

On the day, early in the afternoon, the prominent members of the party, a few notables, Mehmed the photographer who never missed anything of interest, the *kaymakam* and I piled up in a couple of jeeps and went to wait for the Minister at the last hill-top before Bodrum, where there is a café. It was very cold and the café having no glass panes, had its wooden shutters closed. A stove was going, and we all sat in the dark with our overcoats on, drinking tea. The Bodrum party chairman said that he was going to put the question straight to the Minister and see what answer he would get, and the *kaymakam* agreed that it was high time that these things were settled, and not only the road, but the water and electricity problems too. Time passed, we drank more and more tea and everyone became more and more truculent about what they were going to tell the Minister. Suddenly, there was a distant car noise and we all rushed out of the café, just in time to stop two large official black cars. Rather in a manner reminiscent of the old American gangster films, men in formal black spilled out of the vehicles, the Minister, the Regional Director of Highways, the Muğla prefect, a couple of plainclothes policemen and the usual half-dozen minions who accompany important politicians on such occasions. Everyone lined up and the Minister shook hands all round, the Muğla prefect and the Muğla party chairman greeted a few of our party by name, but there was a marked coolness on the part of the Bodrum gentlemen, an important sign for people who have been doggedly partisan for so many years and who swing the prefecture vote in favour of the ruling party at each election.

After the presentation ceremonies were over, we all piled back into the cars and rolled down towards Bodrum, to alight in front of the Municipality. Around the large table in the middle, all the important people sat down, including the *kaymakam;* including the people who were waiting outside came in and sat or stood at a good distance, around the walls, quite cool and rather serious, with a "now let's hear what you have to say" expression on their faces. Along by the walls, in one or two groups, mildly unkind joking was going on, about the road, the water, the road, the road. I was reminded of the wedding ceremonies which are performed in this same room, with people disposed in similar fashion.

The minister began his speech rather unfortunately: he had had "no intention of coming to Bodrum, but had been persuaded to do so, now he was glad, etc, etc... Tourism was very important... look at Spain, private enterprise must help the government...the road is not so bad, but needs repair..." and so forth. He then stopped and looked around him with a pleased expression on his face. At that moment, the Bodrum party chairman, H.O., began to speak and was quite blunt. The road had been promised and nothing had been done. The Tourism Association chairman rose and quoted figures showing that more and more tourists were indeed coming, but that they said that they would not drive on such a bad road again. The *kaymakam* then chimed in, and in the stilted official language of the capital and the bureaucracy, pointed out that there was not enough water and electricity in the town. All this time, there was no sound from the people and no one smiled. The Bodrum men had spoken bluntly and without the usual flowery compliments. When the Minister rose to go, very few people came forward to shake his hand and when he went to visit the Castle, no one went with him except his suite. The Bodrum men, clustered in a café, cursed the government and again decided that the kind of promise made by this Minister was very much like the other promises made before. The road would not be built this year. To make matters worse, the Regional Director of Highways, who preferred to sit in the café rather than visit the Castle, announced loudly that Bodrum was tenth on the priority list for road-building, and that furthermore there was only money in the budget for the first seven.

That evening, in almost every café, revolt was brewing. The Minister was called names and it was decided to "do something". In the Town Club, the notables gathered in small groups and whispered to each other, papers were circulated, people were asked for and fetched, even the telephone was resorted to.

The next morning, the townspeople were startled to find that the revolt had started. People greeted each other in the street with guffaws, slapped each other on the back, even the women were discussing the situation with satisfaction: the party council had decided to tender its resignation.

This was tremendous news, it had never happened before, in

Bodrum or elsewhere, and the people were all behind this decision, praising and congratulating the council members. There was no danger that a rival group would put up for election, since no one would dare endanger their future political career by going against such clearly expressed popular sentiment. The really important members of the party, the two or three men who held no official position in the party council, maintained absolute silence in public, but it was known that they had telephoned the party branch in Muğla, to keep them informed.

The revolt spread like wild-fire. By evening, the eight *muhtars* had resigned, a petition circulated by the doctor asking for safe water, the road and electricity, had been signed by 2000 people, and the next day, solidarity telegrams began to come in from the surrounding villages, while the Women's Union circulated another petition. Telegrams explaining the resignation were sent to party headquarters in Ankara and to the Prime Minister, and the local newspaper correspondent, young H wrote a despatch entitled "Bodrum Party Council Resigns", which was consigned to outer darkness by the national press.

The municipal council waited for a day or two, the mayor did not resign, but many members of his council did, thus upsetting the balance of power in the council. While the JP had been in the majority, the outgoing members were now replaced by their PRP substitutes, and the strength of both parties was just about equal in the Municipality.

As the days passed, enthusiasm did not wane. The party chairman from Muğla came and left town after twenty minutes, the local party people refusing to talk about anything until the road was started. The townspeople congratulated themselves on their behaviour and discussions went on in the cafés in the evenings as to what politicians are for and the significance of voting. Even the writer was appealed to for consultation on political behaviour in such cases. Everyone really enjoyed the occasion, and people waited for results. Old grievances were aired and defiant words and threats were uttered against the municipal set-up. The party council held firm and promised the townspeople that they would not withdraw their resignation until graders from the Highways Department could be seen at work, on the road.

A few days later there was a *coup de theatre*. The Prime Minister himself had been on the phone to the local JP headquarters and had given his personal word of honour that the road would be started immediately. Under these conditions, he asked the party council to take back their resignations, which they did. So did the *muhtars*, but the members of the municipal council did not, with the result that the mayor today has a council of 13 members, of which six are from the PRP.

The townspeople were impressed with the Prime Minister's interest. It was the first time in living memory that someone so exalted had taken any notice of them and the party council was not criticized for going back to work. The opposition and the more enlightened citizens, however, kept their counsel and told each other that the road was not going to be built, not this year and not next.

Unfortunately, they have been proven right. It has been a full year now, and there are no signs that Bodrum will ever get its road. When questioned about it, the party chairman reassures people and tells them that studies are being made and that soon the road will be contracted for, but no one really believes him. On top of this, a very hard winter brought damage to the town and the municipality was unable to cope with the problems, seaweed, mud, and pebbles invaded the streets, and breakdowns in water and electricity supplies occurred. Bodrum is ready for a change, but the local party structure and organization are not of a nature to produce an alternative candidate for mayor as yet.[1]

The JP organization, like all organizations in Bodrum, is weak and, therefore, at the mercy of a few men. A few years ago, a law was passed, obliging mayors to resign the party's chairmanship. When this happened, the present mayor resigned and a new chairman was elected. He is a solicitor by profession and has no other source of income. The party council includes eight people, all of them graduates of the primary school. Two of them have tangerine groves and one owns property in town. There are two tailors, two sponge-boat owners and traders, one boat craftsman, one tinsmith, the owner and operator of the local cinema and the owner of the larger of the two pastry-shops. Only one of the members is Cretan, a tailor. Since 1963 and until the road crisis of 1967, the members of the party council were also the elected members of the municipal council.

---

[1] There were no municipal elections until 1968 when a new mayor, also from the JP, was elcted, the solicitor who became party chairman. The road was finally improved and surfaced in 1969 but not rebuilt.

No one believes that the party chairman wields any real power and, over the years, a carefully managed rift has occurred within the council. This rift came out in the open at the time that the independent candidate was encouraged to try his luck, but the mayor and the powers-that-be soon mended the rift and the joint efforts of the two groups defeated the independent candidate, as was seen earlier.

Party life

Today the rift has widened. The mismanagement of the town has begun to adversely affect the interests of those who earn money from tourism and the road incident is taken seriously by the tangerine growers and trades. This winter, two fifteen-ton trucks overturned. One driver was killed and the crops were lost. Foreign firms which were sending their forty-ton trucks to Bodrum have stopped doing so after seeing the state of the Bodrum-Milas road. The tangerine growers are very upset, since this kind of on-the-spot sale is ideal, given the very delicate nature of the fruit and the fact that a great deal of money goes to middlemen and a lot of time is lost before their money comes to them. Also there is a certain amount of lassitude. Younger men have come to the age when they can become mayors themselves and have a council which "will do something".

The partisans of the rebel group on the council blame the mayor and the council for not being able to make the Bodrum voice heard, either in Muğla—which has produced a Minister—or in Ankara. Muğla is accused of looking after its own interest and the development of the rival resort towns is quoted as an example. The fact that the people of Bodrum are faithful party followers, that they do not give up their votes to the PRP when incensed in often quoted: "Those higher-ups know that they can count on us and that we fight clean", they say, and feel even more angry when they are reminded that it is Bodrum which swings the whole prefecture vote in the "right" direction.

In view of the mounting opposition, the mayor and a few of the old guard have looked for ways of diverting discontent and getting public endorsement for the JP, the coming elections being, of course, an important consideration. When the Prime Minister started a tour of the west, they used their influence in Muğla to get the Prime Minister to come to Bodrum. After many days of feverish excitement and rumours, the great day finally arrived. It was the first time in history that a Prime Minister was coming to Bodrum.

The party council, old grievances forgotten, began to organize the reception. A committee was set up under the chairmanship of the *kaymakam*, including the Tourism Association. Money was raised to buy a sacrificial calf and Ramazan's restaurant was reserved for lunch. It was decided that since the Prime Minister was accompanied by his wife, some of the ladies of the town should be present too, such as P, Chairman of the Women's Union, and the wives of the *kaymakam*, the judge and the mayor. Bouquets of flowers were hastily made, and the menu for lunch pondered over at length. The visitors were to eat Bodrum dishes, the famous fishsoup and the stuffed pastry, and were going to be entertained during lunch by the singers and dancers of the folklore group.

However, this enthusiasm did not make the people forget that they still did not have their road, and the young blades of the town began to prepare banners to hold up during the ceremony. They felt that the Prime Minister, due to travel on the bad road, would see the point. However, before night fell, the news came that the Prime Minister would arrive by boat and consternation was widespread. Angry at this change, some of the members of the reception committee who were meeting in the Artemis Restaurant for a business dinner abundantly washed down with *raki*, thought up a slogan which was to appear next day, to the delight of the populace. The banner said: "Take in hand the road that your eyes would not contemplate", this last sentence meaning, "that you did not have the courage to travel". It was the most successful banner of all.

On the morning of the visit, people began to congregate on the pier, which was filled to overflowing; boats were hired and people went to spot the Prime Minister's boat and escort it. A small platform was erected in front of the Customs Department and the calf, bedecked with red and white ribbons and flowers, was paraded through the market streets and brought to rest on the pier to await the moment of the sacrifice. Towards lunch-time, women began to flock down with children in their arms or holding on to their skirts, enveloped in their black and white *futas*, curious to see the wife of their beloved Prime Minister.

It was getting hotter and hotter. The boat was nowhere in sight. Children began to cry. Ramazan worried about his pastry, the folklore group waited in a shop, boys and girls not knowing what to say to each other and not daring to say it. The calf, quietly chewing the cud, was once again paraded around the pier. Finally the boat and the escort rounded the breakwater, moored alongside the quay, and the Prime Minister and his wife stepped ashore.

Suddenly there was a great surge, shouting and greeting, and the Prime Minister was propelled onto the platform, surrounded by the people holding banners saying "The Road, the Road, the Road"; "Why did you come by SEA?", and "The votes of Bodrum are repaid by services elsewhere". There was a large banner prepared by the religious people which boldly demanded "religious instruction in the lycées". The Prime Minister looked at the banners and then said they could be taken down as he has seen them. He then made a speech about the beauty of Bodrum and the region.

The visit of the Prime Minister gratified the people of Bodrum and confirmed, as was expected, loyalty to the JP. This kind of visit, where a top-level political personality can be seen, heard and touched, with no intervening cordon of police or gendarmerie, is no mean event and a confirmation that a new style of politician has arrived. The fact that the Prime Minister and his wife are both the children of peasants plays also a big role in the identification of the people with the JP. But the fact remains: politicians do not keep their word. The Prime Minister and ministers are not blamed as a rule; "they have too much on their hands", people say, "it is our local party which should do something about the situation."

The party meets rarely. Some of the "old hands" meet with the mayor a few times a week in the tumble-down café below the party office. It is impossible to have members pay a regular contribution. When I asked for the membership, no one knew for sure and the party chairman confessed that the "books" were not up to date. This was another way of saying that as long as the vote was delivered, little else mattered. He himself is well aware of the weakness of his position but is caught between two alternatives: either join the rebels and almost certainly lose his chairmanship, or side with the mayor and the old guard and be deprived of real power and be the butt of all criticism. This last is the more serious of the two because it endangers his future political career.

Today, on the eve of the elections, the JP exhibits no qualms. They know they will win, here as well as in the other parts of the country. But on the level of local politics, they are in a quandary.

The rebels want the municipality and the government to deliver the goods, while the old guard is still only concerned with votes.

In the meantime, the PRP goes about its daily business. The hopes of ever getting into power again in Bodrum are slim, although the party chairman thinks that they may score a rise in votes that may go up to 10%. He is a youngish man, the owner of a prosperous stationery shop and a man of property. He is the only PRP *muhtar* of Bodrum, owing to two facts: one that he hails from the well-to-do conservative quarter of Tepecik and two, that the JP candidate for *muhtar* was patently no good. As a *muhtar* he has to register births and deaths and counter-sign various papers brought to him by the inhabitants. As the local party chairman, he intercedes for them whenever he can, in official or municipal business. He is energetic and ambitious and follows the family tradition of PRP support and business acumen. The other stationer is a staunch JP man. "In spite of this", says the PRP chairman, "80% of the people come to me". He would like to become mayor and "take the town in hand", but he does not want to be beaten in the election and "lose face".

He, likewise, was unable to quote membership figures and was as frank about it as the PRP chairman. "Forget about things like registration and subscriptions in Bodrum", he said, "you must be content with the votes". According to him, many people are going to vote PRP this time, as they are disgusted with the way the town is run. But people accuse him of dreaming; "he is saying all this because he is PRP" they say and add, "you cannot blame him, after all, for praising his own party". It is obvious that the relationship of the local PRP with Muğla and Ankara is no different from that of the JP. At election time, a few visitors come to the town and a few posters are sent. The PRP feels almost as isolated from the centre of PRP policy as the JP man. The very small PRP vote of Bodrum is not designed to stir interest in the Ankara PRP. The PRP chairman had no difficulty in making propaganda for the independent candidate, all the more so since the latter belongs to an old PRP family. Like all the people of Bodrum, he thinks of local politics in terms of national politics. The fact that as of next year all elections will take place simultaneously will confirm this attitude.

The PRP chairman is helped by a board of ten, out of which only one finished intermediate secondary school, as he did. These men all have tangerine groves and property in town and belong to a higher social category than the members of the JP board. Among them are one yard-goods merchant, three tangerine traders, one large tangerine producer, one truck owner and a clerk. Again there is only one Cretan in the group, a boat-owner and sponge trader. Most of the men, except for the Cretan, live in the two most prosperous districts of the town.

The PRP chairman confessed that it took him some time to understand what the new national policy was, at the beginning. A few months before the national elections of 1965, the leader of the party announced the new direction of PRP policy: left-of-centre. This expression, considering the ingrained attitude of the Turks towards anything which is even faintly remiscent of communism, frightened away a good many voters. In Bodrum, the usual vote went down. It is only in the last year, after a split in the party and the election of a new Secretary-General that the expression was explained: it means a welfare state based on a mixed economy, partly private and partly state-owned. "Now", says the PRP local chairman, "I am more able to explain this left-of-centre thing to voters". This again explains to some extent the neglect into which small party organizations are left by the national and prefecture centres.

POLITICS AND THE PRESS

The party papers could, to some extent, enlighten the board and party members. Oddly enough organs of the ruling parties are not the most popular papers in Bodrum. The main PRP organ, "ULUS", sells a mere six copies a day, and the JP organ "ADALET" also only eight. It is the national independent popular paper "HÜRRI-YET" which leads all others by a wide margin, selling 250 copies a day in Bodrum.

The parties do not send brochures or policy booklets. Administrative circulars compose the bulk of the party correspondence. At election times, posters are distributed. This is another factor which leads the people of Bodrum to confuse national and local issues, and to think of politics in local terms. In a small survey conducted to find out which were the most popular articles in the newspapers, news about the country, not political news, and criminal stories came a good first, as they would, given the nature of "HÜRRIYET". The more or less intelligent comments on politics are to be found in the national liberal "CUMHURIYET" and the mildly opposition, or rather neutral papers, "AKŞAM" and "MILLIYET". The following table gives an idea of the circulation of these papers in Bodrum:

Table 9

No. of copies sold daily

"Hurriyet"	(independent)	250
"Cumhuriyet"	(independent)	90
"Milliyet"	(neutral)	80
"Akşam"	(slightly opposition)	10
"Ulus"	(PRP)	6
"Adalet"	(JP)	8
"Son Havadis"	(JP)	40
"Yeni Asir"	(Izmir-JP)	40
"Ekspres"	(Izmir)	40

The cynicism which pervades the talk about politics extends to newspapers as well. No paper is believed on a serious issue. This attitude was confirmed when Bodrum, becoming known as a touristic centre, it was visited by some newspapermen who wrote articles about it. Their exaggerations and sometimes inventions confirmed the people of Bodrum in their attitude. Newspapermen are considered no better than politicians and bureaucrats.

Under these conditions, wider national issues and foreign policy issues are scarcely taken notice of. The dislike of Americans has by now trickled down to small places, and Bodrum is no exception. Europe is not really known. England is known because of the part she played in the Aegean is the Second World War, and Germany because of the past and because a few men have gone there to earn a living. The French and the Scandinavians are popular as tourists. The only issue which stirred emotions was Cyprus. In this question, the PRP blamed the JP for mishandling the crisis, and the JP retorted by saying that they had inherited the mess from the PRP. When things got really bad, in the autumn of 1967, people were alarmed at the prospect of a war and all politicians were roundly cursed, with little discrimination.

Only once did it happen that a few men considered the time had come to enlighten the community about wider national issues. The occasion was the establishment of the first and last Bodrum newspaper, the BODRUM POST. The paper was founded in 1952 and lived for a few months. It was a weekly and was owned by

Teoman's two uncles, members of one of the most respected families in the town. Teoman himself, with two other young men, wrote the paper and dealt with all its business side. Four hundred copies were printed in Milas, but only two hundred or two hundred and fifty sold in Bodrum, while a few copies were subscribed to by Bodrum people living in Istanbul and Izmir.

In its first issue, the paper announced its policy: it was going to be politically independent and act as a watchdog of the government and the administration. The country had just emerged from the authoritarianism of the one-party era and all over the country freedom of the press was an exciting issue. However, the Democratic Party, flushed with its first sweeping victory, did not like the paper's declaration of independence and from the first the paper came under heavy attacks from the town's political leaders, among whom were friends and relations of Teoman's own family and the paper's owners.

The paper's third issue took in hand the problem of religious reaction, which had also spread all though the country owing to the—at first permissive—attitude of the new political leadership. This issue, which disclosed the fact that religious literature of the worst kind was being smuggled into Bodrum by itinerant merchants from the centre and east of Anatolia, was a big success. For the first time, all four hundred copies were sold, to the indignation of the powers that be and the then *imam* [1] of the Old Mosque. The uproar was such, and the correspondence which ensued between the paper and the *imam* was so exciting that even some Istanbul papers reprinted passages of the controversy. One of the editors, who had PRP sympathies, was threatened with physical violence and the gouging out of his one good eye. The Democratic Party then started a regional paper which began to systematically answer the BODRUM POST, getting its information from its followers in the town. The paper in the meanwhile sold well, because the townspeople were interested and curious about the outcome.

Very soon, however, the political independence of the paper was automatically interpreted as partisanship of the PRP and Teoman's uncles considered that his work on the paper took him away from his work in their office. Also, they did not particularly like the fact that their Democratic Party friends and business associates conti-

---

[1] *imam*: incumbent priest of a mosque with the status of a government official.

nuously put pressure on them. Teoman left the paper, which was taken over by the one-eyed PRP sympathiser and soon became a PRP organ. This sealed its doom. Thirty-eight months after its founding, the BODRUM POST died a natural death.

So, politics remains an intermittent activity, confined to the corralling and delivering of votes at election time. The agricultural labourer or unqualified worker vote with the landowners and the merchants. The people who have least reason to be antagonistic to the PRP, the Cretans, are the most vocal JP partisans, helped by their women who are even more violent in their political preferences than the men. Neither the JP partisans nor those of the PRP have come to the point where politics are used as a means of getting things done, on the local or national level, although the road crisis has been a tiny step in the right direction. Since 1950, when a choice was finally given the people, the people have contented themselves with using the opportunity. It must be expected that, as the years go by, they will not only exercice the privilege of choice, but see to it that the people they choose work for them. It is a realization which will come to the whole country and to Bodrum at the same time.

In the meantime, the people of Bodrum do not let politics interfere too much with their day-to day life. There are no quarrels splitting families or groups, based on political differences. The differences which exist antedate the two-party régime in Bodrum. In buying and selling daily commodities, party differences are not a factor which influence the customer, as was seen in the case of the PRP stationer. Well-to-do merchants and tangerine producers, sponge-boat owners and fishermen, pension and restaurant owners do not let politics interfere with their business. When the Tangerine Cooperative, the Sponge Cooperative or the Tourism Association meet, the members talk business and not politics.

In the light of all these circumstances, the people of Bodrum have made their choice, for better or for worse. They have chosen the JP for the reasons explained above and show no tendency to change. They are quite prepared to blame the parties in power and their own party leaders, but are not prepared to organize themselves better in order to achieve results. They want a minimum of red tape, but put up forever with a large amount of it. They want to be consulted ,but not bothered all the time. They want help from the government, and expect the government to think about them as a matter of course. When all that they want is not forthcoming, they grumble and criticize and either put up with it, or do without. After all, things are better than what they were, and what do you expect of politics, anyway?

CHAPTER FIVE

RELIGION

The Müftü and Nedime Molla

The entire population of Bodrum is Moslem or, as the *Müftü* [1] puts it, "holiday Moslems", that is Moslems who do not live by the rules and who remember their religion only on important feast days. Indeed, compared to other parts of the country, people in Bodrum are much less conservative and observant in their religious practices. Although there has been a kind of religious revival in the country as a whole during the last decade or so—as a result of the establishment of the multi-party system—older people in the town consider that religious conservatism is on the wane. By this it is usually meant that attendance at the mosque and all other external forms of religious behaviour have diminished; only five or six years ago, the shops did not sell alcoholic drinks and no one smoked in public during the month of *Ramazan*. The young as well as the old fasted, and women wore long sleeves and stockings even in the summer, with their *futa* wrapped closely around theirs heads and shoulders. The *imams* were consulted quite often about matters of everyday life and their recommendations were followed.

When the Republic was proclaimed a secular state in 1928, the religious *Sheriat* courts which rendered judgments in all civil affairs, were closed and replaced by secular tribunals dispensing secular justice. The important arbitration functions of the *Sheriat* in matters of marriage and divorce, property and contracts were abolished and people realized that only the state institutions could confer legality on their actions. However, with the legal functions ended, the moral power of the *Sheriat* had no longer institutional channels through which to operate. In their private life people did not act any longer as a community of Moslems but as individuals, making their own rules or following custom. On the other hand, the one-party state in the first two decades of the Republic frowned on religious practice, without forbidding it. With the advent of the multiparty state, some parties—and especially the first opposition

---

[1] Government official with a religious training, in charge of the regulation of religious life in a district.

partyadopted a more sympathetic attitude towards religious practices and the religious training schools began to receive more students, usually poor boys from the country who found this way of
getting an education and a guaranteed livelihood attractive. However, the religious establishment which had been steadily deteriorat-
ing, along with the other Ottoman institutions throughout the 19th
century, never recovered its vigour and distinction. Poorly trained
immas and *müftüs*, with an education roughly equivalent to the
intermediate secondary level, took in charge the moral and religious
life of a population which was for the most part poor and semi-
literate. It is true that they did not have at their dispostal punitive
legal instuments and that thousands of young people were being
turned away from an Islam-oriented life towards a western world-
view through the new education system, but the activities of *imams*
continued and found some sort of an echo among the communities
living away from the large urban centres. For increasing numbers,
secular education was the way to a better life and even conservative
parents are eager to send their children to schools with a programme
in which religion has a minor part.

Bodrum is no exception to the general situation and the fact
that it belongs to one of the most prosperous regions of Turkey
encourages the tendency away from what has largely become religious obscurantism. Religious life in Bodrum is at best a matter of observing Ramazan as well as possible, at worst, a tissue of stories
and superstititions; in between it does not impinge on daily life,
except briefly and on very important occasions, such as birth or
death.

There are four mosques in Bodrum; one in the market, one on
the harbour, one in Tepecik and one in Yeniköy. Not one of them
was built in the last thirty years, when hundreds of mosques were
being built elsewhere. Out of these four, two were built in the eighteenth century and two in the twentieth. Each mosque has an *imam;*
all the *imams* are supervised by the Bodrum *müftü* on matters regard-
ing their professional activities, while all this personal is supervised
by the *kaymakam*, as are all other civil servants. The *müftü* and the
imams are appointed by the Directorate for Religious Affairs in
Ankara. Although the *müftü* is not required to preach, the Bodrum
müftü delivers sermons quite often at the Friday noon prayer, the
most important prayer meeting of the week, which he elaborates
in his office near the old Mosque in the harbour, a simply furnished

room which looks like any other minor civil servant's room anywhere in the country. He has no telephone and agrees that he does
not need one, although he is responsible for all the villages in the
district as well as Bodrum. The caretaker of the mosque runs his
errands. He has no typewriter and agrees that he does not need one
very much, asking people in the market for the use of their typewriter on the rare occasions when he has to write to the Directorate.
Like other government offices in Bodrum, his office communicates
with Ankara through the prefecture in Muğla.

The Bodrum *müftü* is the son of a landless peasant, and did not
go to school after he finished primary school. He received his call,
he says, while he was doing his military service, and as soon as he
was discharged he went to the village *imam* and learnt to read the
Koran and the rudiments of arabic grammar. In 1960 he entered,
as an external candidate, the examination for *müftüs* conducted by
the Directorate, passed and was appointed to Bodrum.

The Directorate sends a few books, he buys some himself from
dealers who import them illegally from Egypt. When someone comes
with a question, he looks it up in the relevant book. When I asked
him about interpretation he said, as I knew he would, "the door of
interpretation" was closed in the tenth century. The *müftü* was very
proud of the new building which is to house the new religious school
this year. It has seven rooms, which means that they will be able
to take in girls, a kitchen, a bathroom and three toilets, for it is
intended to keep the village children in town while they are receiving instruction. He was impatient to start, but had to wait for
the Directorate to give authorization.

This made the *müftü* start complaining about the general situation
in Bodrum; he did not dare start the courses right away, as is done
elsewhere, because the Bodrum miscreants might inform against him
in Ankara. The young people are not interested, the old are dying
off, the rich, whether local or Cretan, equally unwilling to undo
their purse-strings for the propagation of religion: "We had to mix
our own cement, and do our own painting and carpentry in the new
school. The town did not contribute as much as 5000 liras; no rich
person gave more than 50 liras, while one man gave 500 and one
as much as 3000, although neither is rich. The villagers are more
pious and generous. The people of Bodrum are immoral and the
men drink too much".

The *müftü* is not provincial-minded. The recent Arab-Israeli war gave him the opportunity to preach a sermon. The reason why the Arabs lost is because they did not "abide by Moslem principles", which demand that "one returns victorious from the wars, and in that case one becomes a *ghazi*, or dies defending one's faith and becomes a *şehit*. They did not fight to the end, and lost". And he further added, "they were not united, as brothers in religion ought to be".

The *müftü* seemed pleased about the newly formed "League against Communism" but did not seem unduly put out when it was pointed out to him that the Arabs had allied themselves to the Russians: "Oh well, when you fall into the sea, you cling to a snake", he said.

The *imam*, who was sitting next to him, was a little old man who had been born in Crete and spoke Turkish with a strong accent. He recalled the day when a Turkish community in a Cretan village had decided to burn themselves to death in the Mosque if the Greeks attacked them again. But it appeared that just at this time, Atatürk had liberated Anatolia from the invading Greek armies, and thus the small community was saved. While the little *imam* agreed that it was wondrous indeed how Atatürk saved even a small remote community of Turks, the *müftü* kept silent. After all, he is a *shafi* and his sect forbids him to touch a woman—except his own— and he had no reason to admire Atatürk!

The *imam* of the New Mosque is a young man and his wife uses lipstick, a fact which is appreciated by the women of Bodrum as "truly modern".

It is men who go to the mosque and talk to the *imam* and *müftü*. Women can go to the mosque provided that they sit in the upstairs gallery built for them. If they sat downstairs, they would "induce the men into temptation", and the value of the prayers would be lost. But the women of Bodrum do not go to the mosque except at *Ramazan* for special prayers. They say the five daily prayers in their homes and, when they feel they need guidance or inspiration, they go to see Nedime Molla.

Nedime Molla—*molla* means a person who possesses religious knowledge and can read the holy books—is seventy, very handsome and lives with her husband, her married daughter and her three grandchildren in a large house at the back of the Cretan quarter. He husband was a shoemaker and now looks after their tangerine grove and the vegetable and fruit garden around the house. Although they are people of substantial means, the house is simply furnished, with hand-woven rugs, a couple of carpets and *sedirs*[1] running the length of the walls. Nedime Molla's daughter cooks the family meals on an old-fashioned wood stove and they all eat sitting on the floor, out of communal dishes.

Nedime Molla went to the old primary school and learnt to read and write the arabic script, since there was no other in those days. She was a bright pupil and her teacher wanted her to go on with her schooling but there were no schools in the vicinity she could attend and, she adds: "In those days no one dreamed of sending a girl to Izmir or Muğla like they do today". But her grand-daughter, a bright pupil at the secondary school, will go and Medime Nolla approves and is glad that she can do what she her-self and her daughter could not. She went on reading after she left school and her father bought books for her, the Koran, religious text written by old priests and stories about saints and holy men. She also wrote letters for people in the neighbourhood. As time went by, women began to ask her to come and say prayers in the houses, or they would come and ask about a religious rule, such as whether it is permissible to bathe when fasting, or whether cursing a neigh-bour is sinful. Little by little her house became a meeting place for the Friday prayers, and although she never preaches formal sermons, she explains and exhorts with quotations from the holy books.

Nedime Molla's talks are about good neighbourliness, help to one's relatives, charity towards the poor and occasionally the duties of a good wife. She reads the punishments meted out to the sinful and they are so horrible that the women can be heard wailing "Oh God, preserve us" every now and then. Nedime Molla really believes the stories she reads, even if sometimes they are very far from the intentions expressed in the Koran itself. Many of the pray-ers are sung in Turkish and are of obvious Bektaşi origin. But the women do not know this and, even if Nedime Molla grudgingly admits this, she is prompt to add that although the founder of the sect was indeed a holy man, his sect later on became heretical.[2]

---

[1] *sedir*: wooden settee covered with a thin cotton mattress.

[2] This reputation was the work of the Ottoman religious establishment who disliked the sect for its liberalism, its mysticism and the equality it granted women. There were also political factors involved. For a long time, about three centuries, this region was suffused with Bektaşi-ism as a result of the conversion of the Menteşe *beys* to the sect.

The Cretan women remember that there were many Bektaşi shrines in Crete, which is not surprising since the island was occupied by the Janissaries who were all converts to the sect. Indeed, there is the tomb of a holy Bektaşi "father" in Bodrum, on the west side of the inner harbour.

FESTIVALS AND MEETINGS

Religious fervour increases at the approach of the two great Moslem festivals, *Ramazan* and *Kurban*. While men usually attend the mosque in their fives and tens, attendance reaches a hundred or so during *Ramazan*, whipped up by the frequent sermons and the arrival in town of itinerant preachers.

Ramazan, the last month in the Hegira calendar, the "sultan of eleven months", is the most important religious festival of the year. During this month people have to fast from sunrise to sunset. Since the date of *Ramazan* follows the movement of the moon, *Ramazan* goes back eleven days each year. When the fast occurs in the winter, it is bearable and pleasant, the days are short and people do not feel thirsty. But when it occurs in the summer with the sun rising at four-thirty and setting at eight-thirty, then the people find the fast painful and tiring.

Ramazan is a month of penance and rejoicing. It is a time when people should examine their actions of the past year, repent and rejoice in the hope of forgiveness, and adopt good resolutions. One of the five "musts" of Islam, it is observed by people who normally do not pay any attention to the other four. "We live like infidels all the year", said Ismet's sister to me, "I should at least fast at *Ramazan*", and this fairly well sums up most people's attitude to the fast. Consequently, even younger women fast and younger men are seen attending the mosque and refrain from smoking in public. A few years ago, not a glass of alcohol could be bought and no one smoked during *Ramazan*. But nowadays this is changing. The cinema which stopped its after-lunch matinées last year did not do so this year, and even the bearded and devout owner of the best grillshop did not close this year. Everybody is surprised, since he has been doing so for years and he is such a good Moslem that he foregoes the interest on his money in the bank.

Ramazan, being also a month of rejoicing, the evening meal, *iftar*, is usually better than during the rest of the year. The rich buy and eat all sorts of delicacies brought down from Izmir, such as smoked and marinated fish, sausage and all kinds of sweetmeats. As for the poor, they eat meat then, which they will not eat again for a whole year. They also feel it is their religious duty to have a dessert now and again and feel that they are not celebrating *Ramazan* properly if they cannot buy cakes or *helva*.

This year, on the eve of *Ramazan*, the two brothers who own the Gulf Restaurant, stopped serving drinks and went to the mosque at lunch-time, leaving the place to the apprentices and the cook. But they did not cover the windows with newspaper as they did last year. Next door, Kasa, the owner of a drinking and eating place beloved of tourists did not stop serving drinks, but he hung heavy curtains in the front of his shop and lowered the lights. In the evening, at aperitif time, the town's intellectuals and miscreants, such as the museum staff and a few civil servants, complain that it is worse drinking under those conditions and that they almost feel guilty. But Kasa keeps his counsel, afraid to antagonize the town's *softas*, or religious cranks. "Wait until *Ramazan* occurs in the tourist season", said a shopkeeper to me, "and then we shall see whether their religion will weigh more than their desire for money". But until then, it is felt by most that those who do not sell drinks at this time must be given the benefit of the doubt!

As *Ramazan* progresses, some people get tired. "Djange" is getting bored by the not very interesting sermons preached by the *müftü* or by a young itinerant preacher who appeared one day from nowhere. Ahmet Kaptan, who is a gay old dog, misses the evenings when he can drink, sing and dance. Many watch their waistlines and wonder whether *Ramazan* helped or not. "The devil take it" said Ismet's sister to me, "Every part of me got thinner except this behind of mine", and she gave it a big smack.

As the fast proceeds, wills get weaker. Children, who do not have to fast until they are seven, give up, attendance at the mosque dwindles, to rise again towards the end. People's complexions get sallower from either over or under-eating. Tempers get short, civil servants in their offices become impatient with the public, mistakes are made by the bank clerks, discipline gets laxer in the schools. In the meantime, new clothes for the women and children are made at home, the tailors do their briskest trade of the year and the grocers bring in bags of sweet sin preparation for the *Şeker Bayram*, the Sweets Festival, which brings *Ramazan* to a close.

While the men have been going to the mosque two or three times a day and have rarely stayed for the sermons, the women have continued to pay and fast. While all the women fast, it is only the older women who observe *Ramazan* by constant prayer. The younger ones just pray the required five times a day. The older women say additional ritual prayers and are directed in their devotions by Nedime Molla. She tells them what prayers to say on each day and what other devotions have to be performed. Thus, Fridays are especially well-attended at her house.

As early as eight o'clock in the morning women begin to come in, leaving their shoes at the door, treading softly on the floor covered with hand-woven rugs. The first comers sit cross-legged on the *sedir* all around the room, while Nedime Molla sits by the window, with her books propped up on a roughly made stand in front of her. On that day, the women have gone to the market earlier and those who have not, come later, in their ones and twos, and settle themselves on the floor, in circles, facing Nedime Molla. When an old woman especially known for her religious knowledge comes in, like Aunt Zubeyde or Deli Ibrahim Kaptan's old mother, room is made for them in the centre and Nedime Molla turns her head and greets them formally, calling them also "*molla*". All the women drape their heads with their white prayer scarves and the older women show the henna stains on their palms, a ritual which takes place in the fasting days preceding *Ramazan*.

Nedime Molla reads from the Koran and from other holy books and explains obscure points to the audience. Only the women called *molla* know how to read the arabic script, most of the others are illiterate and rely on Nedime Molla to tell them what to do on these special occasions. Now and again a prayer is said or chanted in chorus, asking God for his mercy and welcoming the month of *Ramazan*.

As time goes by, the air gets stuffier, some women get drowsy, others begin to gossip in the back, usually about the prices of things that morning at the market, and some others become exalted. The singing is more in tune. At around twelve, women with small children go back home where they will say the midday prayer, while other stay until *iftar*, the evening meal, when the men will be coming home. As the women leave, they put a small piece of money on the table among the books. Nedime Molla protests but the women leave the money anyway. Usually the sum is a quarter

of a lira. At sunset, when the difference between "a white thread
and a black" cannot be detected, a shot is fired from the cannon
on the Castle, which saw more martial service in the eighteenth
century. The cannon is fired by Dalavera Mehmet, the odd-job
man of the Cretan quarter, at sunrise as well. At sunrise, also Ali
Dayi, the piper, goes around the town in the rain and wind playing
his drum. The drum awakens the people who have not been awaken-
ed by the cannon shot and hospitable houses invite Ali Dayi in and
give him some soup and a piece of *helva*. After the fifteenth day, he
stops in front of each house and recites traditional *Ramazan* verses.
Some people who do not fast give Ali Dayi a tip so that he does
not stop in front of their house, which is easy in most quarters, but
difficult in the Cretan quarter where the houses are small and closely
pressed together.

At last, the month-old fast comes to an end. After the early morning prayer, there is the *Bayram* prayer in the mosque to which
almost all the men in Bodrum go, even those who have not fasted
and who have not gone to prayers during the fast. They are all
freshly shaved and wearing clean and new clothes. After the sermon,
which exhorts people to continue praying after *Ramazan*, and the
collection, people come out and the elders stand along a wall
nearby and receive the wishes of the younger. Hands are kissed or
pressed and then everyone goes to the cafés to await the first lunch
in a month. The restaurants all serve drinks again and that night
all the inveterate old drunkards will drink twice as much as usual
"to celebrate the *Bayram*". Children will be going round neighbours'
houses dressed in colourful new clothes and with new shoes on,
kissing hands and receiving sweets or money in exchange. Ali Dayi
goes round one last time in full day-light, playing his drums and
followed by bands of children, and collects his pay for the month,
as he has been doing for the past fifty-two years. But no one knows
who will do the job when he is gone, for no one plays the drum
any more or knows the ancient verses.

The other important festival is the Feast of the Sacrifice, *Kurban
Bayram*, which commemorates God's mercy in sparing Abraham's
son. Every household, rich or poor, has been keeping a lamb,
which is pampered and spoiled by all for months until it becomes
a fat sheep. Barka Mehmet, who is the *muhtar* of Yeniköy and a
blacksmith, is raising three beautiful sheep two of which he hopes
to sell for at least 250 liras to people who have not bothered to

raise a sheep themselves. He is so afraid that envious eyes will bring harm to his animals that he has hung blue beads and amulets around their necks and they look for all the world like old dowagers.

Most heads of households sacrifice the sheep themselves on the morning of the Bayram. Teoman and his family cannot bear to see the spectacle and get their gardener to sacrifice a sheep at the back of the house and so do many other people who find the custom out of date and distasteful. But the average person does not think so. The sight is familiar and the poor people especially are thankful that they will receive platefuls of the meat by lunch-time. A smell of slaughter and roasted flesh pervades the streets after the sound of the wailing sheep has been stilled. Children run to and from one house to the next, bearing gifts of liver and brains, legs or heads wrapped in newspaper or lying in copper dishes.

On this day also, special prayers are said and the children get new clothes, this time for the coming season. And they go round again, getting their share of sweets and coins in exchange for kissing hands.

The festivals are also celebrated in the large cities, but in small places like Bodrum they retain their full flavour and a genuine air of festivity prevails. The people of Bodrum who usually go around slovenly dressed are resplendent at the *bayrams*. The expectation of better food and sweet things brightens the faces, and the excitement brought on by the special cooking and the hurry to get everything ready on time pervades every household. The women, of course, can really enjoy the *bayram* only in the afternoon. They are much too busy before that. But after lunch, with the children out of the way and their husbands back in the cafés, they have time to dress up and go visiting, beginning by the eldest relatives and ending with their contemporaries. It is only the very old who do not go visiting but wait for greetings at home.

The month of *Ramazan* is the third of three months which precede the birth of the Prophet. They are holy months and some very religious people fast for all three months. Others fast for three days each week, Tuesday, Wednesday and Thursday, and break their fast on Fridays. During these months it is customary to hold prayer meetings called *mevlut*, which means nativity. The *mevlut* prayer tells the story of the life of the Prophet. The prayer was written in the fifteenth century by a Bektaşi scholar and poet, in Turkish.

The local women hold the *mevlut* prayers in the early summer, in the months of June or July, rather than during the "three months".

They rarely invite Nedime Molla because there are two or three younger women in the local quarters who have gone to the religious instruction course and it is they who read the prayers, although they do not enjoy the prestige that Nedime Molla has. *Mevlut* meetings are as much a localized activity as visiting. Rarely do women go to a meeting held in the Cretan neighbourhood and the Cretan women participate more in the prayers and recitations. Nedime Molla—who is a local—and many local women agree that the Cretans are more knowledgeable than themselves in religious matters but less God-fearing.

Mevlut meetings are held by men and women, but in separate groups. Often the men have the meeting at the mosque, but the women always hold it at home. These *mevlut* are held either as a way of earning God's good will, or in order to thank Him for a favour. They are always held at a death or for the souls of dead relatives. A generation ago, say the older women, scarcely a Friday passed during the "three months" without a *mevlut* being held.

Money used to be collected from the women in the neighbourhood, an *imam* or Nedime Molla were invited and the meeting took place in the houses which were most suited to such large gatherings. Nowadays, there are fewer such meetings, although one is still held every ten days in the Cretan quarter during the three months preceding *Ramazan*. But the attendance is not as large as it was of old. The *mevlut* is attended by women of all ages.

When a woman decides to hold a meeting, she invites her friends and neighbours and sends word to Nedime Molla. The house is cleaned, the husband and small children are sent away. Before the meeting starts, incense, apple peel or cloves are burnt and the smell greets the guests as they come in. All the women leave their shoes at the door and go to the largest room in the house, where rugs and flat cushions have been prepared. The women sit cross-legged on the floor and put on their white prayer-scarves. The scarves of the younger women have embroidery and lace on them and have come out of the trousseau chest for the occasion. A place is prepared for Nedime Molla against the wall, and a small stool is placed in front of her cushion to hold her books.

The prayers are spoken or chanted, one after another, and forgiveness is asked for. Then the long story of the birth of the Prophet is read in a singing voice by one of the younger women, or by

one of Nedime Molla's pupils. At the point where it is related how
a white bird touched Emine Hatun, the Prophet's mother, on the
back to announce to her that birth was at hand, there is a great
movement and the white-veiled women lean towards each other
and touch each other's backs with their right hand to commemorate
the event. After the birth, the news was spread far and wide,
Moslems rejoiced and to illustrate this part of the story, the women
again lean towards each other and shake hands and then touch
their faces with their hands, saying "merhaba", which is the traditional form of welcome and salutation.

After this prayer, sweets and lemonade are passed round and
rose-water sprayed on the guests' hands: it is the smell of Paradise
and the women greet it by exclaiming "Grant it to us, oh God". The
meeting is usually brought to an end with more prayers and then
it is broken up and informal discussions take place. On one occasion
the talk had been about the *zekat*, the prescribed one-fortieth which
every good Moslem must give the poor and the discussion turned
around whether or not taxes are included in this; some of the richer
women, like Aunt Zübedye, argued that the government takes as
much as 45% of one's income and that this should be counted as
zekat, or at least part of it. Fureyya who was there did not agree
at all: "that is money given to the government, not to the poor".
The discussion went on for quite a while, each source of income
being examined in turn; income from cattle, or from fields or trade.
All though the discussion Nedime Molla kept silent. She is inclined
to believe that *zekat* is one thing and taxes another, but she would
not want to contradict Aunt Zübeyde, who is verry religious and
her constant partner in all religious meetings.

There are other religious ceremonies in Bodrum designed for
the special purpose of asking God for a favour. It is the women who
organize these, never the men. Only women and girls attend. One
of the most popular is called the "Night of the forty-five Sultans".

When a woman has a wish to make, she asks her relatives and
as many of her neighbours and friends as she can get hold of to come
one evening for the "Forty-five Sultans". The forty-five are all holy
figures, saints and princes who have attained oneness with God. It
is obviously, again, a Bektaşi ceremony, but the women do not know
this and they hold and attend this ceremony simply because they
believe that it is effective. Nedime Molla is the guest of honour on
all these nights, as well as Aunt Zübeyde, her sister-in-law Fatma

and Ibrahim Kaptan's mother. These women will assist Nedime Molla in reading the lengthy prayers.

One evening, Ibrahim Kaptan's wife, an alert housewife who runs a family pension in the summer, invited me to the ceremony. She wanted to ask God to help her daughters, who are away at college in Izmir, to pass their examinations. She had already had one sitting for one of the daughters and now it was the turn of the second. The two girls are very bright and have never failed an examination yet, but their mother still holds these ceremonies.

The older women were all sitting on the *sedir*, with Nedime Molla at the "head corner". They were murmuring the prayers, pushing chickpeas to one side of a small plate to keep count of the pages. The younger women or girls were sitting on chairs or on cushions on the floor. There was utter silence except for the murmur of voices and the sound of pages being turned. In the meantime, the mother was in the kitchen cooking the traditional *helva*, a mixture of semolina, butter and sugar. Tradition demands that the preparation of this sweet should begin and end with the prayers because the smell is pleasing to the forty-five holy men. After the prayers, the special invocation to each of the forty-five is read, each holy man being addressed by his name. At this time, three leaves are brought from the garden, a spoonful of the sweet is put on each and the leaves thrown on the roof, so that the birds "may carry the news to heaven". Then the sweet is dished out to the guests. As many people as possible should eat the of sweet, wishing the hostess good luck and asking God to grant the favour.

Teoman's sister, who lived for many years in Istanbul, invited us one evening to another ceremony called "Zachariah's Supper". No one had ever heard of this ceremony, and therefore many women were eager to be present. At this ceremony, anyone can make a wish and, if it is granted, then the recipient must hold another "Supper" come next November. In this case, Teoman's sister wished for a happy marriage for her daughter. Teoman's sister is a woman who is quite sophisticated, but she believes in these ceremonies all the same.

This time a long table was prepared in the dining-room of the rather modern flat, and on this table were arranged forty-one kinds of food, ranging from nuts to cooked dishes. Poor people usually trick the prophet Zachariah by counting all the ingredients in a dish as so many items. But this was not the case this time. Before we ate, the prayers were said and Teoman's sister took a candle and lit it, making her wish while Aunt Zübeyde read the special prayer. Then the women who wanted to make a wish each took a candle and lit it from the first, while Aunt Zübeyde tirelessly recited prayers for each. After a unanimous "May God accept this", all crowded around the table and a lot of joking went on as to whether people had actually eaten something from each dish. Some just bit on an onion, some ate half an olive, cheese was sprinkled with parsley and all kinds of subterfuges were resorted to in order to get through the forty-one kinds. For here the custom demands that everything should be eaten. What is left must be thrown into the sea or buried.

While the women are eating, stories of past favours granted by God are related and as the evening advances, it turns into an ordinary gathering. Aunt Zübeyde and Nedime Molla are usually the first to leave because they are so old and because their services are so much in demand.

Yet a third ceremony is often performed for wish-granting. It is connected with the wish-granting gift of a holy man who is buried on on a small hill overlooking the inner harbour. Although there is no historical evidence of his life and death, he is called Murat Baba, this appellation testifying that he was a Bektaşi. Beside him are buried the founder of the naval shipyard in the eighteenth century, Mustafa Paşa and his son, Cafer Paşa. The tomb is covered with a small white dome, indicating that this is a holy place. When a woman or a girl wishes for something, she promises to go and thank Murat Baba if the wish comes true. When it does, she takes a candle, or a piece of cloth, as a gift to the Baba, and asks her friends to come with her and light a candle too. On these occasions, prayers and the *mevlut* story are read.

These ceremonies are pleasant and, for the older women, an edifying way of spending an evening. However, they do require a certain amount of money. Although Nedime Molla never asks for a fee, she is usually given money and the food can be very expensive. The poorer and more ignorant families do not resort to these ceremonies, but to the casting of spells, which is a cheaper and quieter way of asking for something.

Casting spells

The casting of spells is an activity which lies in the twilight zone between religion and superstition. It has religious overtones while it is applied and becomes openly religious when the spell is exorcised. It is different from other forms of wishing, in that God is not appealed to; a spell addresses itself directly to the person whom it is intended to touch, for good or for evil. The vehicles of the spell are things, such as animals and plants, and products derived from these over which incantations and prayers are read. Incantations by themselves are ineffective.

The casting of spells is an activity almost entirely resorted to by women, no doubt partly because women are a repressed group in Moslem societies and as such have a restricted range of possibilities at their disposal. Usually deprived of open means of action and control and yet experiencing strong desires and feelings, the use of spells is, for them, a shortcut to the attainment of limited goals. In a culture which puts silence, discretion and obedience at a premium as far as women are concerned, spells are a way of expressing strong feelings and a means of direct action. Spells alone may be resorted to, but often more open and socially acceptable forms of wishing, such as those described above, are applied in conjunction with the spells. It is a matter of not neglecting anything that may help.

It may be that spells are of an extremely ancient origin, pre-Christian and pre-Islamic, and that these two religions have provided the wherewithal. The use of such ingredients as olive oil, honey, almonds, wax must have been known in very remote times and resorted to by women of all ages. These ingredients are met in spell casting all around the Mediterranean basin, with Islamic or Christian accretions according to the area. In Bodrum, spells show a mixture of pagan, Christian and Moslem elements, which is not surprising since the Aegean coast has always been the scene of inter-cultural contacts.

Spells are cast by old men and women who used to make a tidy income out of it. Nowadays, almost all of them have died off and it is extremely difficult to get to know one. People are reluctant to introduce you to someone who casts spells, first because this would be to admit that they have resorted to one, and secondly there is a law which punishes anyone "who obtains money by false pretences".

But talk of spells, cast for good or evil, is constant in Bodrum. Madness is often attributed to spells, unless it is attributed to a great sorrow. Any kind of psychological disorder is invariably attributed to a spell. Although no one believes that spells can do the work of the bank or the cooperatives, it is believed that they can do the work of the doctor, when medical care has failed. While men do not resort to spells, even the brightest among them are reluctant to deny their effectiveness. Such men as Foto Mehmed, "Baggypants" the grocer, and "Djange" who can talk most intelligently about politics and the world situation are among these. Baggypants will tell you how his mother-in-law was bewitched a few years ago. One day, out of the blue, she began to act strangely, throwing herself about, breaking things and talking nonsense. Her husband, one of the best old sailors in town and who was at the time a handsome, drinking and wenching man, had to hold her down to keep her from killing herself. One night he heard her talking in her sleep and she was saying that she had been treading on a piece of stone in the courtyard and that the stone was beneath a certain flowerpot. Intrigued, he went out and found the stone. The stone was smeared with grease and there were hairs in it. These proved to be boar grease and hairs, two ingredients widely used in casting spells and especially abhorrent to Moslems since pig is considered a most unclean animal and its flesh forbidden. Be that as it may, the minute the stone was found, the woman woke up and was again her normal self, a sensible and loving wife.

Another instance was told me by Aunt Zűbeyde. The occasion took place many years ago, when her husband engaged in smuggling and making fig alcohol in secret, at nights in their grove house, beyond the city limits. One day, this most sensible of husbands began to act strangely and nearly set the house on fire. Aunt Zűbeyde was young at the time and she became terrified. Her mother and an old neighbour were called in for consultation and it was felt that a spell must have been cast. They began to search the house and sure enough they found a handful of black earth beneath the mattress in the bedroom. This earth come from "either a tomb or a prison" and had been put there to ruin the marriage. In other spells, pieces of soap and wax are used, pierced with needles, amulets concealed in clothing containing poisonous seeds, pieces of paper on which curses are scribbled hung on trees or hidden in the house.

In each case the spell is exorcised by calling in an *imam* and having prayers read. Sometimes the bewitched person recites a religious formula. The Cretans on these occasions get sea-water "from forty waves" and pour it everywhere in the house, while the locals burn a mixture of sesame seeds, blue stone—sulphate of copper—and thyme, and fillthe house with the fragrant smoke.

Spells are not always cast with evil intentions. They are quite often resorted to in order to bring about something good, such as getting back an erring husband or wife or inducing, at a distance, some young man to ask for a certain girl in marriage. One day, coming into Baggypants' shop, he told me half in kest that that was the way he came to ask for his future wife. She was the most beautiful girl in Bodrum—and by the way, still is—and he was not too well off. Knowing the plight he was in, his mother apparently cast a spell on the girl, so that "her eyes would not see anyone else anymore". Baggypants' wife laughts at this, but she believes in spells since her own mother had a spell cast upon her twenty years ago. But she is glad that those who can cast spells are dying off "so that we can now begin to breathe in peace". Fureyya, the woman who does my laundry, is so afraid of spells that she only accepts food and drink from people she knows well. "I have enough to eat at home, thank God" she says," without taking the risk of having a spell cast". For in many instances people are bewitched by drinking or eating somthing which has been "read over"—like a tangerine over which the Korean is read backwards, or a glass of water over which incantations have been said.

In the case of "good" spells, those who cast them are better known and respected. If the thing that has been wished for occurs, then prayers of thanks are given and Nedime Molla does not mind saying them, but she will have nothing to do with the "bad" kind of spell, even to exorcise them. "I do not deal with such devil's work" she says with finality.

The attitude of young girls and boys towards spells is no different to that of their elders, although girls are a little more inclined to believe these stories than boys. Among the simpler and poorest people, the tendency to believe in and resort to spells is almost universal.

The local community does not seem to resort to casting spells as often as the Cretan. It is not that spells are not believed in but that they are feared and considered sinful. The locals think that one of the things which is wrong with the Cretans is their interest in spells. Indeed, I have never heard locals mention an instance when a spell was cast, while the Cretans talk about it constantly. However, both sides are quick to attribute spell-casting activities to someone they do not like or with whom they have quarrelled.

The festivals of *Ramazan* and *Kurban*, the wishing ceremonies and the *mevlut* meetings are special occasions. In everyday life religion is not a very important factor. It is true that about a hundred men between the ages of fifty and eighty go to the mosques regularly and that almost all older women pray at home for the required five times a day. For the rest of the population, the practice of religion is ignored and it is only at such important times and at births that religious ceremonies are performed. At weddings, the religious content of the celebrations is slight and, as we shall see, more cultural than religious in character, even if the people themselves are not aware of the difference. The introduction of religious instruction in the intermediate school was not greeted with enthusiasm either by parents or the *imams*. The first felt that this "could not hurt" and the *imams* believe that this is best given in the Koran school, although they were pleased to see the course introduced. When religious instruction was introduced lately into the lycée curricula—largely, it is believed, to please the more conservative element of the national electorate—the attitude was the same. Young people nowadays have other preoccupations, such as the raising and education of children and the most important matter of earning a living. Although the twin formulas "with the help of God" and "Thank God" are constantly heard in everyday life, the people of Bodrum rely on themselves, on the bank and sometimes on better-off relatives, in order to achieve their aims.

PART TWO

THE PEOPLE

CHAPTER SIX

INFANCY

Birth

Each year, between one hundred and thirty and one hundred and sixty babies are born in Bodrum, which is slightly lower than the national census figure of 2.7% for the district, a difference between town and villages which is to be expected. The figure has not changed in the past ten years. Except for five or six, they all survive, to be followed quite soon by a brother or sister; a third child may follow, but rarely more than that because the people of Bodrum do not want more than two or three children and see to it that they do not have more. When a girl marries, she is not given information about contraception since "she will have to have her first anyway" and then, "before she has turned round, she has her second"! It is after that that husband and wife begin to take precautions. The young woman learns from an older sister or sister-in-law what to do—unless her husband has begun to practice *coitus interruptus*—and starts to use some of the time-tested devices, such as a piece of sponge or cotton-wool dipped in lemon juice or oxygenated water, pieces of soap or quinine. Since the government has embarked on a fairly discreet birth-control campaign, women have heard about the pill and the spiral or "loop". The pill is as yet too expensive, costing T.L. 7.50 a month and women fear that it may bring on sterility. Only a few school-teachers use it, under medical supervision. But many women want to be fitted with the spiral. If they do not, it is because this can only be done at the hospital in Milas, and this is too far. Both the doctor and the two midwives think that if there were a clinic in Bodrum, women would cease to resort to the harmful products they now use.

Be that as it may, the expectation of a child is a happy time; the poor hope that "God will provide" and the rich are not worried. Husbands and in-laws usually want a boy for the first child, but the future mother and her family say that either a boy or a girl will be welcome, since it is "God who sends them both". This does not mean that a mother of sons will not be proud of the fact and look with some sympathy upon a mother of daughters. At the same time, at least one daughter is always wished for- especially by women because a daughter will become, in time, a helper, a confidante and can be relied upon to look after her parents when these get old. Boys have a reputation for being ungrateful after they marry and too ready to forsake their own family for that of their wife.

The birth of a child is still enveloped in ceremony in Bodrum. Many changes have occurred in the past few years and some of the most "primitive"—a term used by the midwife—habits have been discarded. The midwife recalls the days, not over six or seven years ago, when a woman in labour was made to lie near the door in order not to soil the rugs, or was violently tossed in a sheet so that "the child may turn". When the baby was born, it was salted like a fish and left like that all night, to cry in pain, because the process was supposed to "toughen its skin". Nowadays these habits have been discarded, but a pinch of salt is still thrown into the water with which the new-born baby is washed.

When the labour pains begin, the husband and the mother of the pregnant woman go out of the room, the mother because she is not supposed to witness the suffering of her child. Older women, the grand-mother-or the mother-in-law, stay behind and begin the pre-parations while the midwife is being fetched. About five years ago there was a Cretan midwife catering to the Cretan women, but then she left to go to Izmir and two midwives take care of the Bodrum women, one who is appointed by the government health services and one who works on her own. The midwife only calls in the doctor when there are complications. Otherwise she works alone, helped by the older women. This was not easy when she first came here seven years ago, and she often had to threaten the older women with government action when they insisted on employing a custom which she considered harmful to the mother or the child. Today she rarely encounters such difficulties in town, only when she attends a village woman who has married here.

Various customs are followed in order to hasten the birth of the child. The local women drop a cake of soap to the ground through their dress and the soap is then given to a widow. The Cretans fetch a woman whose delivery has been quick and this woman gives the woman in labour water to drink out of her hand, so that she too may have a quick delivery. Sometimes, although this custom is becoming rare now, a plant called "Mother Mary" by the Cretans and "Mother Fatma"—after the Prophet's daughter— is put in a dish of water. As the plant, which is the Rose of Jericho, expands the woman is told to look at it and that her womb is expanding and opening out in the same way. The Cretans also given the woman a drink of sweetened water flavoured with cloves and cinnamon, to relax the muscles. The midwife and doctor do not mind these practices because they believe they are psychologically helpful and reassuring.

When the baby is born, it is washed in the salted water, into which the Cretans usually throw some money, as a gift to the midwife. Rich families also give the midwife presents, in addition to the coins and her fee. The midwife cuts the baby's umbilical cord. intoning a religious formula, and gives the child its "navel name". This name is taken from the names of the Prophet's family, and it is by this name that the man or woman will be called on the day of Resurrection. The baby is then tightly swaddled so that "its limbs may grow straight" and laid beside its mother. All the Bodrum women swaddle their children although they know this is no longer done in the cities. They also know that this is not done "in Europe", and wonder how the tourists have straight limbs in spite of this. The younger women are ready to stop the practice, but can hardly do so since the older women in the family and especially mothers-in-law, do not allow them to. On very hot days in the summer, the swaddling leaves the arms free, when the baby is over two months old. This is when the family decides upon the every day name of the child. In the case of a first boy, it is always the paternal grandfather's name, in the case of a second, that of the maternal grandfather. The *imam* is called in, the call to prayer—"There is no god but God and Muhammed is his Prophet"—is said into the baby's right ear, and this ends the rites of birth. The name-giving ceremony is the same for all Moslems, Cretan as well as local.

After three prayer periods—eight or nine hours—the baby is ready for the first feeding. A prayer is said while the baby is given some sweetened water first. The mother has her breast cleaned with raw onion—onion is believed to be antiseptic— and then washed with soap and water. The local women give the child the sweetened water in an olive-leaf, the Cretans in a spoon. Sometimes a little boiled aniseed water is added "to clean out the baby's insides". From now on the child will be fed whenever it cries.

In the meantime, the room is prepared for visitors. Embroidered scarves and towels are hung on the walls, the young mother is dressed in her best nightgown and jacket, embroidered sheets are put on the bed, and the best quilt in the house. For the next forty days, the young mother is a *lohusa* (a woman after confinement), resting and receiving guests and congratulations. On the first day, the visitors and the relatives bring her gifts of milk, yoghourt or sweet biscuits. The child receives gifts of gold coins, lengths of material, and knitted garments. When the visitors leave on the succeeding days, they find that their plates have been filled with nuts and raisins, which they take back home. The mother and the baby are never left alone "so that the evil spirits don't come" and in case where she has to be, a broom is left by her bedside to keep watch. She must never turn her back on the child and, in order to keep the baby from catching jaundice, a yellow ribbon or a yellow scarf is tied to its swaddling. A blue bead or a small "hand of Fatma" is also tied to the swaddling to keep away the evil eye. The Cretan women do not leave a broom, but a small child, and they tie a red ribbon in the mother's hair "to keep the devil away". Actually these are all devices to make sure that the young mother is not left alone in case something happens to her or the child, although this is only realized by the more modern and intelligent women. The others truly believe that these customs do indeed keep evil at bay.

After seven days, prayers are read and "the bed is taken down" that is, the embroideries are put back in the chests and the young mother gets up. Visitors begin to come often because she is getting bored and many young women even go out "unofficially" to the next door neighbour. On the fortieth day, the young mother is no longer a *lohusa*, and is expected to resume her daily work and look after her family unaided. On the morning of that day a cauldron of water is heated and into it are thrown forty olive leaves or forty small stones gathered from the sea, or from the roof if the family lives inland. A short prayer is said over each stone and the child and mother are washed with this water. As the mother comes out of the tub, she is made to step on something made of iron, like a pair of tongs, so that she may become as "strong as iron", and the stones are put in a piece of cloth and placed under the baby's pillow so that he may "sleep like a stone". The mother and the baby dress up and go on their first visit. This is usually to the midwife, who has been calling frequently to keep an eye on the baby. The midwife seizes upon this opportunity to make her last recommendations to the mother. The midwife finds that men are readier to accept her advice and that they can often be heard admonishing their wives and telling them "to listen to the midwife". She also finds that Cretan women are more difficult in childbirth "because they are spoilt", she says.

Babies are breast-fed for quite a long time; a year and a half for girls and two years for boys are periods considered to be the "right" for children as decreed by God. But as from the fourth or fifth month, liquid foods are given, rice or wheat broths, vegetable and meat broths and, among the more prosperous, ready-made baby foods. Weaning must take place on a Saturday. On that day, if the mother has been wearing a milk-stone or a spindle-whorl on a string around her neck, the throws it back so that "the milk may go back". The local women then boil an egg, sweep it to the door and, taking the baby by the hand, make it pick up the egg, saying "from now on, my child, you are on your own". The Cretans do the same, except that they hide the egg behind a door and make the child look for it.

Toilet-training begins very early. From the second fortnight on, the baby is stripped of his swaddling a few times a day, and made to lie on the extended legs of his mother, who then coaxes him with appropriate noises. At three months, the child is taken out into the courtyard and held over a stone and told to relieve itself until it does. After a time the child comes to associate the noises with the action and begins to make the noises itself to warn the mother. This gradualy becomes a habit and eventually babies will toddle out or even crawl out on their own to the accustomed place in the courtyard, until they are old enough to go to the family toilet, which is always built away from the house in the yard. Nappies are not used, but a piece of cloth is put around the child in case there is an accident.

All the while, the baby has been sleeping in a swing cradle slung on ropes between two walls. Only when it is very cold is the baby put to sleep next to its mother. Little by little, the child becomes accustomed to sleeping on the floor and by the time it is three, it is put in the cradle only as a special treat. The cradle is rocked when the child cries and the mother does this easily, as the cradle ropes are fairly low and the cradle is placed near the fireplace where she prepares and cooks the family food. If the child cries too long, then it is thought that it has a pain. The swaddling is unravelled and a little sage-oil is rubbed on the stomach and the baby is picked up and petted or given the breast.

TRAINING

Children are not expected to behave "reasonably" until they are five or six. Until then they may be scolded, but are rarely beaten. They are threatened with "the doctor's needle", which they all know since they all get their shots regularly, or with being thrown into the sea for the fishes to eat. Threats such as this last one are not taken seriously, nor do they believe their mothers when they say "I shall beat you until you die". The doctor's needle, however, is a definite possibility. They are never deprived of food as a punishment, even when they are quite grown up. Also, when a child has been scolded it can always run out of the house to a neighbour's. The neighbour, not knowing the cause of the tears, will immediately pick up the child and fondle it, and if the mother arrives and explains what happened, the neighbour will apologize for the child and ask for forgiveness in the child's name. If there are no neighbours around, the grandmother or even a passer-by will do the same and young mothers complain "how can I train this child to become reasonable when everybody spoils him?" Although the extended family represented by the immediate neighbourhood prevents strict disciplining by parents, on the other hand it constitutes an area of security. Should a child fall and hurt itself a neighbour, passer-by or a shopkeeper is immediately at hand. Knowing this, mothers do not worry about their offspring out in the street, as long as they turn up for their meals. Small children are quite independent in the Cretan quarter and start roaming the neighbourhood as soon as they can walk. They have no gardens in which to play and the alleys are too narrow. In the local quarters the roads are wider, but the children play in the gardens and fields surrounding the houses. They go over stiles and barriers to other children's gardens and play there. Their mothers can then watch them from the window or the doorway.

Little children start talking when they are about one. By the time they are one and a half, they talk incessantly and begin to ask questions about everything. People attribute this precocity to the constant attention the child receives the whole time from everyone.

When a child asks too many questions, people tease it and say that he is "worse than the prosecutor". But an answer is always given. When a little boy cries, he is invariably told "he is a man" and that "men don't cry", while a little girl is told that "it is shameful to cry"; however, children are not left to cry, sooner or later they are picked up and consoled.

Quite early a sense of money and property is inculcated into the children. They are asked, albeit jokingly, to pay for a tangerine or a piece of bread, and when they touch something are told "Dont' touch, it is not yours". When a small child asks about an object in a house or shop, the grown-ups will say. "This is mine, do you have one in your house?", and the child will be led to boast that his parents, too, have one of these, whatever it may be. When I asked my neighbour why she always asked for money in exchange for what she gave the visiting children, she said, "We all do it, the child must know the value of things, how else will he learn that he will have to work when he grows up?".

Although they are trained to go to the toilet, no other rules of cleanliness are inculcated. While mothers always scold the children for getting themselves dirty, they are rarely given a handkerchief and their noses are often wiped on the corner of their blouse. Until they go to school, they do not wear pinafores, although their clothes are changed quite often. In the winter they wear plastic shoes and in the summer tongs. Before these existed, they use to go barefoot in the summer and wear rubber boots over woollen socks in the winter. Their clothes are mostly knitted when they are small and one can see that the garments of older children or grown-ups have been unravelled and knitted again, because most of the clothes are knitted of multicoloured wool. On the occasion of the two religious festivals of the year, *Ramazan* and *Kurban*, the children are dressed in something new, a pair of shoes or pants or a dress. These will be worn "for best" during the year and become everyday clothes the following year.

Until the ages of three or so, boys and girls play together with a ball, or with pieces of wood and stone. Toys, except some cheap plastic guns and dolls, are not sold. The wealthiest people buy toys for their children when they go to Izmir. So the very small children play at imitating their elders: boys go "fishing" and girls go "visiting". As they grow older, they begin to play in separate groups. The boys go fishing with real rods, the girls have rag dolls, they play hide and seek, hopscotch, and a variety of skittles which is played with a ball and heaped bricks. Boys take to the hills where they catch birds with glued sticks, or play at guerillas. Sometimes they ask the girls to act as Red Crescent nurses. But both the girls and the boys go swimming most of the year. In the local quarters, very few little girls go swimming, as the sea is relatively far from the house, while in the Cretan quarter they all do.

By the time the children are six, they are asked to do some work; they fetch bread from the baker's ,tea from the grocer's, water from the street fountain. They are often asked to mind a child. When they are seven, it is time to go to school and by this time, although the little boys and girls will play together during the breaks, they will not play any longer in the streets or gardens. The girls will be expected to come home right away, in preparation for their segregated life, while the boys will be shown more tolerance.

CIRCUMCISION

There is no special event which marks the end of infancy for girls, but for boys there is. This is circumcision, and its attendant ceremonies and festivities. Circumcision *(sünnet)* is the act by which a male child is formally made a member of the Moslem community, and this usually takes place when the boy has reached the age of seven or eight. If there is another boy in the family, the two children are circumcised on the same day in order to save money, as a circumcision festivity is quite expensive. The most modest celebration will cost something like T.L. 600 or 700 and can run into thousands in the case of rich families. At that age the boys are at school and most circumcision ceremonies take place in the summer or during the winter vacation of February. In Bodrum, the winter vacation is preferred, as it is for all activities which require an outlay of money.

Ömer, who is a sponge-diver and a friend, asked me to come to the circumcision of his two sons, Mehmed Ali and Alim. Alim is only three but since Mehmed Ali was going on for nine, the family decided to have the celebration and "do" Alim at the same time. Weeks beforehand, Mehmed Ali and Alim were congratulated by everyone and asked to tell about the preparations at home and everyone impressed upon the boys the fact that the day of circumcision was going to be an eventful one and they were going to receive lots of money. For in Bodrum it is not toys which are given to the boys on such occasions, but money, and the children spent hours telling their friends and me what they would do with their money. Mehmed Ali wanted to put it in the bank "for when I grow up", and Alim wanted to buy a small camel, because he wanted to become a cameldriver. Everyone laughed at the idea, and they kept telling Alim that the should strive to be something better and not live all his life "with the camels in his backyard".

The day for the great event was set on a Sunday and the day before, the boys were dressed in new clothes and the tinsel-embroidered cap worn on such occasions was put on their heads. "Don't let the lady tourists see you"people said, because these ladies have been known to buy the caps as cocktail hats, to the vast merriment of the locals. The boys also had a red sash tied across their chests and were given sweets to be distributed to their friends. Salim, a little friend and son of the baker who had been circumcised the previous winter, kept telling Alim about what would happen to him, "they will cut you" he kept repeating, and the little boy would look at him and say, "no, they will only put a bandage on". while Mehmed Ali would listen in silence, for he knew exactly what circumcision meant. The boys visited the neighbours' and their two uncles' houses, where food was being prepared for the guests, and received congratulations and kisses from everybody. Women had tears in their eyes at the thought of Alim being so small and of their own boys, who would have to face the ordeal sooner or later.

On Sunday morning, Ömer hired two jeeps in the market and asked Ali Dayi the Piper to come with his drum. Ali Dayi brought his "middle" son-in-law, the fiddler, and they got into the jeeps with all the little boys of the neighbourhood together with Mehmed Ali and his little brother. The little girls wanted to go too, but they were not allowed to do so; they went to Ömer's house to wait for their return. Ali Dayi played his drum and the son-in-law played his fiddle and the two jeeps went round the town, to come back about half an hour later. In the meantime, we were being entertained in Ömer's house, which has two rooms with a separate kitchen and a fireplace. The two grandmothers were sitting on the floor on either side of the fireplace, dishing out the food in bowls. There were chick-peas cooked with meat, beans in olive oil, stuffed pastry, pilav, and sweet pastry. The main room had been reserved for the men and the *imam*, and the room where Ömer and his wife slept had been decorated for the occasion. The double bed was covered with embroideries, carpets hung on the wall and embroidered towels and napkins had been pinned on the carpets, above the grandfather's portrait and that of a brother lost at sea. The boys were to be circumcised in this large room and put to rest in the large bed. On the wall were hung two stuffed animals made of rags for the occasion. Ömer's sister-in-law was there, and since she is a Cretan, she said to me: "We do not make all this fuss, the embroideries and the animals, and all this food; the music is enough", implying that there was a good deal of wasted money and energy involved.

Since there was no room for the women in the house, except the kitchen, a next-door neighbour had lent her house and all the women settled there on mats and cushions on the floor, in a circle around the fire. A loudspeaker had been fixed to a tree outside, so that the prayers could be heard in the neighbourhood. Soon the *imam* began to recite the *mevlut*, and food was brought in. A cloth was spread on the floor and a large round tray was placed in the middle, with the spoons and a few forks arranged in a cicrle. Bowl succeeded bowl, and we all dipped in while the prayer went on. No woman recited the prayer and the ritual hand and shoulder-touching which occur during the *mevlut* was very perfunctorily performed. "These locals", said the sister-in-law, "they do not know a thing about religion". It is true at that a Cretan *mevlut,* no food or drink is served and no one talks during the reading. After the *mevlut* was finished, the circumcision prayer was read and this was a signal that the boys were to be prepared.

Some of the women went next door and the boys were given a piece of Turkish Delight and told to go and "kiss hands". They did so and held out their embroidered caps and people dropped in money. I was told later that something like T.L. 300 was collected in this way. Then they were undressed and dressed again in blue flannel night gowns and taken into the room. The boys' mother stayed at the neighbours and began to cry, and so did the sister-in-law, thinking of her own boy and saying, "you need a heart of iron to look on while they are being cut up". The boys were held, each in turn, on a strong relative's knees, and Ali the barber, who is the town's circumciser and leech-applicator, did his job in two deft strokes. Little Alim cried for a long time, but Mehmed Ali was congratulated by everyone because he did not say a word or cry. The boys then were put to bed and everybody congratulated the father and the uncles of the children. In the meantime, some young girls ran to bring the "good news" to the mother and were given handkerchiefs in return.

After that, all the men left and the women and girls came into the room. It is customary to keep the children awake all day and all night and to entertain them with shows and games. But here there are no such shows; the boy's uncle bought his *darbooka*, a small earthenware drum, and began to fool around and play it, pretending to be a donkey or a camel. Alim then began to smile and to play with the coins which had been dropped by his pillow. This was the end of the first act, and all were invited to come back in the evening for the dancing and singing. The evening celebration is an opportunity for the father to display his generosity to his friends and neighbours, and everyone is welcome.

In the evening the house looked quite different. A long table had been set in the yard andall the men were sitting on three sides of it. It was a "raki" table bearing all the usual snacks of white cheese and olives, melon and tomato, cold bean salad and fried squid and octopus. Ali Dayi and the fiddler were playing and the men sang and got up to dance the *zeybek*, the regional dance, while the other men clapped hands and encouraged them with shouts of "hoppa". Inside the women were talking and now and again came to the windows or the doorway to look at the dancing. Ömer and his two brothers often came into the room and danced there to entertain them. The two boys were asleep in bed, coins surrounding their pillows, unaware of the tumult of the drum and the shouting. On this occasion the fathers dance with their daughters and the girls among themselves, whenever Ali Dayi struck a "modern" tune. The smallest children followed their elders around the room, looking at their feet and trying to dance the *zeybek* too. When Ömer's brother wanted to dance with his wife, she refused, saying that it would be a shame to dance when she had two grown girls dancing there. "He insists, as if he did not know that it is only young girls and brides who dance", she said to me. Eventually she rose, but put her white veil on her face and sat down after a few steps. At local celebrations it is extremely rare to find a woman over thirty dancing, but the Cretan women dance, even if they are past forty.

As is the custom in Bodrum, the young girls danced together and asked each other to dance quite formally, one leading the other, like a male partner. I was aksed to dance by a young girl there who was home for the holidays from Teachers' Training College, but not directly, as she did not want to risk a refusal; her aunt conveyed the invitation, also quite formally. All through the evening, the grandmothers, more tradition-minded than the mothers, kept shaking the boys to wake them up, saying that they were grown men now and should not sleep. But the children did not wake up for a long time. Alim finally woke up and watched the proceedings without too much interest. Before midnight the men had departed and so had most of the friends and relatives. The parents would sleep on the floor that night and the following few nights, until the boys were well enough to go back to their room, where they slept on the floor with their two sisters. Visitors would come and go for a few days, and the boys would go round the neighbourhood with their caps on for the next seven days. When school starts again, this will be the great news, everybody will be told that the boy has been circumcised and other children will ask Mehmed Ali how much money he got and what he will do with it. The next day he had given up his idea of putting the money in the bank and thought he would like to have a bicycle instead.

On these occasions, parents watch their children and comparisons are constantly made. Such and such a child is weak, the other looks like a "top", this little girl dances well, that other one has a weakness—already!—for her neighbour. The children's health and looks are discussed freely by all concerned and only in cases where there is something really wrong with the child are people discreet. Everyone in the immediate neighbourhood knows the children from birth, and although they have a fierce attachment to their own, they are generous and kind in their praise of other children. On an occasion such as circumcision, fathers are as much involved as mothers, because by now their sons have become old enough to share some of their father's interests.

Fathers do not see much of their children as a rule when they are small, and do not play an important role in their upbringing. The small children share the social life of their mothers, going to the cinema with her, or visiting. The fathers often have breakfast at the market and return home after the children have eaten their supper. Since most of the men work in the evenings or go to the café after supper, the children are left with their mother. During the short times the men spend at home, they are inclined to spoil their children and women often complain that their husband undo in the evening the disciplining work they have been trying to accomplish during the day. No matter how naughty a child has been in the daytime, by the time the evening comes, all has been forgiven and forgotten anyway and the children are petted and kissed by their fathers who tell them how beautiful and good they are. It is only when the children are old enough to accompany their fathers to the shop or at sea that a real relationship is established and it is then that the fathers begin to play a real role in the child's life. Even so, once the child is at school, it is the mothers who will attend the parent-teacher association meetings and who will come to enquire about the child's progress. This situation is especially noticeable among the families of fishermen and sponge-divers, who spend long months at sea.

The mothers of Bodrum are realistic women. They will talk about their children's faults quite openly and ask for advice from each other and even strangers without reluctance. When the child is at school, they frequently ask the teacher about the problems they meet at home in making the child work or behave properly. They rarely talk about these problems with their husbands who are, they say, "too tired to be bothered with the children". At the same time, they are quite possessive about the children and quick to spring to their defense when a serious quarrel breaks out between children in the street. This is especially noticeable among the Cretan women and the quarrels between children often end up as a quarrel between grown-ups, ending up in front of the *commissaire de police*. Local women are more reticent about their children and more inclined to let quarrels between children go at that. School teachers agree almost to a man that as a result of the difference in upbringing, Cretan children are more lively but less stable than local children. It may very well be that the fact that few of the local men are away from home for long periods makes the children more subdued and more secure.

However, the cultural differences between the two communities which are vividly felt in the home will be mitigated when the children go to school and are subjected to the same educational system.

CHAPTER SEVEN

CHILDHOOD AND SCHOOL

Little boys and girls in Bodrum await with impatience the day when they will be going to school. They look with envy upon their brothers and sisters putting on the black overalls and carrying their satchels, and pretend they are going to school too by taking a book and reading it upside down. As soon as they are six they will tell you right away that next year they will be going to school.

The Bodrum children go to three primary schools which take care of something like seven hundred children between the ages of seven and eleven. Two of the schools are very old, having been established in the early eighteen eighties. The last one, in the Cretan quarter, was opened in 1957 to relieve the other two. Now, all the children in the Cretan quarter and in Umurca go to this school; the children of Tepecik, Yeniköy and Eskiçeşme to the C school and those of the market quarter, Yokuşbasi and Türkkuyusu, to the B school.

Primary education is compulsory and free and heavy penalties, extending as far as imprisonment, are inflicted upon parents who do not send their children to school. All the same, the literacy rate for the district of Bodrum is 59.5%, slightly higher than that of the prefecture. However, in this town, as in the rest of the region, this very rarely happens because parents have accepted the necessity of education for girls as well as for boys. But it does happen that in the poorer quarters of Eskiçeşme, Yeniköy and Türkkuyusu a few children, especially girls, are not sent to school after the third year. The parents in this case avoid punishment by sending the child to relatives in a village and then bringing it back again, and this may last until the child is fourteen, when penalties are no longer applicable.

PRIMARY SCHOOL

The primary school has five grades and one teacher for each grade. This year there were so many children, that for the first time the Bodrum Education Officer had to do what has been done for years in Istanbul and Ankara, that is to have two shifts a day. In this way, no class-room has more than twenty or twenty-five children. More teachers were also requested from the Ministry, but in some cases this was not granted and many teachers now have to teach the same class twice a day, so that the school day starts earlier and ends later.

Schools in the country are all built according to a regulation which prescribes the number of windows, the colour of the building—grey or yellow—and the materials for the roof—red tiles. Only the A school in the Cretan quarter conforms to these specifications, because the other two are very old and were built in the days when such regulations did not exist. Besides, the vicissitudes of the town made themselves felt in the school buildings too, and much pulling down and rebuilding has taken place. Each school has a largish playground, with bushes and trees, where the children spend their recreation periods and do their physical training exercises. Inside the rooms open out from a large corridor and each room is very much like the other, the walls decorated with the children's drawings or maps, and an Atatürk Corner. This latter contains a portrait of the great leader, and some photographs; flowers, green branches and a flag add colour to the arrangement. Before the shifts were introduced, the children were sitting three to a bench; only the classes for the smallest children have a stove, fed with wood which is brought in by the school caretaker. Since the schools are totally supported by the government, many amenities are lacking. Each school asked the parents to organize themselves into a School Aid Association and the money collected thus went to pay for a telephone, or a typewriter, a record-player and even chairs and tables for the headmaster's room, as was the case for the A school. The Aid Association also provides money for the purchase of books and children's magazines. In each school there is also a Teachers' Room and a meeting-hall.

School starts on the 27th September and ends on 1st June, and there is a fortnight's holiday in February, but in the meantime there are many other holidays—religious as well as national—and relatively speaking it is a short school year. It is made even shorter by the fact that preparations have to be made for many of these holidays, such as the 29th of October, Republic Day, or the 23rd of April, Children's Day, and the day on which the first National Assembly met, or again the 19th of May, Youth Day, or even for the 10th of November, when speeches and poems are recited to commemorate the death of Atatürk. Days in advance, the children are organized into groups, taught appropriate songs, speeches and poems and rehearsals take up most of the day. This year, for Republic Day, the B school had children dressed as craftsmen in the parade and this took many hours away from instruction.

For the first day at school, great preparations take place. School for the Bodrum child is a familiar landmark in his neighbourhood and he is used to seeing the playground empty and fill at the sound of bells. He or she has also been taken to school many times when the mother and father went to enquire about an older child and has met many teachers in this way. Early in September he is taken again, his father or mother carrying all the necessary papers for registration: birth certificate, small-pox vaccination and health certificates, and the photograph which was taken a few days earlier by the town's photographer, Foto Mehmed. But still, on the great day it is difficult and the little child is taken to school by an older brother or sister, or more often than not, by the mother. Sometimes, in the case of a shy or nervous child, the mother is allowed to sit in the class-room for a period or two and the pains of initiation are thus alleviated. In the days to come, a neighbour's child will take it to school until it can go by itself.

On the first day, the children are dressed in their new shiny black smocks, little girls wear a large white bow like a butterfly in their hair, they all wear new shoes and carry a brand-new satchel, which will sooner or later burst at the sides or lose a handle. But none of this is thought of, the thing that matters is that now everybody, at home, in the neighbourhood, in fact everywhere, will compliment the child on going to school, on being grown up and will say invariably, "now that you are at school, you won't be naughty any more, will you", or, "now you will work hard and be a model pupil, wont' you?", and he or she will feel important and grown up.

On this first day there are no lessons. The newly arrived first grade will watch in awed silence while the other four grades all sing the National Anthem in the school playground. Then they will all file in, led by their teacher, and the rest of the time will pass with the teacher asking their names, complimenting them on a ribbon or on clean nails, telling them about school life, and teaching them a story or a little song.

On the second day, school starts in earnest. Since there is no nursery school, much of the first year's programme consists of games and manual work, like paper-cutting, moulding, and needlework. The alphabet is taught, according to the new method of block-reading, and addition and subtraction. After four months, the children can read and write simple sentences.

Schools begins every morning at 8.15. The children assemble in the school playground and on Monday mornings and Saturday at noon they sing the National Anthem. Then they go into the class room and each morning all recite in a chorus the Children's Pledge:

> I am a Turk, I am straight and hardworking;
> My duty is to protect the small and respect my elders,
> and love my people and my country more than myself.
> My aim in life is to better myself, to go forward.
> I promise to devote myself to my country.

This *credo*, printed and framed, is hung in the Atatürk Corner and is part of every Turk's childhood memories.

After that, for a quarter of an hour, the "news" is discussed, such as a new calf, someone who became ill during the night, a visitor from out of town, the return of a fishing or sponge boat. At 8.30, formal work begins. For half an hour the day's work is planned by the teacher together with the children and the work is distributed. From 9 until 10.30, each child works on his or her project. There follows a break of half on hour. Milk and buns are distributed, out of the funds provided by the Aid Association, but sugar and cooking money are contributed by the children themselves. The windows are opened in the class-room and the place tidied up under the supervision of the class prefect. From 11 to 12 o'clock, formal instruction in Turkish, or arithmetic, singing and listening to music on tape take place. At 12 p.m. the children go home for lunch, except the poor ones, who eat at school supervised by a teacher; the meals are provided already cooked by the townspeople who had promised to help earlier in the year. Some housewives, too busy to cook for twenty or thirty children, ask their husbands once a fortnight to take the children to a restaurant in town. When the children stay at school, they eat in the meeting hall if it is not too cold, or in a class-room. They all bring a plate and a fork and spoon, and the duty teacher supervises the meal and teaches them table manners. The children are free to talk and joke, but few do so, feeling uneasy and ashamed. Many of the townspeople think that meals ought to be provided by the school for all the children so that the poor ones will not feel embarrassed, but the expense for the government would be so heavy that the day when this can be done is very remote.

At 1.30 p.m. formal instruction continues for another hour. There is a twenty-minute break with games and then, for the last hour, each group spokesman presents his or her group's report; this is checked and the next day's programme is prepared by the children under the guidance of the teacher. This method, a version of the project method, is only used in the A school and has given good results. But the number of hours each subject is given does not vary for the other schools. The number of hours per week devoted to each subject is given below:

Table 10

	General Knowledge	Turkish	Arithmetic	Manual	P.T.	Music
1st Grade	5 periods of 45″	8 × 50″	4 × 60″	3 × 45″	90″	45″
2nd Grade	6 × 45″	5 × 50″	4 × 50″	75″	90″	45″
3rd Grade	6 × 45″	6 × 50″	5 × 50″	75″	90″	45″

	Social knowledge, Civics History, Geog.	Turkish	Science	Mathematics
4th Grade	3 × 90″	5 × 50″	5 × 45″	4.5 × 45″
5th Grade	2.5 × 90″	6 × 50″	2.5 × 90″	4.5 × 45″

These last two grades have 45 minutes each of music, 60 minutes of drawing, 45 minutes of physical training and 45 minutes a week religious instruction, which is attended by all children, even though it is not compulsory.

Put in a different way, this is the total amount of hours per week that the main subjects are taught in each grade:

Table 11

	Turkish	Mathematics	Science
1st Grade	6 hrs 40″	4	—
2nd Grade	4 hrs 10″	3 hrs 20″	—
3rd Grade	4 hrs	4 hrs 10″	—
4th Grade	4 hrs 10″	3 hrs 30″	3 hrs 45″
5 th Grade	5 hrs	3 hrs 45″	3 hrs 45″

At 3.30 p.m. in the afternoon school ends. In the spring, summer and autumn, the school children run home and then go swimming. They clamber in and out of the boats and fish with a hook and line. While the sea in the Cretan quarter is near, for the children in other quarters it is a longish run down to the sea and some prefer to play in the courtyards or the street. They also have chores to do, such as buying bread or fetching a pail of water from the fountain, while girls have to look after a baby while the mother prepares the supper. Since supper is eaten early in Bodrum, there is plenty of time to do the homework afterwards.

In the winter, when there is wind and rain, the children drag their feet disconsolately on the way home, because they know that they will be told to start on their lessons right away. Usually all the children are in by nightfall, which comes at five-thirty in the winter.

Before the new teaching programme came into operation, the Ministry of Education published a programme which was followed throughout the country. Now teachers have been urged to give emphasis to subjects of special regional or local interest. The children begin with the immediate environment of the home and then, as they progress from grade to grade, the sphere of interest is enlarged to take in the country and eventually the world. A project may last from two to eight weeks and every child is left free to do his research as he thinks best. Some will think of going to the public library for additional information and some may not. Many of the teachers complained that the teaching materials had not been prepared to suit the new method, which requires a different arrangement of the subject-matter and many books. In the A school, the children are contributing one tenth of a lira per week towards the purchase of an Encyclopedia for each group.

This year a new regulation was introduced, abolishing examinations at the end of the first and second grades and allowing all children, irrespective of whether they can read and write properly, to enter the third grade. This has resulted in inflated third grades and a lowering of the level of learning. Consequently, the children all read and calculate at different speeds and this makes group work extremely difficult and unproductive. Under these conditions, the children cannot cope with the group method, although it is appreciated in the fourth and fifth grades.

The new regulation has incensed the teachers, first because they

consider it unwise educationally and because they were not consulted by the Ministry, whose Methods Division takes decisions without
conducting surveys or sending out questionnaires. The teachers feel
unqualified to teach the new method and do their best to remedy
this. When information is unavailable in books and they themselves
do not know the answer, the children are taken to someone in town
who knows the problem, such as the Agricultural Officer or the Town
Clerk. The smallest children are often seen in a shop gravely asking
an indulgent and interested butcher or shoemaker for information.

The 21 primary school teachers of Bodrum are supervised by an
Education Officer, who reports to the Ministry in Ankara through
the *kaymakam* who in turn channels the correspondence through the
prefecture in Muğla. The teachers are civil servants and they are
answerable to the *kaymakam* for such question as leave, sick leave
and promotion. Most of them are local people, come back to
teach in Bodrum after various posts in other parts of the country.
They teach 18 hours a week and receive T.L. 450.- per month. They
can teach up to twelve additional hours a week, which doubles
their salary. Since many teachers are married to teachers, husband
and wife make a comfortable living and many teachers own their
houses and have invested in some land. Their many ties with the
townspeople make it difficult sometimes to enforce discipline, while
on the other hand their knowledge of local conditions is invaluable.
But being themselves part of Bodrum, they find difficulty in inculcu-
ating into the children a notion about life which would be wider
than local and the most enlightened among them, or those who come
from outside, confess that they find their training inadequate. Their
relationship with the people of Bodrum does not mean that they
take part in the city's problems other than as townspeople. As teachers they are dissatisfied with the way the government treats
them and would like to receive more recognition.

On the other hand, parents have a tendency to surrender the
children to the teachers. They rely on them to make the child
work hard and even allow them to resort to giving them a hiding,
if need be. The traditional saying "the meat is yours, the bones
are mine", fairly sums up the situation. Most of the parents are
barely literate and are not able to supervise homework or to control
the child's activities. Teachers can be constantly heard telling the
children not to loaf, not to gape, not to spit, all the things which
parents do naturally. However, the Parents-Teacher Association

meetings are well attended, mostly by mothers. At these meetings, the teachers try and explain the new method or changes in the regulations and to help parents with their problems. But most parents are interested in marks and in knowing what the prospects are for the child to pass to the next grade. Even the poorest are very willing to contribute small sums to help in buying books or buns for the snacks, but the expense of buying books and school materials—a sum of T.L. 100.- to 150.- per year—is a real sacrifice for the poorest parents. Hence the extreme anxiety to have the child pass at all costs.

As things stand, the anxiety is well founded. At all educational levels throughout the country, the achievement rate is extremely low and Bodrum is no exception. Many children remain in the same grade for two years, or three or even four. It is only at fourteen that he or she will be given up and the parents relieved of the expense. Over the past ten years, both Schools A and C did not reach an achievement rate over 39%, whereas School B reached 67.7%. Moreover, it is A School which provides the best graduates, according to the Secondary School headmaster. The achievement rate is better in the fifth grade. The following tables give an idea about the situation. The first shows the failure rates for the three schools for the two five-year periods and the second the failure rate for the fifth grades:

Table 12

	Has entered 1957	Graduated 1962	% Failure
A School	51	26	49
B School	46	29	37
C School	64	18	71.2
	Has entered 1961	Graduated 1966	% Failure
A School	58	27	53.6
B School	58	42	27.6
C School	46	28	31.3

Table 13

	A School			B School			C School		
	Ent.	Grad.	Fail.%	Ent.	Grad.	Fail.%	Ent.	Grad.	Fail.%
1956-57	—	—	—	74	62	16.3	46	39	15
1957-58	27	24	10	38	31	18.4	51	47	7.9
1961-62	30	26	13.4	33	29	12	37	18	50.6
1965-66	60	27	55	42	40	4.8	44	28	34.1
1966-67	58	58	—	39	39	—	39	36	5.4

Girls, as will be seen later in the case of the Secondary School, make better students than boys, but in that of the primary school, the percentage is small. In the Secondary School, the percentage will be considerable. All the teachers, including those of the Secondary School, agree that there is a marked difference between the behaviour of Cretan and local children. The Cretans adapted quicker to school life, were more lively and more quarrelsome. The local children, or the other hand, were shy and reserved and while they did not display the same interest, they were steadier and more hardworking.

The Ministry does not conduct achievement surveys and the government has not appointed a committee to look into the problem of education. The headmasters and the teachers know that the system is deficient, but do not usually conduct surveys themselves. As for the parents, they know who among their neighbour's children have passed or have stayed in the same grade. Therefore the extent of the problem is not known with accuracy. Even the figures shown above are only rough estimates. In the case of the percentages of success, they do not indicate how many years it took those who eventually graduated to do so. Some took the normal five years, others may have taken seven or eight years. But once teachers and parents are told one or two figures, they are appalled and the causes for this loss of energy and money are asked for. While many of the teachers recognize that their training has been inadequate—three years of Teachers' Training School after Secondary School, barely reaching the educational level of a lycée—they are at a loss to know how to remedy the situation. They would like the government to improve their methods of training, but they do not feel, for the most part, that they themselves can do anything about the situation. Self-improvement as a continuous activity is practically unknown. Few read anything beyond a newspaper, very few subscribe to a good weekly or monthly publication, and not one attended one of the rare refresher courses which the Ministry runs at remote intervals.

The books which the children use have to be approved by the Ministry, and are all written by schoolteachers, active or retired. A quick perusal of these reveals that the subject matter is either not up to the age level of the children for whom it was written, or much too complicated. The books praise hardworking and clean children, always mention the schoolteacher as a "gay and smiling" person and inculcates into the children some basic notions about

Atatürk and the nation. From the third grade on, the child is "nationalized", made to memorize poems about national victories, the greatness of the Turkish nation, the glory of the Turkish army and love for Atatürk. This covers about 10% of the reading matter. However, the rest of the book reveals a serious lack of imagination and child psychology. The stories are usually suitable for five-year olds, and the vocabulary throughout is extremely limited. On the other hand, the civics book for the fifth grade imparts administrative and legal knowledge about the election and tax systems, the structure of the government and administration, which are well beyond the grasp of an eleven-year-old. No information at all is given about children in other countries, or about different ways of life. Animals and plants are ignored. Instead of teaching children the extremely poetic and linguistically rich folk-lore of the country, simplistic little poems are taught, using a vocabulary which is always the same and which is moulded into half a dozen clichés. Under these conditions it becomes increasingly difficult to keep the teachers and children interested and the tendency to memorize the material is encouraged.

Parents, themselves the product of this system of education and bent upon making a difficult living and both ends meet, cannot provide the child with the necessary stimulation. Teachers all agree that sooner or later the government will have to introduce nursery-schools so that children can be removed from the home influence at least at the age of five and thus be better prepared for the primary school programme, provided that this latter is properly revised and teachers better trained.

The boys who leave school at eleven will be placed as apprentices or become deck-boys on the fishing and sponge boats, or begin to work in the fields and tangerine gardens. All but a few will forget Ottoman history, the structure of the government or three-dimensional geometry. Few will remember how to calculate a percentage. But then, it may be argued, they will not need this knowledge since they will rarely read a book or write a letter. They will sign their names, read a popular newspaper and get someone from the town to write an application to one of the government offices for them now and again. And the cycle will begin again, for they will want their children to acquire the same education which has been of so little use to themselves.

GIRLS' TECHNICAL SCHOOL

After graduation most of the boys go on to the Intermediate Secondary School but fewer girls continue. The girls will enter the Girls' Technical School which was started thirty years ago. The school is located in the basement of the A School in the Cretan quarter and does not have to pay rent.

There are ninety girls attending the school, which teaches embroidery, sewing, cutting out, lingerie-making, flower-making and home economics. Each course lasts two years. The girls come especially to learn to sew and embroider in order to prepare their trousseaux; they do not take other courses, since these do not represent a potential source of income. There are two teachers, graduates of one of the large Girls' Technical Institutes distributed throughout the country. About twenty girls who graduated from the School set up as seamstresses, earning from TL. 5.- to T.L. 50.- per dress. A wedding dress costs from T.L. 75.- to T.L. 100. When a girl sets up as a seamstress, she has no paid assistant, the whole family helping at odd times, turning up hems, finishing seams, sewing on buttons and ribbons. Only two of the best seamstresses are officially registered and therefore pay taxes.

The Home Economics course is not too popular and never has more than a dozen or so girls learning to knit, mend and repair, etc. There are no cooking, infant care or budgeting lessons.

In one week the girls have 8 hours of sewing and cutting-out lessons, 8 hours of lingerie-making, 8 hours of embroidery and 4 hours each of home economics and flower-making. But few girls can take all these courses because of the high cost of materials, especially for such things as lingerie and flower making. The poorest children are helped out of a tiny fund allocated by the Ministry of Education, T.L. 200 a year. This year the School ran a lottery which brought in T.L. 2000.

The school has a typewriter and a telephone, paid for by the Ministry, but fashion magazines have to be bought jointly by the girls. It costs the Ministry T.L. 5700 a month to run the School, rent being free. There is a Director, two teachers and two cleaners. There are not enough teachers for all the courses, so the two teachers teach supplementary hours for which they are paid T.L. 10 an hour.

The Director, who is the wife of one of the district officials, complained that the diploma delivered had no market value and since there is no compulsory attendance, girls tend to be casual about coming to school and completing the courses. If the school became an Institute, then a lot more could be done.

The Director also said that there were slow changes in the last three or four years, more attention is paid to fashion, skirts are getting shorter, heels are now worn, materials are brought from Istanbul and Izmir, or smuggled in from Cos. The Cretan girls are more alive, more fond of fashion, but less hard-working and persevering. The Cretans send more girls to the School, there are 20 Cretan girls to 60 local girls. Most of them are girls from poor or middle-income families, those who have finished primary school but who do not have the means of going on to further study outside Bodrum, or whose parents consider that the girls ought to be married early. Later on, during the days of the wedding festivities, the embroidered sheets and pillow slips, tray-cloths and bedspreads will be exhibited for the visitors to admire. From now on, the bride will not have time to embroider, but her sewing, knitting and mending skills will be an important contribution to the family budget.

SECONDARY SCHOOL

Every afternoon around four, droves of boys and girls dressed in black pinafores and a black rather ugly peaked cap, invade the town streets. They are the Intermediate Secondary School children, all 420 of them coming out of school. The Bodrum Secondary was established in 1949 in its modern form, although there had been a secondary school in the town since 1880.

The Bodrum Secondary School has three grades and grants a certificate upon graduation. It is considered as a preparation for further study, that is the lycée or a technical or professional school, and very few parents send their children to secondary unless they intend to continue spending money on their education. For the certificate given to a boy or girl of fourteen qualifies them only for a minor clerkship in some local office. The return is considered too small for three years of upkeep and expenses, for although there are no fees, the money spent on books and materials amounts to about T.L. 175.- a year and this represents an important sum to a peasant or a poor fisherman.

Although Bodrum Secondary has been functioning for the last eighteen years, it is only since the early sixties that it has acquired its full establishment of teachers. Before that, teachers from the primary schools used to be called in. Foreign language teaching was always a problem until the Peace Corps sent one of their volunteers. German and French did not meet with any interest and instruction in those languages has ceased.

Compared to the last grade of primary school, there are more hours of teaching in secondary. There is no school on Wednesday and Saturday afternoons. These are devoted to group activities such as the Tourism Group, the Music Group, the Cooperative Group or the Cultural Activities Group. The weekly programme shown below is taught from the end of September to the end of May, with a fortnight's holiday in February:

Table 14

	1st Grade	2nd Grade	3rd Grade
Turkish language	6 hours	4 hours	4 hours
History	2 ,,	2 ,,	2 ,,
Geography	2 ,,	2 ,,	1 ,,
Civics	1 ,,	1 ,,	1 ,,
Mathematics	5 ,,	4 ,,	4 ,,
Physics	0 ,,	3 ,,	3 ,,
Chemistry	0 ,,	0 ,,	2 ,,
Biology	3 ,,	3 ,,	2 ,,
Foreign language	3 ,,	3 ,,	3 ,,
Commercial subjects	2 ,,	2 ,,	2 ,,
Music	1 ,,	1 ,,	1 ,,
Drawing	1 ,,	1 ,,	1 ,,
Physical training	1 ,,	1 ,,	1 ,,
Religious instruction	1 ,,	1 ,,	0 ,,
	28 hours	28 hours	27 hours

It was only 27 hours until voluntary religious instruction was introduced by the government in 1956. This subject is taught by a teacher who considers tourism bad for morals but who turns his house into a *pension* every summer and who founded last year a league to fight communism, with a total membership of five and no activity whatsoever, so far. This subject is voluntary, but if a child attends religious instruction, then it must sit for an examination and failure results in remaining in the same grade for another year, even if the child has received high marks in all other subjects. This rule was introduced this year, and it will be interesting to see parental reaction; for many parents tell their children to attend so that "people won't say that my child is an infidel's child", and will probably experience a mental tug-of-war between their tendency to conform and their desire to see the child graduate as soon as possible.

The regulation about religious instruction was followed by new rules governing passage from one grade to the next. Until now, a child had to take a make-up examination in September for subjects failed in June. An average was calculated of the marks received for all subjects, on the basis of which the child passed or not. Even with this relatively easy rule, there was an impressive number of failures. The new regulations are even worse—from an educator's point of view. Now a child, instead of trying again in September for his failed subject, can sit again for a subject he has passed already to try and raise his average. One can envisage a child receiving a Secondary School Certificate without having ever received a mark higher than 30% in Turkish, mathematics, and science, precisely those subjects which give the poorest results in all tests and examinations anyway. Since this rule is applied to *lycées* as well, it is foreseen that very few children will be able to pass the State *Lycée* Examinations and equally few qualify for university entrance. All teachers are incensed about the new regulations, while parents have not yet grasped their significance, although these are being explained to them at the Parent-Teacher Association meetings. "Vote-hunting, that's what it is, catering to religious emotions", or "this is certainly a manoeuvre to restrict the number who want to go to college", "this is only to make parents believe that their children will have an easy time from now on and will succeed", are the kind of remarks overhead these days. One teacher said to me: "How can I fail a brilliant child because he has been unable to memorize the pidgin Arabic of religious instruction?"

However, to an outside observer, the situation could hardly become worse since so few children manage to graduate anyway:

Table 15

	Has entered			Graduated			
	Girls	Boys	Total	Girls	Boys	Total	Failure%
1957	42	75	117	30	23	53	44.7
1959	41	77	118	19	29	48	60.0
1963	44	59	103	24	18	42	69.3

Table 16

	Has passed to 3rd Grade				Graduated same year			
	Girls	Boys	Total		Girls	Boys	Total	Failure%
1956	7	29	36		5	17	22	38.9
1957	19	27	46		9	22	31	32.7
1960	34	52	86		30	23	53	38.4
1961	35	63	98		19	29	48	51.1
1965	37	48	85		24	18	42	50.6

In the school year 1965-1966, there was a loss of 78%: 191 children entered Secondary in the first grade, 27 did not make the 2nd grade, 20 left school, 85 were able to go on to the third grade and eventually 42 graduated. There are also indications that as the years go by and attendance increases, failures also increase: there were 117 entrants in 1957, out of which 53 graduated three years later and 191 entrants in 1963 out of which 42 graduated in 1966: an increase of 38.8% in numbers was accompanied by an increase in 33.3% in failures.

A perusal of the figures show that Bodrum reflects other national characteristics. For the situation described above is by no means particular to this town, it is the rule throughout the country, since education is a state monopoly. The other characteristics are the increasing attendance of girls and their relatively better record when compared with that of boys.

Table 17

Year	Girls	Boys	Total
1956	29	70	99
1957	42	75	117
1958	41	77	118
1959	36	81	117
1960	28	83	111
1961	30	81	111
1962	30	48	78
1963	44	59	103
1964	42	77	119
1965	85	108	193

In ten years, the attendance of girls has increased by two-thirds, that of boys by one-third and a look at the preceding tables will show that there is a higher achievement rate for girls. It is only when one looks at the number of children who go on to secondary after primary school that it becomes evident that parents still favour boys' education:

Table 18

Graduating from Primary				Entering Secondary		
Girls	Boys	Total		Girls	Boys	Total
49	53	102	1958	25	46	71
42	31	73	1962	28	29	57
47	50	97	1966	36	49	85

While in many parts of Eastern Anatolia parents still refuse to send their children, and especially their daughters, to school, in Bodrum, in the most developed region of the country, education, including girls' education, is increasingly sought as a thing good in itself—"It do not want my daughters to be "blind ignorant like myself'"—and also because of the salaries it will bring later. At the same time, a culture which segregates the sexes in practically all social aspects of life favours girls from the point of view of achievement. After school, girls have to come straight home and, after doing a little housework, have nothing to do but study; while boys are free to run around, they rush home to drop their satchel, snatch a piece of bread and rush out again to go swimming or fishing, or to play ball in the street. Very few of them have to help their fathers in the workshop or the fields. They have less responsibilities towards the family than girls. "Be careful," one teacher is fond of telling his boys, "lest the girls take over this town and rule you, like in the days of Artemisia!"

However, there are more serious reasons for the large number of failures. About 40% of the children who attend secondary come from the surrounding villages. If the village is near town, they commute, but if it is not, they have to find lodgings, unless they are lucky enough to have relatives living in Bodrum. It is not unusual to find a boy of 12, or two girls of the same age, who have rented a *dam* or a room somewhere and who do their own cooking and laundry. Away from the warmth of village life and home, alone in what is for them a large city with shops and bicycles, cafés and a cinema and lots of people they do not know, these children—who are in any case at the age of puberty—have great difficulty in adjusting and working. Some give up and go back to the village to become peasants like their fathers, some begin to explore corner street games and the cinema. Failure in the first grade often leads a parent to reconsider prolonged expense. But those who survive, by sheer ability and courage, do as well at the final examination as their city counterparts. However, a large proportion of those who leave are village boys. Parents are reluctant to take girls away after the second or third year, because it is easier to find an occupation for boys. Among those who give up, there are as many Cretans as locals.

For a Bodrum child to succeed is no mean achievement. Parents are unable to provide either the guidance or the control they should, since most of them are barely educated themselves. The child, even in a well-to-do household, does not have a room to itself, and the ingrained habit of thrift of this rather poor community precludes the provision of such things as proper lighting and desks, books and magazines, trips or travel. The parents, however, display considerable interest in the progress of their children. It is usually the mother who enquires about the child, as is the case in the primary schools.

On market days, when peasants come into Bodrum, they rarely fail to come to school and ask about the progress of their children. During the recreation, the Teachers' Room fills up with their white and black *futas* covering their heads, waiting their turn to ask about marks. After that they will go to their children's room, and empty their bags of beans and lentils, chestnuts and a few almonds, and cook a large pot of food that will last the child for a few days. If they spend a night in town, they will do the laundry and go away the next morning, exhausted but reassured. They beg the teacher to be severe with the children, so that the boy or girl may grow up to be a teacher or a government servant, and dress like a lady or gentlemen, with a secure salary coming in each month. For the poor peasants of Bodrum, labour at T.L. 10 a day in the August heat or in the wind and rain is becoming increasingly distasteful and hopeless.

The Parent-Teacher Association meetings are well attended, also by a majority of mothers. At recent meetings, the largest school-room was not enough to hold them all. But few of the parents display what could be termed an informed interest. They ask about marks and rarely, if ever, ask for guidance in helping the child. On the other hand, few parents can be asked to help their children in a positive manner and the teachers know enough about their home conditions to realize the futility of suggesting improvements. In many cases, they themselves grew up in a similar way and their own children study in similar surroundings, with the wireless on, people dropping in and conversation going on non-stop. The connection has not yet been made between conditions in the physical environment and achievement in the case of most parents and teachers. The child is always accused of "laziness", "unruliness" and "disobedience". Teachers' training institutions do not teach the ways in which interest can be aroused, discussion stimulated, abilities explored and nourished. There are no laboratories, only the most simple experiments can be carried out in the class-room and the textbooks, though of a better standard than those of the primary school, are still not interesting enough. The teachers are aware of the problems and at a loss for solutions. The Ministry is a remote bureaucracy showering them with circulars and then "explanatory circulars", concocted in the capital without consultation or relation to every-day teaching experiences. And they do feel that they are responsible, in the last resort, for the children. The years they have spent training recede, and what they learnt appears as more and more disconnected with reality. So the pattern of the primary school is repeated, a garden of tangerines is acquired or the house turned into a *pension* in the summer. Teaching becomes a routine, the Teachers' Association Club takes on the aspect of any café, with men playing cards and drinking tea: "it is not a place where *we* can go", say the women teachers, who are busy anyway with their homes and husbands and the supervision of their children's work. The only thing that changes is that prices and the number of pupils increase with every passing year.

After graduation, the children are faced with the second choice of their young life. What to do next? And they opt for one of the openings shown in the following table:

Table 19

Year	Graduates		Lycée & Business lycée		Technical Schools		Military Schools		Teachers' Training Schools		Public Health School		Nowhere	
	G.	B.	G.	B.	G.	B.	G.	B.	G.	B.	G.	B.	G.	B.
1956	5	15	4	7	—	2	—	5	—	—	—	—	1	1
1961	23	30	—	10	—	9	—	—	12	2	—	—	11	3
1966	18	24	6	11	—	10	—	—	6	1	1	—	4	2

In all cases the children are leaving home for good. They will find employment in another town and marry away from Bodrum, or in the case of boys, come back and marry a childhood friend or a relative and leave again. Mothers cry and say "Now the girl has gone, I have to start working on her trousseau", and letters from the children are read aloud to relatives and friends.

But there are those who stay. And the parents are divided between a feeling of joy at not losing them and a feeling of shame because their child is not going to become a teacher or a government servant. For those who stay, it is time to look for a way of earning a living.

CHAPTER EIGHT

ADOLESCENCE

When the people of Bodrum talk about the "youngsters", they mean boys and girls who are not yet married. Adolescence is the period which extends between leaving school and settling down in one's own home. Since most of the boys go to intermediate secondary school, the range will cover the ages between 15 and 25 or so and for the girls from 15 to 20. As far as boys are concerned, there is a nuance: young men are not considered adolescents once they have come back from their military service and every boy knows that after he has left Bodrum to serve his two years in the Navy, his carefree days are pretty much over.

Work

Boys and girls do not leave the parental home until they marry, even in the rare cases when this carries over into adulthood. As soon as they leave school, they are put to work and begin to earn money. There are peculiarities about holding a job in Bodrum; like their elders, it is rare to find boys who have only one job and it is a current feature of the town that many jobs are tried out and discarded, sometimes in quick succession. If the boy cannot work with his father, on the land or in a shop or workshop, then either he is apprenticed or has to fend for himself, doing one thing for a few months and then another. In rare cases, fathers are well enough off to start the boy in a business of his own. Suat's father, who is not a very rich man, rented a shop in the market and set up Suat as a jeweller. But the boy preferred to have a good time with the tourist girls in the summer and after two seasons, the shop was shut. Now Suat does nothing, or finds himself odd jobs around town to earn some pocket money. He does not have to worry about his keep since he lives at home, but his mother despairs of getting him married and settled down, since no girl in town will have him. Ahmet is a rich man and his son was able to go away and learn pharmacy. Now his father has financed him and his pharmacy does a brisk trade. People prefer to go to him because he is a local boy and is more inclined to give credit. The other pharmacy, which was started by "strangers" is losing much of its customers. However, these are rare instances. Most fathers can just about keep their family and there is no room either on the land or in the workshop for another man. The barbers, tailors and shoemakers can take in only a limited number of apprentices and usually do not pay them a wage, but give them pocket money, such as T.L. 10 per week. Also, they are not willing to teach the boy seriously, since they know that as soon as the boy can find a better job, he will leave. Since the building trade has increased in Bodrum, carpenters and builders have taken on a few boys, likewise the boat-builders. In these cases the boys earn T.L. 10 a day and their lunches, less than what they would earn as casual labourers, but at least the job is secure and they are learning a trade. Another occupation which has recruited boys is the hotel and restaurant business. With the development of tourism, hotels and restaurants need additional waiters and workers and many boys like that, earning something like T.L. 150 a month. This income is supplemented by tips—a new institution in Bodrum—and many boys consider themselves lucky. However, some of them are dismissed in the winter and have to look for other jobs, the establishment concerned only keeping on one or two of the hardest-working boys to have them available the following season.

Therefore, many of the youngsters in Bodrum have no alternative but casual labour or going to sea in a fisherman's *tratta* if they want to remain in Bodrum. Casual labour includes anything from carrying loads and messages to making wooden packing cases for tangerines, doing paint and repair jobs or hauling boats on shore with the coming of the first storm. There barely amount to a hundred working days in the year and the income from these days will not exceed T.L. 600-700 in the year.

Hence the extreme anxiety of the townspeople to have a factory built in Bodrum which will process the tangerines and tomatoes, the olives and the fish. Otherwise they see no hope for the young except exile. The Cretans, who occupied the whole of the Kum-bahçe quarter two decades ago and amounted to one quarter of the population, now do not constitute more than 10%. Their younger people constantly emigrate to Izmir in search of employment. The Cretan youngsters do not have the advantages of the local boys, which is a piece of land from which the income of the family is supplemented and cannot stay at home for years without helping the family make ends meet. Another development of recent years is fishing and sponge-diving. While these were almost exclusively Cretan trades a decade ago, now many local boys have become fishermen and sponge-divers. If employment in a trade is impossible, then the favourite work of boys is fishing in the winter and tourist work in the summer. In these cases their income for the year may reach T.L. 3000 a year, which is considered enough to keep a family on. Parents would accept a bridegroom employed in this way, but the fact remains that only a third or so of the boys are fully and gainfully employed in Bodrum from one year to the next.

In spite of this situation, boys do not want to leave Bodrum, or if they have to, they do not want to go far. Izmir and Instanbul are the favourites, sometimes Ankara is accepted, but only one boy said that he was willing to go east, even with a good salary. They say they could not live in a place where there is no sea and where it is cold for many months on end, and sometimes add that the people in the rest of Anatolia—meaning those living beyond a line roughly cutting the country in two—are not "civilized". They are really dissociated from the rest of the country, while quite well informed about the Agean region and Istanbul.

The fact that some of the young men have gone away to study has created a rift between boys who had gone to primary and secondary school together. Those who stayed talk about "that student crowd" and say things like "I do not sponge on my parents, I work for a living". When the students return home, there is the pleasure of coming back, a kind of euphoria sets in and the young men become friends again. But it is not only the boys who study who settle down away from Bodrum; those who stay for a year or two after primary school eventually go out in search of work. The Cretans adapt more easily to conditions outside Bodrum, and it is they especially who go away. But no one leaves Bodrum "cursing", all leave it with regret, and the beauty of the place, the intimacy of daily life, the fact that all are known by all make going away a sad experience.

LEISURE

Boys who work, regularly or casually, are expected to help the family, in all except the most prosperous homes. They are reminded that their sisters have to get married and the trousseau bought, and that younger brothers must study as long as possible so as to acquire a profession or a trade. Pocket money is left them and each boy spends it as he likes. The amount of pocket money that a boy spends rarely falls below T.L. 20 a week or exceeds T.L. 40. This money is spent on the cinema, where they go three times a week, every time the film is changed; at the café, where they drink tea, and sometimes coffee, and where they play cards—the stakes being more tea and coffee, and in the summer the more expensive carbonated drinks or Coca-Cola; on the football pools; on papers and detective magazines and on cigarettes. The young men will rarely drink, and never in public. They may get a bottle or two now and again and drink in some secluded spot among themselves, or at weddings. But drink is not part of the normal leisure time expenditure.

All the young men can dance the local dance, the *zeybek*, and sing the local songs. But it has been impossible to keep a folklore group together, even though the groups can earn good money in the summer singing and dancing for the tourists. Conflicts occur in the group and it breaks up. Also, folk dancing is so much a part of everyday life that the thought has not yet dawned on them that it can be exploited for commercial purposes. Some young men go hunting, but very few take it seriously and fathers disapprove of a youngster having a gun and keeping a dog before they are "grown up". They all go to the weekly football match and bet on the outcome, but very few actually play. Many of the young men say that what they need is a "leader" who will organize them and teach them new activities and ways of passing the time. But they add right away that this would not work because "we cannot act as a group". This happened with the Youth Club which was established four years ago. They received sports equipment and hired a man to operate a small canteen. But the Club rented a small house far from the centre of town, and boys preferred the cafés where they could more easily drop in between jobs and at breaks. The Club finally split into two over a play that was to have been produced in aid of the secondary school. In due course, two plays were produced and performed, with a great deal of enthusiasm and a strong desire to do better that the other side. The young men today congregate in two different cafés, roughly corresponding to the two groups; upon enquiry there is nothing to distinguish the two groups from each other, except the personalities. The Youth

Club split occurred because two or three young men found it difficult to hold together the whole group. It was certainly not a case of two rival leaders pulling the Club apart, just a general inability to act as an integrated, organized whole. If anything, the young men in one group seem to be more regularly employed than the boys in the other.

Another way of enjoying oneself is going to weddings. During the wedding season, young men go from one to the other, for the few evenings preceding the last day of the wedding celebrations. They complain of the fact that they can never dance with girls: even the girls who come to the folklore group come "to find a husband" and not for the dancing. As to modern dancing, they would not invite a girl, be refused and earn the reputation of being "irresponsible". After all, they say, "these girls have brothers and we might get into trouble, and we have sisters too and would not like a boy to come and "take them lightly". Even boys who go to a *lycée* or the university in Izmir or Istanbul share this sentiment.

Reading is not a popular pastime in Bodrum, though young men, like adults, complain about the boredom of life. The few good novels which the paper-seller brings in are bought by school-teachers or the few "strangers" who have retired in Bodrum. The boys read newspapers, usually the most popular one in the country and an Izmir paper or two; they buy weeklies, of the sporting or detective kind. When the Peace Corps girl announced that she was going to run English classes, 45 registered but after a few weeks attendance had dropped to 13, and these were all people connected with the tourist trade. Education is considered as a way to better one's condition in life and education for education's sake is not appreciated. As we have seen, the educational system does not awaken intellectual curiosity or stimulate the acquisition of productive hobbies.

A dozen or son young men have fun in the summer with the tourists. The European or American girls arrive in Bodrum, either via Izmir or more often via Cos and strike up friendships with the young men here. The fact that there is no common language does not seem to affect the development of love affairs and a good time is had by all. However, although the girls rarely stay longer than two or three weeks, they are succeeded by others and for some of the boys, the summer is one long session of *dolce vita*. After four months of this kind of life, some of them have found it difficult and even impossible to settle down to the normal routine. They wait patiently all winter long for the summer to come round again. As to their parents, they hope that the boys will lose these habits once they go into the army and will come back chastened and ready to settle down. There are three boys, however, who are considered well "lost" to the Bodrum girls and who agree themselves that they could not marry a Bodrum girl and settle down to a normal life again. They expect to go abroad or even to marry one of the foreign girls some day and to emigrate.

Sometimes there are serious sequels to the holiday romances. One boy fell genuinely in love with a foreign girl and followed her to Europe somehow, only to return after a month, completely crushed. He had been unable to share in the girl's life, understand her friends or her way of life, take pleasure in her hobbies. Another boy was informed by his girl-friend, upon her return to Europe, that she had decided to divorce and was coming to him. He rushed to Teoman, who had to write a long letter in French to try and dissuade the girl from going through with her plans. The people of the town do not frown upon what they consider as foreigner's folly or young men's pranks. But they are concerned with something else, and that is the police incidents which have grown since the arrival of tourism.

To the young male of Bodrum, the idea that a girl can choose a companion for love and that she may also have male friends is not understandable. They tend to assume that if a girl "goes" with one boy, she will with another, and that if she speaks freely to them, it is a sign of special favour. Hence fights among the young men and unpleasantness for the girls. In the last two summers there have been five such cases, where the story ended in the courts, much to the scandal of the population. "This tourism is ruining the boys", say the town people, "they are turning into hooligans, we never knew such disgraces before".

ATTITUDES

One evening sitting in a café with some of the young men, relationships with parents were discussed. In the matter of "do's" and "dont's" the attitude of all parents seemed the same: cigarettes are forbidden, drinking is forbidden, girls are forbidden, and even the cinema and football are frowned upon. Not one of the boys ever smoked or drank in the presence of his father or even an older brother. Although they criticized their parents freely, they obviously needed their approval. They expected their parents to help them get a start in life, find a suitable girl for them to marry, show them affection and understanding. They did not want their parents to interfere with them after they were married.

This word "understanding" kept recurring. They all complained that their parents and especially their fathers did not show understanding. When they had a problem with a girl, such as wanting to marry her, or falling in love with a girl from afar, they confided in their mother or an elder sister, or a brother's wife, never in a male relative "who would not understand" or who would "make a joke of it".

While they expected the young girls to come to marriage absolutely innocent, they complained that their fathers and elder brothers had not helped them to understand sexual life or did not even tell them about fundamentals. They were determined to tell their own children, but did not think "it was their place" to enlighten a younger brother. They wished that they could have a drink now and again with their fathers, but all agreed that this was out of the question.

When the conversation turned to religion, they laughingly agreed that they were bad Moslems. Only three out of this group of twenty-odd young men went to Friday prayers, and this not even regularly. Most of them did not fast during *Ramazan*, and only one, a boy who had left school at eleven and was apprenticed to a barber, went to the religious instruction course conducted by the *müftü*. They did not mind contributing money for religious purposes but here some heated teasing went on; it appeared that they only did so when people were looking. They did not go to the *imam* or the *müftü* for advice about problems which arose in their everyday life. "I have as much sense as he has, haven't I?", said one, and another boy said that the *imam* did not understand about the problems of daily life that they were facing. "My father gives me lessons in morals" said another, "I do not have to hear the same thing from others". As for spells, they said that this was something that women resorted to, but they knew that some of their friends had gone to the *imam* to have a spell broken.

They laughed at the idea of having a religious ceremony performed at weddings instead of a civil marriage. This way of marrying is often resorted to in the villages of the hinterland by men who want to marry more than one woman. Though illegal, it is socially acceptable. But they all agreed, even the university students, that they did not mind having prayers said before the wedding; "after all, everyone would like a prayer said when entering a new life", and everybody did have the prayers anyway, as well as when the children were born.

In politics, the young men follow the opinions of their fathers and group as a rule. The left and communism are considered as the same thing and dangerous. There is little outspoken criticism of religious practices, although less than half of the young men ever fast during *Ramazan*. Faith is vague, the following of religious precepts limited to not drinking or having sexual intercourse during *Ramazan*. The need to believe in something is apparent, and this goes for educated boys as well; they all seem to like the social approval which they receive when seen going to the mosque at *Ramazan* or on Fridays. However, it is difficult to say that religious and political convictions are linked in Bodrum.

In marriages, it is usual to see the "rich go to the rich, and the poor to the poor". Marriage is recognized by all as a step in life, bringing responsibility. It is considered as a social necessity and also as a proper way of regulating sexual life. For the first two or three years of married life, the young man still sees a lot of his friends, although he attends café parties less often. The parents expect the boys to marry, and marry girls of the parents' choice. They want the bride to look after them, to be "respectful" to her husband's family, and to be chaste and simple. That is why sometimes a girl from the village is preferred. They all thought that it did not matter if the girl was rich or poor, but "one does not look at a girl's wealth" and even if you did, "the girl's parents would resent it".

In this issue of marriage and the choice of a girl, there was quite a heated discussion. After agreeing that they would marry an educated girl, that is a girl educated beyond the secondary level, they got into discussion with each other and all the boys, university students included, came out with the admission that they preferred girls who had not left Bodrum, that is girls who had not gone to Izmir or elsewhere to attend *lycée* or college, because "the girls get spoiled in the large cities. We know, we have our spies and we follow their movements, we know where they go and with whom".

The boys, at heart, do not mind the girls studying, because there is respect for learning in this part of the world, but they know that once the girl has gone away to study, she is lost to them, for no educated girl has been known to marry a boy who had not had the same education, while quite often an educated boy will marry a girl who is only a primary school or a secondary school graduate. The new ways that girls bring back from Izmir or Istanbul are accepted, as part of further education, the girls have become "modern" and that is an inevitable part of higher education.

The girl they would like to marry should be a good housewife, faithful and possess commonsense. She should not use too much make-up and should be able to "appear in society with credit", this from the university students. She should not be too gay, as this is a sign of light-headedness. Not one boy mentioned that the girl should be pretty. "Of course she should be pretty, this is understood", they said, or "every girl has something pretty about her, her eyes or her hair", said another. It did not matter to these young men if the girl was Cretan or local, only three boys who were local said they would not marry a Cretan girl because Cretan girls "cannot leave the shops alone" and are "spoiled". But they all agreed that a girl from Bodrum was to be preferred to a girl from another part of the country. One of the boys said, "anyway, a girl from outside would not marry us." They wanted to stay single until the age of 25, or even 30, until they were "properly established", but asked the writer laughingly not to tell the girls that. They did not think there was anything wrong in marrying a girl of twenty or twenty-one, but after twenty-two, they said, "you wonder what's wrong". There should be a difference in age between men and women, say seven years.

Three or four boys said that they would not mind marrying a rich girl, even if she were richer than they, and these were the boys who were university and *lycée* students. All the others agreed that it was a bad thing and that it would lead to unpleasantness in the home, "she would think she is better" is the way one of them put it.

The same thing went for education; no one wanted to marry a girl who had been educated to a level higher than their own, and certainly not a girl who had been educated away from Bodrum, "they are all trollops" was the verdict of some. As for foreigners, i.e. girls from other countries and even from Istanbul and Ankara, "they are all right for fun" the Turkish girls being deemed just as bad as the foreigners. Five or six young men went to Germany as workers and married there but only one brought his wife back, and she did not like it so they returned. A marriage with a foreign girl would not work "because of the difference in religion". Further discussion revealed that what they meant by religion was culture, a way of doing things. Also, they would not know how to treat their parents correctly and it would be difficult for the children. One or two boys ventured the opinion that foreign girls "went with everybody, were immoral". Anyway, the parents would not approve of such a match.

Life after marriage is supposed to be more "serious", more "organized". There will be "responsibilities", work will be taken more seriously, "everything will change". Very few of them wanted the traditional seven-day, seven-night wedding, it was too expensive and too much trouble, but some of them said they would have to go through with it because their parents would want it. Only the simpler boys ventured to say that the traditional wedding was fun. The others preferred to spend the money on a trip, or on a boat.

GIRLS

If adults agree—albeit tacitly—that adolescence for the boys is a time to sow one's wild oats, this is not so for the girls. As soon as a girl has left school, her life is almost completely segregated. She will see the elder men in the family freely, but rarely such close relatives as a first or second cousin. She will not be allowed out on her own after dark and a close check will be kept on her movements. In the house she will share all her mother's work and help look after the younger children and in her spare time she will work on her trousseau. When she goes visiting with her mother or a sister or a sister-in-law, she will carry her embroidery or her sewing with her. Young girls are expected to be busy with something all the time and not to sit idle. A reputation for idleness is soon made and is to be avoided. When there is more than one girl in a family and the elder girl helps the younger with a piece of embroidery, there are endless discussions and teasings about whose trousseau the piece concerned will go to.

The life of the young girl is centred in the home. She will go to the cinema as often as is the fashion in her family and be able to look at the young men there, and be looked at. She may go down to the market to buy embroidery thread or materials in the day-time and be looked at by the young men through the windows of the cafés and by their fathers from the doorstep of their shops. She will also go to the "visiting days" of her mother and have a "day" herself, when girls of her age come with their embroidery. And she will go to the weddings and dance and sing there moderately, so as not to acquire a reputation for "wildness".

Adults appreciate the following qualities in young girls, and in this order: chastity, industry and sobriety. Young girls never smoke or drink and most will display signs of horror or disgust at the suggestion. They are also expected to be discreet and modest, not to talk out of turn and not to laugh or joke too much. When a mother catches her daughter having fits of laughter with a friend, she will apologize to any stranger present by saying "What do you expect? Girls are silly", and half-seriously rebuke the girls for laughing like "fools".

Young girls are expected to contribute to the family income. Some of them may take in sewing, knitting or embroidery, but then the money they earn in this way is used for the trousseau, unless the family is very poor. In the poorest families, girls go with their mother to earn money at seasonal jobs such as sorting tangerines, gathering olives or stringing dried figs. In this case they earn T.L. 10 a day, or a little less, but they cannot expect more than two months work in the year. They may also go to trim sponges, with some older women, and will get the same wage. But regular employment is out of the question for girls, and would be so, even if it were accepted socially. It is only the daughters of the Museum Director—a "stranger" from Istanbul, and of B, who is one of the most prosperous and well-known merchants in town, who can work in the Bank without incurring disapproval. The reason is that work outside the home brings girls in contact with men and these may "turn her head". This expression "turning a girl's head" is constantly heard. It is not imagined that a girl may be willing to share the company of men, or talk to them. It is assumed that if such instances occur, the girl's head has been "turned". The tutelage that parents have over their daughters conditions the latter for the tutelage of the husband.

Young girls do not have control of their money, when they earn any. The sums they get for their work are discussed in the house and the money given to them there. There is no secrecy attached to these transactions, while boys may earn money outside and parents have no way of finding out how much was received. When the girls do not earn any money, their expenses are part of the household expenses and they have to ask their fathers for any extras, such as a magazine or a novel, or a piece of fancy jewelry. In poor families, these demands are for clothing or shoes. Since the girls have no outside life and no club to go to, they do not, in fact, require money. The girls do not read more than the boys. They are fond of magazines which specialize in serialized picture-novels and in weeklies which describe the love life of well- known actors and entertainers. Vicari ously, through these two media and the cinema, they taste the forbidden pleasures of flirtation, romantic love and secret assignments, and rejoice in and approve of the happy endings and the punishment of the wicked. While they hope that they will be able to marry a handsome young man, and experience a love-marriage, they know that real life is far from resembling that of the magazines. What they recognize in the magazines—which for some unknown reasons are always translations of Italian picture-strips—is a familiar pattern of relationships: the mother-in-law, the jealous husband, the thwarted young girl, and all the aspects of "bad luck" and destiny which can beset human beings. To that extent, the world of the picture-strip is like the real world and the magazines are a lesson in chastity and morality given via Latin melodramas.

In politics, the young girls, like the boys, follow their parents. one of them told me that she voted differently and that she did not like to tell her father, for he might have disapproved. But they are not interested in politics, any more than the boys are. They share the general scepticism and follow the general trend of the towns-people, which is to vote at the requisite time for the party which is favoured. But in religion there is a marked difference: almost all of them fast during *Ramazan* and like to pray at least a few times a week. They do not go to Nedime Molla's Friday sermons—or to the other women preachers—although three or four of them receive religious instruction from her. Many of them accompany their mothers to the *mevlut* meetings, enjoying these social occasions which have religion as a starting point, but which end as a pleasant evening among neighbours.

Many young girls know that their life will really begin with marriage and feeling that girlhood is a time free from responsibility, they are not in a hurry to get married. But they all expect to be married not later than twenty and are only slightly worried about being "left on the shelf". This is a remote possibility, but they do not want to be left in a position where they will have to accept any boy just because time is running out. They all expect to be consulted when suitors appear and strongly deny that they may be tempted one day to elope. They want to marry with their parents' approval and not to "run to a stranger and be looked down upon by a mother-in-law".

Looking at some figures, it can be seen that in the last ten years there have been changes in the ages at which girls marry: while as many girls married between the ages of 15 and 19 a few years ago as they did between the ages of 19 and 24, the tendency since has been for fewer girls to marry in their middle teens. As far as boys are concerned, the same trend is observable, most boys marrying after 24. This may be attributed to the fact that in the last few years, life has become more expensive and agricultural products have experienced a fall in prices.

Table 20
Ages of Marriage

Age Groups	1955		1960		1965		1966	
	Girls	Boys	Girls	Boys	Girls	Boys	Girls	Boys
15-19	29	3	21	0	16	0	16	2
20-24	17	21	27	20	15	12	26	6
25-29	10	24	6	27	6	20	5	21
30-34*	2	5	2	6	1	5	1	1

* The few marriages after 35 are second marriages, except in two cases.

Another tendency in the last few years has been for the number of girls who marry below age to increase. The legal ages for marriage is 18 for girls and for boys. If a boy is below 17 and a girl below 15, the written permission of the parents is needed and the judge too has to grant permission if the girl is 14 and the boy 15. These early marriages, involving a very young girl, usually take place among the poorest people of the town, the labourers and fishermen.

In any case, marriage for both boys and girls is considered by adults to mark the end of adolescence and is similarly considered by the young people themselves.

CHAPTER NINE

MARRIAGE

LOCAL-CRETAN ATTITUDES

The locals of Bodrum have a saying whenever marriage is mentioned: "Give your girl to a Cretan but do not marry a Cretan girl", and any Cretan girl, asked whether she would marry a local, is sure to exclaim: "and be sent to work in the fields? God forbid!" Indeed, out of the fifty-odd marriages that take place each year in Bodrum—and for the last ten years the figures have barely changed—only four or five are "mixed" marriages. In these marriages, it is the boy rather than the girl, who is a Cretan. Some fairly simple facts explain these attitudes. The local community, owning and getting a living out of the land, needs the labour of women. The incomes from harvests and crops and the sale of animals come once or twice a year in lump sums and are apportioned by the head of the household over the whole year. Except for the religious festivals, which are an occasion for spending more on food and renewing the wardrobe of the family, the standard of living of the locals does not experience ups and downs and is very much the same all through the year and from year to year. Even a particularly good harvest will rarely result in over-spending but the money will be spent on a wedding or a piece of equipment for the land. Also, the Bodrum "local" community, like any peasant community, is used to and appreciates sobriety in dress and thrift in all things.

On the other hand, the Cretans being mostly sea-faring people, get their income in windfalls and this income is subjected to greater hazards than that of the peasants. Their standard of living is accordingly subjected to constant ups and downs. Not having land and rarely keeping a cow, they do not enjoy a continuous supply of such basic goods as the land provides and are much dependent upon grocers and shops. They will eat and drink well for a week and then practically starve for the next. The constant danger experienced by the men at sea, fishing or diving, makes them avid for pleasure when they are on land and safe for a few weeks and the subsequent recklessness pervades family life. The women are just a little less reckless than the men, since they have to think about the children day in and day out. And also, sea-work does not require the labour of women; even if in the old days the women made nets, they made them at home, and when they have to trim sponges this is also work that keeps them at home and which they do at odd moments in the course of the daily housework. Because of these factors, work in the fields, under the scorching sun or in the rain and wind, appears extremely hard to the Cretan women, while the insecure life of the Cretans seems unbearable to the local women. In the mind of a local woman, to be left alone at home for months on end or even weeks, and having to face decisions and emergencies is a distasteful prospect, while the Cretan woman is much more independent of her husband in daily life; she arranges her budget as she sees fit, does her own shopping, and is free to buy herself things if she saves a little money on the side. It may well be that, quite apart from these factors, the mobility of the sea encourages recklessness while the stability of the land encourages steadfastness. To the local ant, the Cretan is the cricket.

This, however, must not obscure the fact that the Cretan is a harder working man than the local. He is also more able to find and do odd jobs and change trades than the local. There are no jobs that he finds distasteful or beneath him. Thus it is that one finds Cretan sponge divers working at all kinds of jobs in the winter, while the local man will spend the winter in the cafés, after having gathered in the harvest.

Hence the attitudes of the two communities towards each other where marriage is concerned has some basis in reality, apart from the antagonism which always pits newcomers and minorities against the established majority; a local knows that Cretans make good husbands who do not overwork their wives, while Cretans dislike the idea of giving their daughter to someone who will make the girl work in the field like a common agricultural labourer.

The unwillingness to marry between the two communities does not apply to marriages with "foreigners", that is with people who live outside Bodrum. Half the marriages on both sides take place between a Bodrum boy or girl and someone from either one of the surrounding villages or from Izmir or any other town in the west. This proportion will increase because of the increasing number of girls who leave Bodrum to get a higher education; once they do, it is not expected that they will return but will marry someone from outside, since the boys of Bodrum who do get a higher education do not come back either but settle in Istanbul or Izmir. As was seen earlier, no educated girl expects to come back to Bodrum and marry in the town.

Marriages are expensive in Bodrum and, like all activities which require money, are tied to a seasonal pattern. Sponge-divers marry in October when their contracts end and when they receive the final pay of the year; fishermen marry in the winter, when fish commands the highest price of the year; people who live off the land marry their children in the spring—to secure some additional female labour for the planting and later harvest—and in January and February, after the olive and the tangerine crops have been sold. Although many young people in the larger cities marry on a joint salary these days, this is not so in Bodrum. Tradition, and the security-seeking mentality of the people demand, and receive, guarantees on both sides. These guarantees are solemnly, if discreetly, discussed by the families beforehand.

Custom requires that the young man should provide the house, gold pieces and gold bracelets to a value ranging between T.L. 1,000 and 3,000, the materials for the bride's personal trousseau, and part of the expenses for the wedding. The bride's family provides all the household goods, materials for the bridegroom's personal trousseau and the wedding expenses. The most expensive item in a marriage is the house. Until four of five years ago, a young man could have a house built on the family plot for as little as T.L. 5,000. But nowadays, with the pressure resulting from tourism, it is difficult to have a house built for less than T.L. 15,000. This is a considerable figure for a group whose annual income rarely exceeds T.L. 4,000. Weddings are therefore one of the occasions when a man gets into debt, to relatives, to the bank or, if he has no relatives and nothing to mortgage, then to the usurers. The easiest way to secure money is to wait for the time when the bank gives out the seasonal credit loans to the tangerine growers, fishermen and sponge-divers and then borrow money on the pretext of getting a new piece of equipment for the boat or for the tangerine grove. Hence the large number of weddings in early February, the time when the bank gives the "management credit" to the tangerine growers.

The expenses incurred by the bride's family are less. For in Bodrum what is meant by "household goods" is slightly different to what is meant in large cities. The furniture may include a double bed and a few upright chairs and a sewing-machine. There will be a good many mattresses, quilts and pillows and a few rugs. There may be a carpet or two, and many copper pots and pans, trays and bowls. There will be linen, cutlery and dishes, and even the brooms and dustpan. These household effects would have been bought over the years and the expense would not be felt all at once by the bride's family. It is in the days immediately preceding the wedding, when many visitors come to eat and drink, that the expenses will suddenly soar. Hence the Bodrum saying, when a man complains that he has no money left, "Have you married a daughter?"

The gold given to the bride by the bridegroom is a guarantee against the future and preferred to a sum in the bank. Any gold piece or gold bracelet can be exchanged for money at any time at the jeweller's. The gold pieces have a rate which is published daily in the newspapers and the bracelets are weighed and the money paid accordingly. An unwritten convention allows women to sell their gold at their own discretion. Attempts by men to sell their wives' bracelets or gold pieces is often a cause for divorce in the villages. Although the Civil Code introduced in 1923 provides for alimony and subsistence allowances in cases of divorce, women in the villages and in the small towns prefer to have gold at their disposal. In fact, the women wear the gold on their person, the pieces strung on a piece of ribbon around their neck and the bracelets on their right arm. A usual sight, barely noticeable after a while, is the gleam of gold among tattered or faded clothing.

THE CEREMONIES

Weddings in Bodrum last "seven days and seven nights", as it is said in old stories, or at least as many days up to seven that the families of the young people can afford. The number rarely falls below three. The week-long celebration is the last step in a sequence of events which may go back a year or even more.

On the girls' side, preparations for the wedding really start on the day she finishes primary school or the evening technical school, for it is then that she begins to embroider the pieces of her trousseau. Her mother and her grandmother will help, the former very often by crocheting yards of lace which will adorn the edges of the pillow slips and the *sedir* covers. When the girl reaches seventeen or so, the father and mother will begin to receive requests from friends and relatives who have a son of marriageable age and status, that is from a boy who has finished his military service and who has begun to earn a living. In some cases, the young man will remember the girl from their days at primary school, or would have noticed her in the market or at family gatherings, or going up and down on the bus to Izmir. In some cases she will be a neighbour and he will have seen her as she flits in and out of neighbours' houses. It also happens that the young man is away at work in another city or even in Europe and in this case his family makes the choice and the young people only see each other's photographs. In rare cases, and this happens especially in the case of marriage between first and second cousins, the young people would know each other a little and reach what they term "an understanding". "Reaching an understanding" is the local equivalent for a love-match, based on the exchange of a few sentences and a great many glances. Since many of the people of Bodrum marry among close relatives, it is rare that the young people do not meet and do not know in advance something about one another.

The girl's family does not have to accept the first comer and girls are rarely informed about unsuccessful candidates. A girl may be told, however, that there have been many "refusals", as a compliment and neighbours and relatives are told the same thing, as a means of keeping away undesirable suitors. But when a suitable offer is made, the girl is informed by her mother and it is only if she likes the boy that the offer is accepted. It often happens, however, that parents are keen on a young man for prestige or financial reasons, or simply on the grounds that the young man will make a reasonable husband. Most girls will bow down to the choice of their parents as the "will of God", but a girl who does not has only one other choice, and that is to say "no" on the day of the civil marriage ceremony. Needless to say, this happens very rarely. Most girls are keen on marriage and enter into it as a normal part of life, with no qualms about possible unhappiness. It is only when a girl has reached an understanding with a boy, and the boy has been unsuccessful in his demand, that custom has provided a loophole, widely resorted to in the villages and quite often in small towns, i.e. eloping.

One of the reasons why more girls run away in the villages than in the towns is that village life is more propitious to meetings between boys and girls. Working in the fields all day, bringing home the cattle at night, fetching water from a remote fountain, provide many opportunities for secret assignments, while in the small towns girls are more severely guarded and such meetings well-nigh impossible. Eloping is frowned upon, but only moderately. The custom is for the boy to meet the girl at night and for the two of them to run away into the coutryside for a day or two. It is assumed that the girl has lost her virginity and then it becomes the boy's duty to marry her, so the wedding duly takes place. In these cases, the parents either give the girl her trousseau or she makes it herself after marriage if her parents—usually the father—are so angry as to refuse her their sanction. The reason why the custom is frowned upon is because it is a flouting of parental authority. Were it not for the extraordinary premium which this society places upon the chastity of women, elopement would lose its meaning. As it is, it is one way in which young people can freely choose each other and marry for love. Usually, after the birth of the first child, even the most adamant parent will be softened. The young couple will bring the baby home, kiss their elders' hands and all will be well. All they will have missed is the long drawn-out nuptials.

In a conventional case, when the offer is accepted, through the intermediary of common friends, the boy's family or "boy's side" pays the girl's side an official visit. This visit is called "giving one's word". Someone from the boy's family will say: "In the name of God and with the permission of the Prophet, will you give your daughter in marriage to our son?", and the girl's side will reply: "We have found the offer suitable and we accept". Then the girl is called in and she meets her future family for the first time. The next day, the boy's mother or his sister come and take the girl's measurements for the ring and the day of the official engagement is decided upon. This must either be a Thursday or a Sunday. On the afternoon of that day the boy's family send over to the girl's house the traditional gifts: gold pieces and bracelets, lengths of material for dresses and underwear, slippers and shoes, and a present of coffee, sugar and Turkish Delight.

In the evening, everyone meets at the girl's house. The men and the women sit in separate rooms, coffee and Turkish Delight are served, and the *fiancée* is brought out. An honoured guest or an elderly relative places the ring, a plain gold band, on the girl's right fourth finger—it will go on the left on the day of the marriage ceremony—and she goes round, kissing hands and being kissed on the cheek in return. It is only after this that the boy is allowed to shake hands with his future wife, quite formally. On these occasions, it is unseemly for either of them to look at each other or smile. The *fiancée* will then sit down and the boy will rejoin the men. After their betrothal, the young couple will not see each other until the day of the civil marriage ceremony.

A week or two later, again on a Thursday or on a Sunday, the fiancée's gifts will go to the boy's house: lengths of material for a suit, underclothing and presents for the rest of the family, such as handkerchiefs and socks, all wrapped in squares of embroidered silk. It is with this embroidery that the *fiancée* will impress the mother and sisters of the groom as to her ability and good taste. With these, two kinds of pastry, one stuffed with cheese and meat and the other with nuts and raisins, are also offered. The boy's ring is also sent on that day. That evening, someone from the girl's family puts the ring on the boy's finger. From now on, the women of both sides will begin seeing each other if they didn't know one another previously. Arrangements for the wedding will be discussed and the trousseau examined and discussed at length.

The next event is the civil marriage ceremony, which takes place at the town hall. Marriage ceremonies are performed by the Chief Clerk and are very brief. The bride and groom have to submit photographs for the register and the marriage certificate, certificates of good health and birth certificates. The banns would have been published and hung for three weeks and an appointment made with the Chief Clerk, who performs the marriage ceremony. This ceremony has replaced the old religious marriage contract of pre-Republic days and, as a result, some of the old customs connected with it. One of them is that such a ceremony cannot take place between the two festivals of *Ramazan* and *Kurban*. In the last few years this period has precisely coincided with the most prosperous period for Bodrum, which is the winter. This is why people have enclined to have the civil marriage performed before *Ramazan*, in the autumn, and leave the expensive wedding festivities until the winter. Eventually, the Hegira calendar will bring *Ramazan* and *Kurban*—separated by nine weeks—to the summer and then young people will have to wait longer for the wedding festivities.

The civil marriage is a very brief ceremony. When Ali Dayi, the piper, married his last daughter—and heaved a huge sigh of relief at the thought of having no more wedding expenses to come—it lasted exactly seven minutes. The bride and groom were nicely dressed; the girl's hair had been dressed and her lips rouged. But everyone else came in their daily clothes. We all sat on the chairs along the wall, provided for such occasions, the Chief Clerk read the legal formula quickly, the young people and the witnesses signed, a box of Turkish Delight was passed round, the young couple kissed the hands of their elders and everybody dispersed as quickly as they had come. Although this part of the wedding ceremony is the least festive, it marks two important events: first, the young people are now properly married in the eyes of the state, entitled to the rights and subject to all the duties thereof; second, the groom can now come and go to the bride's house as often as he likes and they can go out together for short walks, albeit chaperoned by a younger member of the family. They are still not left alone, for as long as the traditional wedding festivities have not taken place, they are not man and wife in the eyes of the community.

Provided that the date of the civil marriage has been chosen carefully, the wedding festivities can begin a month or two later, as soon as both sides can provide the necessary funds. Food and drink must be given to dozens of people in both households and for days on end, dish-washers hired to wash the dishes as soon as people have finished eating, for no one has enough plates and glasses to go round. Music-makers must be brought from Milas and put up for many nights and entertained with food and drink, and camels and jeeps, or boats, hired to convey the trousseau, the bride and the guests from one place to another. Many people on these occasions charge "bride's rates", such as the hairdresser, the jeep or camel drivers and the music-makers. Such a traditional wedding festivity will cost a lower-income family T.L. 3,000, or a little less than their yearly income.

The seven-day wedding used to last from Thursday to Thursday-nowadays termed the old week—before the Republican era ushered in Sunday as a day of rest. The "new week" starts on a Sunday and ends on a Sunday. When the invitations are handed round, people say "our wedding will take place in the old week", or in the new, as the case may be and people know on which day to start their visiting. In Bodrum, invitations are not written. They are issued in the shape of small cakes of soap or small hand towels. Most people prefer the towels, which are useful and durable, to the soap, which is of very poor quality. Ali Dayi the piper bought 180 small hand towels for the wedding of his daughter, and the writer received one, duly wrapped in newspaper, with her name written on it.

One wedding attended by the writer took place in the "new week" and she was invited by the bridegroom's father, a sea captain and the brother-in-law of Aunt Zubeyde. The boy is a sponge-diver and Cretan on both sides, and the bride lived in Cefaluka, on the western tip of the peninsula. Her mother is a local woman and her father Cretan, the Cefaluka lighthouse keeper and uncle of the boy. The grandfather had emigrated from Crete and had prospered as a carrier of goods between the islands. He had bought the largest and handsomest house in Cefaluka, which had been vacated by some departing Greek seaman. The bride's father and the bridegroom's mother were first cousins and so these two knew each other from childhood. The boy's mother thought that a girl from Cefaluka would be less spoiled than a Cretan girl from Bodrum and pleased to come and live in Bodrum, which is a large city by comparison.

On the first day of the wedding, a camel was brought to the boy's house and loaded with the "bride's load", a chest and a deep basket. The chest was a bright affair of wood covered with gilt tinsel with grenadine velvet insets and contained the wedding-dress, the wedding shoes, the veil, and small gifts of clothing for the bride's family. The basket contained loaves of bread and *helva*. When the camel arrived at the harbour, a boat was waiting to take the "bride's load" to Cefaluka. In the bridegroom's house, there was a lot of activity. The window-shutters were being painted blue and the yard walls being white-washed. The bridegroom's mother was in the kitchen, starting the preparation of the many dishes which would be eaten in the next few days. The camel went on its way, swaying slowly along the narrow streets to the harbour, and its special bride's bell boomed sonorously, announcing to all Bodrum that a trousseau was on its way. People came out in their doorways or looked out of windows, admiring the chest. "May God grant them happiness" said matrons to each other across the street. At the harbour, a boat was ready to take the chest to Cefaluka because there is no road there. In the days to come, there would be a constant coming and going of boats between Bodrum and Cefaluka. The boat, which belonged to a friend of the bridegroom's ,was an old *tirandil*, with its paint flaked off and its compressor pipe neatly coiled on top of the cabin. We all embarked and the engine was started. The wind was with us and within the hour we had passed

Cos and were in sight of Cefaluka, a huddle of white houses set along a sandy beach. The writer counted thirty-three houses and a school. As we drew near, we saw the bride's house, the tallest of them all, built a little to the side of the pier. It had double doors of wrought iron and a few people were standing in front of it, waving their arms to greet us. We came off the boat and were inside the house in a minute. The downstairs *sala* was a large room with a high ceiling, adorned by a nice wooden staircase. But the whole place had been neglected and looked poor. It was full of women talking, sewing pieces of cloth and they all greeted us and got up to see the chest. The bride—Selvi, who deserved her name because she was as tall and slim as a cypress—sat on a chair sewing lace on a length of white muslin. The chest was taken into a room on the right and the bride and her friends went in there to see the wedding dress. The writer went with them and we all admired the dress, which was long and white, with trimmings of nylon lace. The veil was adorned with the same lace and everybody was pleased when a pair of nylon lace gloves were found, tucked amid the other things. The bride was urged to try the dress on, but she demurred because she was afraid that the children, who were running in and out, might spoil it.

After a while, plates of food were brought and everybody dipped their spoon in each dish and ate the food with chunks of bread. There were beans and chickpeas cooked with meat, rice, and a tray of sweet pastry. Young girls came in from the village and were soon singing and dancing, but the dancing and singing were desultory. We were told that it would get more lively in the evening. In the afternoon we went back to Bodrum and were there early, because the wind had turned and was with us again.

The writer did not go to Cefaluka again for the next four days. In these days the bride and her relatives and friends would complete the trousseau, the copper pots and pans would go and come back from the tinsmith's, the chest filled with clothes, and the embroidered sheets stitched on to the quilts. In the evening, the women would sing and dance, and the men be entertained in the café or in a room in the house, where they would drink *raki* with hors d'oeuvres of cheese and olives. The whole village will help with fetching and carrying and with the loan of pots and pans.

On the fifth day, which was a Thursday, we again went to Cefaluka for an important landmark in the festivities, the "wild henna" night. This time we left in the afternoon and the bridegroom's sisters and aunts came with us, but not the bridegroom's mother. With us on the boat were the music-makers—paid for by the bridegroom's father—a four-piece band calling itself the Milas Jazz Ensemble and made up of a violin, a drum, a pipe and a kind of banjo. They were wild-looking men and—as is the case with all musicians— suspected of having gypsy blood. They had started drinking in the bridegroom's house and began to play as soon as we took off. They only stopped when the waves got too bothersome and huddled next to the cabin, drinking from a bottle which they passed around.

When we reached Cefaluka, it was cold and rainy. Inside, the *sala* had been straightened up and wooden chairs and settees put against the wall, and the floor covered with rugs and mats. The place was full of women and girls and we were told that the bride was in in the room at the right, being prepared for the application of henna to her hair. It is said that the application of henna is a thing which pleases God and it is believed that it is daughter of the Prophet, Fatma, who started it. There can be no doubt that it is an extremely ancient custom and which was known to the ancient Egyptians. The fact that Fatma used henna has conferred religious significance on the act, although no one knows why. Be that as it may, older women apply henna to their hands during the "three months"— the two preceding *Ramazan* and the month of fasting itself— and it is customary to apply henna to brides. The "wild henna night" is the occasion when henna is applied to the bride's hair. The bride came out after a while, dressed in a red dressing-gown and with her head wrapped in a blue towel and as soon as she came in, the band struck up a dancing air and she began to dance, followed by her friends. In this case, the bride had chestnut hair and the henna would give it an auburn sheen. But this custom is dying out, because most girls do not want to spoil the colour of their hair, if it is fair or dark.

Later that night, after everyone had eaten and drunk, the men in a separate room as usual, the bride was taken into the kitchen for her bath. The henna was washed out of her hair and she was put to bed to get some rest, for the next two nights would be strenuous. That night we all stayed at the house, sleeping on mattresses laid side by side on the floor in the two large rooms upstairs. Most people did not undress, just took their shoes and outer clothing off.

Next morning, after a breakfast of figs, olive oil and olives washed down with weak tea, we went round some of the neighbours' houses, returning dishes and pans. The men had gone back to Bodrum the night before and only the bride's closest friends and two cousins of the bridegroom remained. The rest of the day passed in chatting and desultory singing and dancing. Everybody was waiting for the evening, which is called the "*temel devren*" evening. The *temel devren* is the traditional ceremonial costume of the Bodrum women. It is a long robe of burgundy-coloured velvet embroidered with raised designs in gold thread and a tunic of the same material, also embroidered, is worn over it. The head-dress which goes with it is a red veil embroidered in gold. *Temel devren* means "shaking the foundations" because the dress is embroidered with real gold and used to cost a fortune. Nowadays no one has one made, and if the bride does not have one in the family, then she borrows one from relatives or friends. Osman Bey, who is the Education Officer and very attached to the old traditions, has bought an old *temel devren* for his oldest daughter and is now looking for one for his youngest, but they are hard to come by and are still quite expensive.

When evening came, the bride went back into the room at the right to put on the heavy robe. When she came out, everybody applauded and she danced the Bodrum *zeybek* in it, moving slowly because of the weight of the robe. Later on, she took it off and put on her everyday dress. In very traditional households, the bride keeps the robe on throughout the evening, but in most cases the custom has become symbolical and is slowly disappearing. When Fatma Oktem married her fourth daughter, there was no *temel devren* evening, because the third daughter had taken it with her when she went to live in Holland with her husband, who works in a factory there. All the daughters agreed to this because they wanted the "Europeans to see our customs".

The next morning, Saturday, we were awoken at seven by the music, playing wildly in the *sala* downstairs. It appeared that the music-makers had not gone to bed at all, but had played all night in the village café, entertaining the Cefaluka men and drinking. When the writer came down, the bride was there dressed in her wedding-dress and veil, and wearing her gold earrings and bracelets. Her gold pieces were pinned to her waist with a small ribbon. She was sitting at the side, looking quite pale and exhausted, and drinking tea. Women were coming in and out as usual and the men in her family were sitting in the *sala* also, recovering from the previous night. The kitchen was again full of neighbours helping out with the cooking of beans and chick-peas, rice and pastry. Bowls of yoghourt were standing on the window-sill and a large tray of meat balls in tomatosauce was simmering on the fireplace. In the back yard, three women, the washers-up, were washing the dishes form the night before. All day people came in and out, and some more dancing and singing went on, but without the music-makers. Towards late afternoon, the excitement began to mount. People were rushing to the door to see if the boat from Bodrum was approaching. For on this night the bridegroom would come with all his family and this was the last night that the girl would spend under the parental roof.

The boat duly arrived and, after the bride had kissed the hands of her parents-in-law, she shook hands formally with the bridegroom. This is a new development; in the old days the bridegroom did not come on that night but now, as Mrs. Oral, the owner of the Artemis Pansiyon says, "everything has become mixed up, nobody knows what should be done any longer". She liked the Cefaluka wedding— she is a distant relative—because it was fairly traditional. But then, she is a Cretan; the locals say that the bridgeroom always comes on that night. The bridgroom did not stay in the *sala*, but joined the men upstairs and the bride and her friends sat and talked while the guests were eating. The bride herself did not eat, although people urged her to and many women looked at her and said, "poor girl, how can you expect her to eat, it is not easy ot leave one's home". On hearing this, the mother of the bride began to weep and then the bride also wept. After the meal, which was eaten by everyone out of common bowls and trays with spoons and only an occasional fork, the men and the bridegroom came back and the young couple rose to dance the *zeybek*. This dance is very slow and dignified, with intricate footwork and is believed to represent the gathering and pressing of grapes. At least this is the theory of the Museum Director. It is danced everywhere in the Aegean and is obviously of very ancient origin. When men dance it, in some of the wilder parts of the coast, they do it alone and anyone who would dance at the same time risks his life, or his limbs, when he does so. For the *zeybek* is the dance of the *efe*, the wild mountaineers of the region for whom honour and individualism are the only rule.

All through the dance the bride did not smile, although the bride-groom did because he had been drinking and was excited and relax-ed. Other people rose, including children and, helped along by the presence of the men, all fairly intoxicated, the evening proceeded with a lot of noise and shouting. At two in the morning, people left. The boat took everybody back and the house was hurriedly straigh-tened up, everybody helping. And the preparations began for the "wise henna" night.

The bride removed her wedding finery and a long white nightgown was put on her. A white veil with lace embroidery covered her head and the writer was told that this was not customary with the Cretans. At local weddings in the village, a red wedding scarf is put on the girl's head. Then she sat down. Ali Dayi the piper, who had come that day as a special treat, began to play some gay little tunes. The women and girls sang or recited little quartrains praising the bride and the bridegroom and using metaphors from pastry and sweet-making to describe the sweetness of the bride, the strength of the groom, the quality of their future life together, which would be as "fine as sieved flour", as "sweet as spun sugar", as "tasty as black pepper". A small bowl, filled with the greenish mixture of henna and water, was stood on a chair near the bride and while the women sang and recited, the henna was applied to the bride's hands.

Since this was a Cretan wedding, the bride's aunt on her mother's side applied the henna to the girl's palms. The hands were wrapped in white cloth and after a while the bride washed her hands and went to bed. At local weddings, the custom is slightly different, as was seen at Ali Dayi's daughter's wedding. Since the girl had a married brother, it was her sister-in-law who applied the henna to her right hand and left foot—so that her heels may be like "pomegra-nates", as it is said in the old stories—and then a friend of the bride applied the henna to the left hand and the right foot. In that case, the white cloth will stay on all night and the bride wash her feet and hands in the morning. Also, at local weddings the music is sad and there are no songs. Ali Dayi's daughter told me "the music must be sad and make people cry." When the writer asked her why, she said she did not know, that this was the custom. Her grandmo-ther said that it was to mark the last occasion when the girl would be with her parents. However, in both cases, the guests put coins in the henna bowl and the money was later given to the bride.

Finally, the last day of the wedding dawned. It was Sunday and on that evening, the bride would go to her new home. The last day is the "bride-fetching" day. This time, a boat was hired in Cefaluka and the trousseau, which had adorned the sides of the *sala* on the "wise henna" night, was put aboard. There were thirty-five cushions and bolsters, fourteen quilts, seven blankets, fourteen mattresses, five rugs and one large carpet. There were also the chest and the sewing-machine, which had to be strapped to the top of the cabin. Since the bride had no sisters, some of her friends and cousins went with the boat to "set up house", meaning that they would take the trousseau to the young people's house and put everything in place, the rugs on the floor, the curtains on the windows and the shining copper ware on the shelves and on the mantelpiece over the fireplace. The bed, which had been ordered in Bodrum, had not come to Cefaluka and had gone straight to the new house. Now the girls would put on it the most beautifully embroidered sheets and the pink satin quilt, and the bride's nightgown and négligée of blue nylon would be hung on a nail next to it.

In Cefaluka, the day passed quietly. The bride was again dressed in her wedding dress, her veil and the customary long silver threads were hung on the sides of her head. Through the nylon of her gloves could be seen the stains of henna on her palms. All that was left were a few packages containing odds and ends which had been collected together at the last moment. We were now waiting for the "bride-fetchers", that is the boy's side and his friends. At two in the afternoon, the boats were spotted. One contained the women, who could be seen huddled with lots of children all over the cabin and at the sides, and the other contained the band and the boy's friends and some of his relatives. The bridegroom's father was at the tiller, come to fetch his daughter-in-law in person.

Everybody disembarked and alla except the younger men came into the *sala*. The bride came out and kissed the elders' hands dutifully and then sat down. The band came in and began to play and the girls danced again, but this time the bride danced alone and she was repeatedly asked to dance by all her friends. She danced every time, but always came back to sit at the place of honour which had been prepared for her, and at one point she began to cry. No one took any notice, for as the saying goes, "brides weep, but go". Every woman in the room had to get up once and dance even a few steps, because if they did not, then "the bride would die within the year". After an hour or so it was time to go. The bridegroom was waiting in Bodrum, dancing and drinking with his friends, and we would get there in the evening. The bride got up and her father covered her face with her veil. She kissed her mother's and her father's hands in formal leave-taking and then, supported on each side by her grandfather and her brother-in-law, she came out of the house and walked along the beach to the boat, not looking back. On such occasions it is the custom, in local households, to make the mother sit on the daughter's bed and stay there until the child is in her new house. Again, no one knows how the custom originated and few people follow it in town, although they say it is quite often carried out in the villages.

A large pink scarf was tied to each of the boats' masts, so that people at sea would see a bride was aboard, while a little boat which joined the convoy, having no silk scarf, tied a pink towel to its mast. People waved from the shore and the village gendarmes shot their rifles in celebration.

The bride sat at the prow and a black coat was put around her knees. All throughout the journey she sat with her head bowed and only smiled faintly once or twice. Children began to feel tired and hungry, mothers opened up kerchief bundles and got out bread and olives. In the other boat, the men were getting gayer and gayer, madly dancing on the roof of the cabin, outlined against the grey sky. The music of the violin and the pipe was wafted on the wind now and again. The wind was from the north, cold.

On the way back the old women begged the captain to go by Cos, which some had not seen since the First World War. As we neared the shore, they broke out excitedly in Cretan dialect, remembering old landmarks, enviously pointing out the factory, the tomato plant, the large hotels and the shopping centre, the asphalted avenues built by the Italians after the Balkan wars. On the island, people spotted the pink silk flags and began to run towards the port. The women began to joke: "We are invading Cos, what if we are arrested?". "Never mind, Turks can always take care of a couple of Greeks". The old women had tears in their eyes as we got nearer. We went sailing alongside the quay and into the port. On the other boat, the boys were drinking, the band struck an island *zeybek* tune, the boys danced on the roof. That is how we entered the port of Cos, with the bride standing up at the prow.

The Greek customs-boat put out and came alongside, to escort us out of the port. All stopped, and the captain of the boys' boat passed his brandnew son over to the Greek customs officer, the child was kissed and petted and passed back. The crew were given handkerchiefs by the bride's elder brother, the sailors teased the old women, "You are Cretans, don't you speak Greek?", and the old women joked back.

We arrived in Bodrum at nightfall. A few people had gathered to watch us arrive. The captain got his "bride" money, and the procession formed: the band in front, the bride with the overcoat over her shoulders. leaning on her relatives, and everybody else behind, straggled along the street to the other end of the town, the Cretan quarter. People stopped the bride en route, "blocking the bride's path", and received money and drinks and sweets in return for "opening the way", a custom followed by all in Bodrum.

The bridegroom was waiting close to his doorstep. He shook the bride by the hand, rather shamefacedly, and she kept her eyes lowered. On the doorstep, relatives rushed and smeared the bride's lips with honey, so that married life might be sweet. The local custom is different: the bride is given a small plate into which oil and honey have been mixed. She has to dip her finger into the bowl and touch the four sides of the door, rather like making the sign of the cross, and then her mother-in-law puts some of the honey on her lips.

The bride is then taken inside and made to rest. The bridegroom continues to sing and dance with his friends until the evening prayer, which he attends in the mosque. He then comes back with the *imam*, who says a prayer by the door of the bedroom. From behind the door, the bride, attended by women, says "amen", and the bridegroom is admitted into the room. The custom is that a bowl filled with water is put behind the door and the bridegroom more often than not will stumble over it. At that moment the bride must seize the opportunity and stamp on his foot so as to ensure that she will be mistress in the home.

But the groom's trials are not over: one of the older women will ask him tree times: "Do you take this girl as your wife?", and he has to say "yes" three times. It is only then that the newly-weds will be left alone, only to be disturbed later in the night by the bridegroom's friends clamouring for and receiving a tray of sweet pastry.

The next day the writer came upon the father-in-law, a sea

captain, in the café. He looked exhausted and we talked about the wedding. ."People expect all this but we are worn out. Thank God it's over." The wedding had cost him a lot of money for these parts, about T.L. 5000 not counting the house, for it is he who had bought the bride's jewelry.

But there was a sequel to the wedding, and apparently, not an unusual one. Early the next morning, around six, the bridegroom was seen hurrying towards the *imam*'s house. Knowing smiles and jokes followed him.

Upon enquiry, the following story was told the writer: it appears that there is some one in the village of Cefaluka who puts a spell on the grooms who take as wives girls from Cefaluka. On the night of the wedding, the bridegroom is struck with impotence. A few days before the wedding, the bridegroom was overheard saying to his friends in a café, "and suppose that this happens to me?". And sure enough, this is exactly what happened, and the poor bridegroom had to rush to the *imam* to have the spell removed. As to the nature of the spell, it is reminiscent of that which changed Tiresias from a man into a woman: two snakes have to be caught intertwining, killed and put under the pillow in the bridal bed!

For a week, the bride is not disturbed, No one comes to visit her and she only goes to see relatives at night. On the seventh day, the *imam* is invited to the new home and a *mevlut* prayer is read. This heralds the "opening of the bride's house". After that, everyone may come to congratulate the bride and look at the new house and the trousseau. This custom does not vary and is strictly followed by the local and the Cretan community in Bodrum.

About ten days after the wedding, the writer and Mrs. Oral went to visit the bride. We were greeted at the door by her mother-in-law and we sat down in the newly-furnished sitting room. The bride was wearing a skirt and sweater and had lost her stilted air. She was natural and relaxed, but sat in her own house a little as a guest. It was obvious that her mother-in-law was still her aunt and she was still behaving like a modest young girl ought to, sitting quietly and speaking only when addressed. Her mother-in-law entertained us, telling us about the aftermath of the wedding; "A house after a wedding is like a house which has caught fire", she said, and complained about the rowdiness of her son's friends, who nearly "brought the roof down with their shouting and dancing". She left us now and again, to look after the dinner, because she was cooking for

the whole family, so as not to tire the bride. Indeed, the bride's
fireplace was still as clean as on the day it was white-washed and it
was obvious that no fire had yet been lit in it.

Although this wedding and that of Ali Dayi's daughter were very
traditional, not all the people of Bodrum go through with all the
intricacies and expense. A new custom has come to Bodrum, which
is followed by more "modern" couples, such as school-teachers and
some of the more educated locals. It is still a very public performance, but lasts only one evening and costs infinitely less. This is the
balo, which comes from the word ball. In a survey conducted among
the Bodrum women, half of them said they would prefer a *balo* to a
traditional wedding and many of them said that they had had one
traditional wedding in the family already and they would like to
try the *balo*, which was becoming "the fashion". Only the poorest
and the least educated women opted for the traditional wedding,
"because it is the custom" or because "the other side may not like
a *balo*". It must be pointed out that the traditional wedding is more
fun for people with low incomes, and practically the only entertainment, together with circumcision, that they enjoy. The *balo* is the
Bodrum version of the wedding reception, and the writer was invited
to one such by Ismet. On this occasion, two of this cousins were
being married. Both were the children of prosperous shopkeepers
in the town, and the girl's mother was local.

Since it was summer, the reception took place in the open air
cinema which had been rented for only T.L. 150. Had it been winter,
the reception would have taken place in the winter quarters of the
cinema, a battered old building seating 430 people. This time, the
seats of the cinema had been arranged in a square, leaving an open
space in the middle. The Milas Jazz Ensemble was there, sitting
at a table fitted with a microphone and decorated with bottles of
raki. But there was no drink in sight for the guests. People began
to troop in at about eight o'clock, and the women had their children
with them and their babies in their arms. The men and women did
not sit on separate sides, but in clusters. The men came in and out
of the cinema, and there was a lot of drinking out of bottles put
discreetly under chairs or from hip flasks. At some time during the
evening, glasses of lemonade and plates of biscuits were circulated
and there was no other food or drink. The heavy expense of feeding
dozens of people for many days was thus avoided.

On one side of the open space sat the bride and groom, surrounded by their parents and relatives. They were the only ones to have a table, decorated with a vase of flowers. The bride wore her wedding-dress and veil and she had the customary silver threads hanging on both sides of her head. The groom wore a suit and tie. But everyone else wore their everyday clothes, skirts and blouses or cotton dresses. The dancing was a mixture of modern and traditional. Girls danced with girls, boys with boys; only now and again an older man would ask a daughter or niece to dance with him. However, no women danced with their husbands. The only exceptions were Teoman and his wife, the Museum Director, and the doctor and his wife. People accepted this because the first were notables of the town and the other two "strangers".

The invitation to dance which girls convey to each other only appears casual on the surface. Girls know who they can ask without being "refused" and talk about who they will dance with for days before a wedding, as if a boy was concerned. They all say that if a boy had the "cheek" to ask them, they would refused. Indeed, boys do not dare invite a girl to dance, for this would be in bad taste and he would be considered as not "serious". The one advantage which a *balo* had in this respect, over the traditional wedding, is that there is no segregation between the men and women, and that they all sit and dance in full view of each other; the day may come when, thanks to the *balo*, young men and girls will be able to dance together, even if they are not married.

As the evening progressed, fewer modern tunes were played. People got up and threw money to the band, with requests for *zeybek* tunes and the traditional dancing took over. At one point, the bride's four brothers, three of whom had come from other cities for the wedding, got up and danced the *zeybek* together. They looked so strong and gay that their grandmother rushed onto the middle of the dancing floor and broke a glass there, to ward off the evil eye.

The bride and groom danced a *zeybek* together, and again, the bride did not smile, while the groom did, since he had been refreshing himself quite often a flask brought by his friends. Again, the same atmosphere of quiet pervaded the audience. The fact that this was a *balo* and that the men were there did not make much difference. Except for the younger men and girls, very few people looked as if they were having a good time. Guests sat quietly, the women exchanging a few remarks with their neighbours, the babies asleep, the men talking in small groups. Just as in the traditional celebration, it was only the small group of drinking men who displayed any kind of gaiety and animation. Weddings are a social obligation, entered upon to the best of one's ability and means, and certainly not an occasion for enjoyment. Although all are pleased at seeing a young couple married off and started in life, the different phases of the ceremoney are gone through because it is the custom.

It is not rare, either, to catch, now and again, a look of commiseration for the bride on the faces of some of the women. Married life for the Bodrum woman is the end of careless days and the beginning of hard work and, oddly enough, loneliness. For she will be cut off from her own family, if she has come from other places, and will see very little of her husband; she has been trained to accept her husband's wishes without protest. From now on, the young girl comes out of her father's tutelage to enter that of her husband. Formerly, she had her mother to intercede but now she will be on her own.

Married life

Nedime Molla is fond of reminding the Bodrum women of their duties as wives. She is herself quite imperious with her husband, and her audience of elderly women is long past mending its ways, but all the same, during the month of *Ramazan*, when good resolutions are taken, she tells them the story of the sheperd girl. It appears that when Fatma asked her father, the Prophet, who would be the first woman to enter Paradise on the day of Resurrection, she was told that it would not be her, Prophet's daughter as she may be, but the shepherd girl. Intrigued and not a little scandalized, Fatma went to see the girl and found her sitting under the scorching sun and eating food which had gone bad in the heat. Asked why she did not sit indoors, the shepherd girl replied that she wanted to live like her husband; he was also eating bad food and standing under the sun all day. Fatma succeeded in getting the womon indoors and noticed other evidences of how good she was to her husband; water was heated in preparation for the evening bath, and the bed had been made ready so that the shepherd would not have to wait were he to return tired. Fatma still did not see anything very extraordinary in these things until she noticed a stick standing in a corner. Asked what the stick was for, the shepherd girl replied, "My husband may come home angry and should he so wish it, he will have a stick ready to beat me with". Then Fatma noticed that one end of the stick was wrapped in cloth. Upon enquiry, the shepherd girl said, "I put the cloth on it so that he may not hurt his hand".

The women of Bodrum listen to the story again and again and marvel at what a good wife the shepherd girl was; however, needless to say, not one of them would for one moment dream of doing the same. The story is one thing and reality another. Not content with telling this story, Nedime Molla likes to drive the lesson home by citing the four cases in which a husband is entitled to beat his wife: if she does not say her prayers the required five times a day; if she does not keep herself clean; if she goes out of the house without his permission, and if she refuses to come to bed. "In these cases", says Nedime Molla, "the bad wife will be hung by her tongue and by her hair in Hell". Hearing this, the older women exclaim, "Oh God, forgive us" and remember, presumably, the many times they have sinned against the all-powerful husband. When the writer asked Nedime Molla where she read these stories, she said that they were interpretations of a verse in the Koran which says that "women must obey their husband", but she was unable to quote the source of interpretation.

In Bodrum, as anywhere else, there is no formal training given to girls or to boys to prepare them for married life. Many girls are completely ignorant about all sexual matters until they find out for themselves on the day of their wedding. The taboo placed on intercourse of any kind between grown girls and boys also precludes talk about sexual matters, as was seen earlier. What girls learn at home is not so much how to treat a husband as how to make a marriage work. The Bodrum women consider marriage as a normal part of everyday life, a partnership where the division of labour is clearly defined and where the privileges of each side are clearly accepted. The notion of romantic life does not enter into the matter, even though love often defelops between the young couple as a result of intimacy and a happy coincidence of personalities. All through their youth, boys and girls have observed the behaviour of their parents and relatives and have heard gossip about what went wrong with a neighbour's marriage, about how a bad marriage was mended, or about what a "husband should do", or a "wife should do".

The relationship and the division of labour are quite clearly established: the husband must keep his family and be a good provider, and the wife must help the husband with the work in the fields, in addition to looking after the house and children. In the Cretan community, the wife must help with the mending of nets and the trimming of sponges and she must prepare some of the provisions for the crew, such as cracked wheat, tomato sauce and dried vegetables, but only when she happens to be a captain's wife, that is a boat-owner's wife. In this way, the husband saves on the cost of a trip, since otherwise he would have to buy these things at the grocer's.

In the case of the children, men are not supposed to help but only to wield their authority when needed. Men can go and come as they please and do not have to tell their wives where they are going, while wives are free to go visiting in the neighbourhood but will rarely go to the market or to another quarter of the town without telling their husbands first. And, most important, women are in charge of the chastity of their daughters. An errant daughter, who comes in after nightfall or who has been seen loitering in the street, is blamed on the mother who was not able "to hold her". A father is rarely, if ever, blamed for an errant daughter, although he will be blamed if his son misbehaves.

Apart from these clearly understood rights and privileges, there are a number of unwritten, but oft repeated rules which the girls assimilate as they grow up and which the boys hear in the course of growing up too. These rules are not announced in front of men or even of young men, for these two categories are considered as "the enemy". The strategies involved in the conduct of a peaceful married life are not divulged openly. Men will say things like "the wife must know who is master of the house", or "one should not listen to women", in front of women and to each other, but women will keep their counsel. When they are together, or when they are asked to give counsel to a young bride who has difficulties, the strategies will out. These can be grouped under three headings and are the same in the local and in the Cretan community. It is only in their application that there are variations. One of the injunctions is, "you do not tell a husband everything", another "men are children and must be humoured", and the third "you mustn't spoil your husband or he'll 'sit on your head'". These sentences are constantly heard in conversations between women. They are extremely discreet as far as their own relationship is concerned but are loquacious when they gossip. So-and-so's husband is unfaithful because he was spoiled, or such-and such's husband does not come home in the evening because his wife does not know how to "humour" him. Very often the word "marriage" is used: "you must know how to manage a husband, marriage is a matter of management". In the cases where a husband drinks, and this is a serious problem in Bodrum, then the injunctions do not work and the wife is told to be patient, that sooner or later the husband will cease drinking. One wife is praised in Bodrum because she put up with an alcoholic husband for nineteen years to be at last rewarded with the man ceasing to drink and beginning to lead a normal life. Under no circumstances are drink or neglect considered as a reason for divorce. These are part of "bad luck" or "destiny" and must be put up with. Rebellion in these cases "serves no purpose". In all cases the existence of children is invoked: "You must put up with him, you have children" is a sentence often heard. The fact that it may not be desirable for children to grow up in an unhappy household is not considered. "Children must be with their parents", because the Bodrum people consider that any kind of parents is better than no parents.

The injunctions are rules applied to normal circumstances and represent, at least to the writer's mind, the defence of a down-trodden group. Religious prescription, cultural milieu and the economic status of women make of the husband the absolute master in the household; women can only resort to underhand methods to be able to lead a resonable life, that is to be able to participate as much as possible in the life of their husband, to be consulted when decisions have to be taken, to be considered—as they are wont to put it—as "human beings". The only way to do this is to bring the husband round in an argument, not to discuss the matter directly; to ask for something when "he has a weak moment", and to lie quite often, if this saves conflict, at least about small matters. Brides are also told that the relationship will be established once and for all during the first months of marriage when the honeymoon is still going on and that "the husband must be trained" during that time, otherwise it will be too late. The way to do this is to restrain oneself from showing too much love and too much concern, to avoid "running at his beck and call" so that "he does not get used to it". This is done by being a little difficult, by pretending not to believe compliments, by a thousand and one small coqueteries which are subconsciously absorbed during adolescence and then used automatically in later life. Women who succeed in doing this are praised as being "intelligent" and are pointed out as examples.

In cases of serious conflict, anger is not shown because it will antagonize the husband immediately, but a marked coldness for a day or two "will make him think". No threats should be used because they cannot be carried out. If the wife runs away to her parents' house, they will be the first to remonstrate with her and they will take her back and she would have lost face. In just such a case, the women shook their head in disapproval, "she has no face to show him now", they said, "now he can treat her like a slave".

On the other hand, mothers do not warn their sons about such manoeuvres. They will say things like "you never know with women" or "women are different", as a way of warning them that they will be treading unknown paths. They may also tell a son not to take his wife's coldness too seriously, or her reticence; "you spoiled her, now she will 'sit on your head'", but they will be unable to put the whole quality of women's behaviour into words, because they themselves are conditioned already. The writer has noticed families where even though mother-in-law and daughter-in-law do not get along well, the son or husband is never told about the conflicts that may have occurred during the day: "you do not tell men evertyhing". The small battles between women must not endanger the outcome of the war between the sexes.

After the birth of the first child, which usually occurs in the first eighteen months of marriage, a *modus vivendi* is attained. From now on, a wife will consider herself lucky if her husband does not drink and if he looks after her and the children properly. She will consider herself happy if he comes home for dinner in the evening and spends most of his evenings at home. And a husband will consider himself lucky if she is a good housewife and knows how to hold her tongue. The Bodrum men will not waste time thinking about married bliss; a good wife is a good wife and the matter will rest there.

Of the many decisions which have to be taken in daily life, many are taken following mutual consultation. These are decisions concerning household matters such as repairs to the house, the buying of the year's provisions, whether or not the children must be examined by the doctor, what relatives should be invited to stay—an important economic decision—and what expenditures are needed for clothing and household goods. But in case of disagreement, it is the wishes of the husband which always prevail, even at the cost of hardship. Such are decisions about continued education for the daughters. Only once did the writer hear a woman say that a girl

should not go to school since she was going to be a housewife. All
women are acutely aware of their helplessness as wage-earners and
education represents for them a guarantee for the future of their
daughters. They want to be sure that the daughters will not be forced
to remain at the mercy of a bad husband, that they will be able
to earn their own living; while the men are inclined to think that
girls ought to be married and there is no reason why money should
be wasted on their education, since there will be someone to look
after them. The education of girls is a matter of serious conflict
in many households, but every time it is the father who has imposed
his will.

Another important decision concerns work for women. Most men
will forbid their wives to work because they will be accused in
the town of "losing the end of the rope" in the marriage and of
being unable to look after their homes properly. In rare cases where
wives are allowed to work, as for instance as maids or laundresses
in the hotels and pensions, men demand that there should be women
in the places of work, and that the wife should on no account work
for a bachelor. The exceptions to this rule are the civil servants and
teachers. Work of that kind for women is accepted by the men and
the additional income is appreciated. Hence the many conflicts
which occur concern money matters. In times of stress, the husband
would want to turn the gold bracelets of his wife into cash and she
would refuse, offering to work instead. If the husband persists
and the wife sees that all her gold is disappearing, she may go as
far as divorce. In fact, in the villages around Bodrum, most divorces
have this question of gold at the root.

DIVORCE

There are four or five divorces a year in Bodrum, and these have
been granted for incompatibility, whatever else was the cause. In
the last five years, only one divorce was obtained for adultery. In
a divorce which is being discussed now, the fact that the husband
drinks and which is cited by the wife as her reason for separation,
is not taken seriously by either men or women. It is said that
when the man grows older, he is sure to desist and that the girl
should "be patient" and not behave as a "spoiled child", since
there is a child involved. Adultery is a rare occurrence in Bodrum,
or rather an enterprise fraught with too much danger. Neighbours

are too close and secrecy is well -nigh impossible. One or two women are known to have "put horns on" their husbands at one time or another, but people are fairly discreet about these occurrences and the husbands are not teased, although some joking goes or behind their backs. When adultery becomes public, however, this is a serious matter and the husband has no option but to divorce his wife. In a recent case, although both parties were willing to remarry and let by-gones be by-gones because they are quite fond of each other and have three children, public opinion precluded it. "How will he be able to sit with his friends again?" they ask, or "no one will look upon him as a man if he does". This in spite of the fact that everyone recognizes that the husband is far from being perfect. Where adulterous husbands are concerned, the matter is quite different. He is blamed if he is known to have a regular liaison, but philandering in Izmir or Milas now and again is put in the same category as drink and is certainly not a reason for divorce and "destroying a home". Even legally the definitions of adultery for men and women differ and its strictest version is applied to women.

An interesting aspect in divorce is that the overwhelming majority occurs in marriages which involve a Bodrum person and someone from another town. The reason seems to be that not enough information is available about one of the parties when a "stranger" is involved and also that divorces are more easily agreed to by the respective families when they are not likely to meet frequently in everyday life. Also, the majority of divorces occur in marriages where the man is the "stranger". Here part of the explanation lies in the fact that it is mostly girls who marry "strangers", the Bodrum boys marrying local girls as a rule, and also that the behaviour of boys as husbands is more unpredictable than that of girls as wives.

As far as mixed Cretan-local marriages are concerned, it does not seem as if more divorces occur in this group or that Cretans married to "strangers" divorce more often. In the last two years there has been a slight increase in the number of divorces but the numbers are so small that it is difficult to hazard a guess as to the cause, except to say that this may be a part of the general trend in the country.

In the Cretan community there are relatively fewer divorces. Here the reason is fairly obvious .The Cretan community is small and extremely close. Furthermore, the majority of marriages occurs between relatives and, quite often, between first or second cousins.

In these cases, the young people have had an opportunity to meet quite often all through their childhood and adolescence and marriages of inclination can be said to be the rule. Both sides have a fairly clear idea about the kind of married life which can be expected. So numerous are the marriages between blood cousins that this has become a matter of concern to the doctors in town, who attribute "the wildness" of the Cretan men or the extreme nervousness of the Cretan women to this type of intermarriage. The increasing popularity of higher education for girls, especially among the Cretan community, will sooner or later change the situation since the girls will then marry a "stranger", chosen among the wider marriageable male population of the other cities of the Aegean.

It may be added, as a footnote to the subject, that the Cretan men are often teased in the cafés and drinking places about being henpecked. The locals will constantly refer to the fact, only to be slightly rebuked in return. Local women are more subservient to their husbands than Cretan women are. The latter are more outspoken and enjoy a greater freedom of movement. In most cases, this is the inevitable outcome of the sea-oriented life, with its long absences; but also, it is outcome of a more lively, more unruly and less conservative temperament, "Our men", say the Cretan women, "will go barefoot rather than deprive us of anything we want". To this contention, the local women reply that the Cretan women are spoiled and work their husbands to the bone. This is said without envy, but with a certain amount of reproval. Local women share their husband's respect for money and a sober life. In the months that follow a marriage, both the Cretans and the locals will settle down to adult life and begin to learn to find their feet in a small town where money is scarce and where, in spite of all, a living has to be made and children looked after and educated.

CHAPTER TEN

EVERYDAY LIFE

HOUSING AND FURNISHINGS

All the houses in Bodrum are built in exactly the same way. Along the shore, in the Cretan quarter, in the market area, most of the houses are two-stories high, while in the poorest quarters, to the east of the town and up the slopes they are single-storied. The dimensions of these houses do not vary much, except for a group of a dozen houses which were built lately and which show the influence of other ways of building, brought back from Istanbul or Izmir. The Bodrum house is a rectangle, its width varying between a little under three meters and rarely over four, and a length of seven to eight meters. The height usually follows the width and when the house is two-stories high, it never exceeds eight meters. All the houses are built with stone walls and an earth roof and there are no interior walls. As time goes by, people build a wooden partition on the ground floor and usually a cupboard is put in alongside. When there is a second floor, the horizontal partition is also built of wood, long flat planks supported by narrow beams laid out at even intervals of half a meter. The planks do not fit properly, either in the vertical or the horizontal partitions, but this does not seem to matter since the floor on both stories is usually covered from wall to wall with hand-woven thin rugs called *kilim*. A simple wooden staircase leads to the upper floor. The house has no kitchen and no lavatory. The large room downstairs always has a fireplace and a wooden cupboard and shelves are built near it. The lavatory is built in the farthest corner of the courtyard, since there is no sewage system in the town and drainage is to a pit. Dalavera Mehmet's most regular source of income is the annual cleaning out of all the pits in town. He does the job at night and carries the refuse to the sea.

The courtyard has a fireplace too, where cooking is done in the good season and where water is heated for the laundry, winter and summer. Very few of the houses have running water and this is obtained either from a tap in the yard or from the street fountain. In the poorest quarters, built on slopes, street fountains are quite far from the houses and the women carry a couple of pails of water for distances which may be as much as 300 metres or more. Many courtyards have a well, from which water for cleaning and the laundry is taken, the water from the fountain generally being used for drinking and cooking. The houses on the slopes do not have wells.

In the local quarters, the courtyard is a paved or cemented area built near the house and surrounded by a field where the cow, the lamb and a few chickens are kept. There are a few fruit trees, usually oranges, tangerines and quince, and many flowers are grown, the people of Bodrum being keen and expert gardeners; they constantly give each other seeds and cuttings and grow new varieties for one another. The courtyard area is covered with a vine and honeysuckle and jasmine is trained on the posts. In almost every house there are flowers in all seasons, put in a glass or in a tin. The Cretans do not have fields or gardens, but each Cretan house has a few pots of flowers and a flowering bush or two in the courtyard.

Half the houses have electricity. Some people pay the municipality to have electricity brought to them, but the price of electric current is very high and not many of the poorer people can afford it. Those who do, use the electricity sparingly; they use coal if they have an iron, and a small bulb for lighting. Since almost everybody in Bodrum goes to bed early, around nine o'clock, the amount used is very small and there are bills as low as T.L. 10 a month. The richest people rarely have a bill exceeding T.L. 60. Electricity is never used for heating or cooking, the fireplace is used instead, and sometimes an old-fashioned stove is used for both cooking and heating purposes. The more educated or modern people, the civil servants and the school teachers, use butane gas for cooking, but even then dishes which take a long time to cook, like dried vegetables, potatoes, and cracked wheat, are cooked over the fire or a small charcoal brazier. Coals are not left in the fireplace, but transferred to the brazier and this is put either in the other room or in the corner opposite the fireplace, thus providing additional warmth.

Logs are not used, either in the fireplace or in the stove. The men gather shavings and saw-dust from the carpenters of the boat-builders, but more often than not get their own wood from the hills, cuttings of olive and pine, of ilex, and arbutus, prunings from the tangerine trees and vines. People who cannot do this buy a "load", that is as much as a donkey can carry, from men who earn some additional income this way. Most people use two loads a week, burning the wood carefully, two or three thin cuttings at a time. The women are careful not to use only dry twigs as these burn too fast. On very cold nights, the fire is covered with ashes and ready to be kindled again in the morning.

The average Bodrum house, whether Cretan or local, has practically no furniture. The few clothes and the sheets and quilts are stored in chests or in the wooden cupboard. Small sacks of muslin, containing dried vegetables, are hung from the ceiling, to prevent mice from getting at them, along with bunches of onions. A few earthenware jars, set near the fireplace, contain olive oil, olives and tomato purée and pickles. Other stuff, such as petrol for the lamps, cauldrons for boiling water, pails and brooms, are kept in the yard. The shelves carry the few plates and glasses, and all the copper and aluminium pots and pans, the large copper tray used for the family meal instead of a table is stood next to the fireplace. There is a long wooden settee, the *sedir*, running the length of the wall, covered in flowered cotton, with bands of muslim embroidered and edged with crocheted lace. The upholstered cushions at the back are covered in the same way and a stack of flat cushions *(minder)*, also covered in patterned cotton are stacked on the floor or in one of the deep window-sills, to be taken down and sat upon as people need them. The mattresses are also stored in the cupboard, unless one of the rooms contains the double bed of the original trousseau. The parents and very small children share either the bed or the mattress, while older children have their own mattresses. The walls are bare, with a photograph or two, an illustrated calendar or some magazine cut-outs and most of the houses have no curtains, unless the windows look over the street. Then some net curtains are hung or tacked on to the panes.

In wealthier houses, one finds armchairs with stuffed arms, chairs, occasional tables, sideboards, refrigerators and washing machines; but in the average house, there are never more than two or three straight-backed kitchen chairs and a deal table, which is almost never used, except by the children to do their homework on. People sit on the *minder* by the fire in the winter and on the *sedir* by the window in the summer, and on very hot days they sit, eat and sleep in the courtyard under the vine.

This is the sort of house into which a young couple will settle, the house bought or built by the young man and the furnishings brought by the bride. Very few houses are for rent. Some of them belong to somebody who has settled in Izmir or elsewhere, some are no more than a *dam*, a smaller version of a one-storied house, at the bottom of the garden and rented to the poorest people. But many of the houses are shut because there are not enough strangers in town to rent them. Many of the minor civil servants are Bodrum people who live in their own houses, and so also are many of the school teachers. The judge and the prosecutor have been here for many years and hope to retire in Bodrum and so have bought houses of their own, and so has the town's best and most popular doctor. The museum staff rents some of the very few apartments in Bodrum, which are converted old houses, where a kitchen and bathroom have been put in and running water and electricity installed. Bachelor civil servants, such as the Tourism man and the P.T.T. man have rented houses and have become used to going outside to the lavatory. The absence of a kitchen does not bother them, since they have made arrangements with a restaurant in town and eat there regularly. The Bank manager has a nice flat built on top of the Bank, which comes with the job, and so have the Customs and Forestry officials. Many of the government offices have rented some of the largest Cretan houses and have repaired them, but the people complain that they have to run from one end of the town to the other to get things done and the government constantly promises to build a government house where the Tax, Customs, Land Registry, Birth Registry, District and Court Offices, Forestry and Veterinary will all be in the same building. When that day comes, then many of the larger houses will again be shut up, to maybe await families coming to spend the summer here. The rents charged then will not be very different from those charged in larger cities. At present, rents range from T.L. 15 to 200 per month.

Housekeeping

To keep house under these conditions should not be a very exacting chore. There are no floors or furniture to polish, not many clothes to wash, practically no ironing. The average Bodrum housewife cleans the fireplace and puts on the pan where the single hot meal of the day will be cooked, and she rarely has fresh vegetables to clean in the winter. She will sweep the rugs and wash them in the spring, to replace them with straw mats for most of the year. She has virtually no shopping to do since she goes to the market once a week and gets her other needs from the grocer round the corner. She will have no equipment to take care of, and practically no dishes to wash, since the food is served in the copper pan, put in the middle of the tray on the floor and eaten, usually with only a spoon. There will be no shoes to polish, since most women and children wear plastic shoes, and no windows to wash, since many of the houses do not have glass panes but only wooden shutters.

But the few tasks that the housewife has take four times as long under the prevalent conditions as they would elsewhere. Lighting the fire is not easy, since the wood is usually damp and no petrol is used to help. All the bedding has to be rolled out at night and gathered up again in the morning. She will have to clean out the cow shed, get the fodder, milk the cow in the morning and in the evening, feed the chickens and, if she has a lamb, feed it too. Then she will settle by the fire and clean out the dried beans or lentils, or chickpeas, of little bits of stone or straw, and while the dish is cooking, with a little olive oil and tomato purée, she will set out her dough-board and make bread. The dough will be cooked, after having been shaped in flat rounds about an inch thick, on an iron tray over a fire built outdoors. She will then go to the street tap and bring water home, and draw more water from the well with which she will water the animals, the flowers and few vegetables. At lunch time, the children will be home and she will then, if she is hungry, also eat, and all the while she will be running to and fro to look after the baby in the cradle.

In the afternoon, after having washed the few spoons and the tray, and gathered up the crumbs from the floor, she will have time to rest. She will go to a neighbour's or a neighbour or two will come to see her. The women will sit, with their children around them or playing in the garden, and chat and gossip. But their hands will not be idle. They will sew or mend, or unravel old knitted garments and knit them anew, with a little bit of new wool added. They may also spin wool, or weave a rug, sheets or material out of which underwear will be made. If they have grown daughters, they will embroider the trousseau or make lace. A Bodrum woman almost never embroiders again after she has made her trousseau, unless it is for her daughter. She will weave and knit good strong serviceable things to be worn every day.

The woman who can spend her days in this fashion is lucky. Her husband provides for her and she has the house to look after. But sometimes she has to earn money too. She may get up at dawn and "make wood", that is cut and collect fuel to be sold in the town. In September and October she may spend her days stringing dry figs, in November gathering olives in distant fields, and in December and part of January in sorting and packing tangerines. For these chores she will be paid T.L. 10 a day and, in the case of olives, she may get the equivalent of her pay in olive oil and thus collect her year's provision by working for it. The luckier woman will take in sewing and make a dress for T.L. 10 or less, or weave rugs for T.L. 14 the meter. If she is too old to do work of that kind, she may go out and clean house or do laundry for wealthier women and work the whole day for T.L. 10.

The Cretan women have a much easier time of it, even if they are poorer and have a less secure income. They have no garden and no cow to tend, only two or three chickens. They buy shop - made bread and ready chopped wood. They never go out to pick tangerines or gather olives, but the poorest among them may go out to trim sponges because they know how to do it and get a higher wage for this, T.L. 15 a day . "Our husbands will never dream of letting us work in the gardens or in the fields, no matter how poor we are" they say with pride. However, they will knit or sew for money, even if very few of them do so. Having no land of their own, and no relatives living off the land, they have to buy olive oil, cracked wheat, dried beans and chick-peas from the grocers and must have meat in each dish even if it is the size of a walnut. As a result, their food bills are much higher than those of the local women, and so are their clothing bills. This is one of the reasons why almost all the Cret an sponge-divers and fishermen work in their spare time, at all kinds of odd jobs.

Some of the Bodrum women are married to rich men, who have received a university education in Istanbul or Ankara and their mode of living is not very different to that of thousands of other well-off women living in the provinces. They travel and shop in Izmir and Istanbul, have a woman come in most days to help with the rougher housework, have their shopping delivered and spend their spare time visiting, going to the cinema or reading picture magazines. They do not number more than half a dozen. The twenty-odd schoolteachers may have a woman come in once a week, but do most of their housework themselves, usually on Sundays, and take care of the cooking and laundry in the evening. They all use butane gas and have washing machines. The wives of the middle-level and minor civil servants live very much like the average Bodrum woman and use modern comforts sparingly, combining stovecooking with butane gas, electricity and fires, home-made and shop-bought staples.

FIVE FAMILY BUDGETS

No one in Bodrum is willing to disclose their income except the civil servants, for whom it is an opportunity to complain. Since many of the civil servants have at least one other source of income, such as a tangerine grove or a field rented out for pasture, even then calculating incomes is a fairly chancy enterprise. Getting an estimate of family expenditures is relatively easier, but even this is not easy. Housewives know how much they spend at the market, for fuel, their clothes and the children's clothes. But it is their husbands who pay the grocer, the butcher and the fishmonger, the electricity and tailor's bills, and the women have no idea how much the husbands spend in the market, that is in town, on breakfast and tea and coffee, papers and cigarettes and, for those who drink, on drinks and the hors d'oeuvres that go with it. The following tables will therefore not include the husbands' personal expenditures, but only the family budget as estimated by husbands and wives. To illustrate the point, a few families, from among those which have been interviewed and whom the writer knows well, have been grouped and composite portraits drawn. It is felt that in this way a relatively small margin of error has occurred and that the portraits are fairly accurate.

Fureyya is the wife of a fisherman. They have three children all at school and live with Fureyya's old mother. In return for giving them the house, the mother is looked after by them, since Fureyya's brother is, according to many, just a typical "Cretan drifter". The fact is that he does not contribute to his mother's upkeep. Fureyya feels very badly about not having her own house and is very sorry that her parents married her to a man without demanding that he build a house first. Her husband works on one of the big fishing *tratta* and brings T.L. 50 every week. He keeps ten for himself and gives forty to Fureyya, who has to make do with it. She cannot understand what he does with the money since he is at sea most of the time and is therefore fed by the *tratta* owner, and she suspects him of saving his money to spend later in the season when he is laid off. Fureyya and her husband are not typical Cretans. He is not very hard-working and she does not mind doing all kinds of odd jobs to supplement the family income She "does" for tourists in the summer, goes to whitewash houses and to trim sponges. She is the female counterpart of Dalavera Mehmet, and everybody says that had she married him they would have been millionaires by now. But winters are still a hard time and when the festival of *Ramazan* arrived and the children had to be provided with new clothes, she went and sold one of her gold bracelets. But, typically Cretan, she uses butane gas and does not neglect to have her hair permanently waved twice a year. Fureyya does not make her own bread and buys all her food at the market and in the shops. In the winter and spring, she goes to the hills and, like any poor local woman, comes back with armfuls of edible grasses and roots, such as mustard, daisy stalks, poppy roots and wild celery.

Fureyya's budget looks something like this:

	(T.L. per month)
Rent	nil
Electricity	15
Fuel (wood)	10
Market	60
Grocer	80
Butane	20
Baker	60
	245

This takes up more than her husband's salary, and all other expenses, such as clothes and the children's schooling, have to come out of what she earns. She had a debt of T.L. 120 for butane gas and most of the money she received when she sold her bracelet went to pay for that. Sometimes Fureyya thinks of divorcing and being free to go and work anywhere and free of the fear of having another child. But some security is better than none and, of course, there are the children. All she hopes for is that one day she may have a house of her own, for although she does not pay rent, her self-respect is hurt and this makes her as unhappy as the lack of money.

The situation of Aysel, who is married to an agricultural labourer, is a little brighter, even though her husband does not make more than T.L. 200 a month, and sometimes as little as half of that. Aysel's husband is a good worker and knows how to look after olive and tangerine groves, how to grow vegetables and to plow. But he does not have any oxen and has to borrow his brother's back in the village, and so does not get as much as he should from plowing people's fields. He also does not know how to prune, and does not receive the relatively higher wages that a good pruner gets in Bodrum. Most of the year he is idle and sits in one of the cafés in the market, drinking the cheapest drink there is, sage tea, and reading other people's newspapers because he is very fond of political and criminal news. Aysel's parents and his live in a village about twenty kilometers from Bodrum, a distance easily covered on foot, and they do not have a house of their own. They rent a *dam* in one of the upper quarters and have neither electricity nor water. But Aysel keeps a cow and five chickens and each year they raise a sheep which is sent them by her father-in-law. While Fureyya eats meat once a year and fish every time her husband comes home from a trip, which is twice a week, Aysel and her family of three have thirty kilos of meat a year which they get from the sheep. The sheep is killed at the *Kurban* festival and the meat cooked and stored in earthenware jars to keep for a few months. They very rarely eat fish, only when a neighbour sends them some or when there is a glut in the market and the fish goes for very cheap. On the other hand, the two children and the baby have milk and yoghourt and fatless cheese from the cow and eggs from the chickens. In addition, Aysel's mother sends her cracked wheat, dried vegetables and almonds from the village and she gets dried figs when she goes figstringing, just as she gets olive oil when she goes olivegathering. Aysel does not buy her bread but bakes it every other day, and she often makes flour dishes and soups. Like everyone else in Bodrum, she flavours her dishes with tomato purée, which she makes in the summer when tomatoes are cheap, and pickles a few peppers and cucumbers to relieve the monotony of the diet. Neither Aysel nor her husband spend anything on clothing. They makes do with old things and with gifts and their clothing bill is negligible, T.L. 20 a month for the whole family compared with T.L. 40 that Fureyya estimates she spends. Aysel's budget runs something like this:

(T.L. per month)

Rent	15
Lamp oil	9
Market	40
Grocer	30
Clothing	20
Flour	50
	164

Aysel and her husband do not spend anything on fuel, since her husband brings back wood from his places of work or goes to the hills for it. By and large, Aysel's family eats better than Fureyya's, even though their diet is higher in hydrocarbons. The milk and eggs mitigate the lack of meat and fish to some extent. On the other hand, while Fureyya lives in a two-storied, three-roomed house and has a tap in her courtyard, Aysel, like most of her neighbours, lives in a one-room house with no running water. She herself is very poorly dressed but her large piece of gold is still hung around her neck.

In both families there is no such thing as three meals a day eaten by the whole family together. Fureyya's husband is away five days out of seven, sometimes longer, and when he is in town eats mid-morning and in the evening, the only time when the family eats together. Fureyya never eats breakfast because she goes out to work early and snatches a meal when she can. Since she is quite Junoesque in appearance, she considers that she does not need much food. As for Aysel, her husband goes out just before daybreak—at the second crowing of the cock—and takes whatever there is available in a handkerchief. He will eat when he gets to the fields, after having put the yoke on the oxen and while "the animals get warm to the yoke", and again at around ten or eleven. When he comes home there is always hot soup, which he will eat together with the children. Aysel also eats when she feels hungry and may or may not eat the evening meal with her family.

Families which have an income five or six times as large as those of the people described above have budgets which are just over half as large. They earn a monthly income varying between T.L. 1000 and 1500 a month and come just below the richest category in Bodrum. Their habits and houses do not differ greatly from those of the fairly poor, except that they have more of everything: rooms, clothes, food and fuel. But they still live soberly and are able to save at least half their income and do not spend money continuously on the house. They may do their cooking with butane gas only and have a woman in to do the washing once a month. But they will not buy electric ovens or refrigerators and still use coal in their irons. The wives will buy a picture weekly and go to the cinema twice a week and have a "visiting day", but they will dress modestly and the men will buy a daily paper and spend more money down-town. But these sums are relatively small and do not constitute

an important part of the family budget. There are very few variations and once you have seen one such home, you have seen them all,
as it is with the poor families.

"Baggypants" has a brother, Ömer, who is the owner of a fishing
tratta. In the summer he fishes for sponges and in the winter for
fish. Ömer thus makes a regular income of anything between T.L.
1,200 and 1,600 a month, winter and summer, and some people
say even more. "Baggypants" himself runs a grocery and his other
brother a bakery. The three brothers are known for their industry
and are regular Cretans in their ways. Ömer is never idle for a
moment. In seasons, between sponge and fish, he mends nets, carries loads, drawing the wooden cart himself; or he will work on
road-building. He is dressed in rags and goes barefoot most of the
year and, like most Bodrum men, rarely shaves. He and his wife,
Devlet, have two children and live in their own three-room house
in the Cretan quarter, situated between the grocery and the bakery
and very near the houses of his two brothers. Their mother and
father live further along the street and Devlet's two brothers, both
seamen, live in a street nearby.

It was relatively easy to learn the family budget of Ömer and
Devlet since they have accounts at the family grocery and bakery.
Ömer buys all the supplies for the crew of the *tratta* from his brothers
and keeps a special account for his family. While he goes about his
business of earning money, his wife looks after the house and after
herself. Some people say that she is the most beautiful woman in
Bodrum and she dresses, when she goes out, in nice clothes. Her
gold bracelets are many. But when she is at home, she dresses very
much like Fureyya, with a duveteen dress in the winter, a cotton
dress in the summer, and slippers. Devlet does not have a refrigerator, since she uses that of her brother-in-law "Baggypants" in
the grocery store. She does not bake bread, but buys it at the family
bakery and on Fridays has her shopping carried by a porter from
the market to her house. The only three things she makes at home
are tomato purée, pickles and the local bergamote preserve and
quince jam. She gives the children's clothes, once outgrown, to other
members of the family and knits new wool for them. Her house has
a sideboard and a dining-table, an electric radio, an electric iron,
and a kitchen was installed, with a proper sink and tap in a parti-
tioned-off part of the downstairs room. She never stores anything,
using the grocery as her storeroom and by and large people cite

Devlet as a typical comfortably-off spoilt Cretan woman. Devlet's
budget is like this:

	(T.L. per month)
Rent	nil
Electricity	30
Butane gas	26
Wood	15
Market	80
Groceries	160
Clothing	125
Bakery	60
Butcher	40
	536

Devlet's bill for meat is small, but no different than the bills of other
families with a similar income. In addition to meat, the family
eats fish every other day, brought home by Ömer or some close
fisherman friend. They keep neither cows not hens and have to
buy their yoghourt and eggs from the grocer. The children do not
drink milk, and milk is only bought when a dessert is to be made
from it, such as rice pudding. On the other hand, her clothing bill
is just below that of the richest woman in town. She has two overcoats and three pairs of leather shoes, which is unusual. Local
women with similar incomes may have one pair of shoes and one
overcoat, while the poorer women make do with knitted jackets and
shawls.

Gülen's husband is a master carpenter and earns a monthly
salary of T.L. 1,000 and sometimes a little over, if he works overtime
doing carpentry jobs on boats. They own their four-room house
and have two children at school. Gülen came as a bride to Bodrum
ten years ago from a village the other side of the peninsula, renown-
ed for its olives. The house they live in was built by her husband's
grandfather, who was a cattle breeder, and is decorated on the
outside and the inside with relief designs representing cypress trees.
Gülen would like to modernize the house and have an indoor lavatory and bathroom, but her husband refuses to spoil the rooms
to do it. But he relented somewhat and she now has a kitchen with
running water and a sink. Gülen is a quiet woman, dressed in a
duveteen frock; when she goes out, she puts on a jacket knitted by
herself and throws a woolen shawl over her head. However, she carries a brown plastic bag, a present from her younger brother, who is a
worker in Germany. Twice a year, Gülen's parents send her olive
oil and cracked wheat and the usual dried vegetables. Like Devlet,

she does not bake bread but makes her own tomato purée and pickles. Like most local women, she does not make bergamote preserve, but only quince jam in the season. And she likes to flavour her dishes with herbs, which she crushes into a powder in the traditional brass mortar. She went to the girls' evening technical school as a bride and sews all her husband's underwear and shirts, and all the other clothes for the family, and she has already started to embroider her eldest daughter's trousseau, because the girl is going to Teacher's Training School, and this means that "you may consider her as a bride already, she will only come home to get married". But she hopes that her second daughter will also go on to higher education, and perhaps become a doctor or a lawyer, for the child is very bright and is always the first in her class.

Like all craftsmen and tradesmen, Gülen's husband has breakfast in town, in the market, where he eats the customary breakfast of bread and the tiny Bodrum meat-balls, washed down afterwards at work with tea brewed by the apprentices. People tease him about this, but he is very particular about his tea and does no like the brew of the cafés. Gülen sends him a hot lunch and he has his evening meal at home, with his wife and daughter, after having drunk his customary double *raki* at Kasa's. Gülen eats breakfast and lunch with her daughter and they have milk and eggs, since she keeps a cow and chickens. She does not have to, but she says she used to keep cows and missed them when she came to Bodrum. The cow has a shed in the courtyard. Gülen's budget was easy to learn because she knows how to read and write and can think in general terms:

	(T.L. per month)
Rent	nil
Electricity	20
Butane gas	26
Market	60
Grocer	200
Clothing	50
Meat	40
	396

Gülen does not have a wood bill because her husband sends wood planks and saw-dust from the shop and they burn saw-dust in their stove. She only lights her fireplace "for pleasure" and cooks with butane gas only. But her meat bill is small because, like all the Bodrum women, except the richest, she uses meat more as a flavouring than as a dish by itself, using a little at a time in each

dish she makes. They do not eat much fish, but sometimes a boat-
owner brings some to her husband and then they have it that night,
but she is not too fond of it because she never had it as a girl, her
village being inland. Her grocer's bill is largish, because her husband drinks a lot of coffee and tea, and her daughter gets her copy-
books and pencils there. She also likes to make sweet pastry and they
buy as much as 4 kilograms of sugar a week and more in the jam season. While most women in her group offer their guests shopbought
biscuits on visiting days, she likes to make her own and is often called upon by neighbours to teach someone to make pastry. Gülen does
not read picture magazines and only goes to the cinema once a
week, on Saturday afternoons, because of her daughter. Otherwise
she would not go and says that both magazines and films are "a lot
of silly nonsense". Her husband never goes.

Zeynep is the wife of a lime-kiln owner and her husband's
monthly income varies between T.L. 500 and 600. Her husband
has a field not far from the western part of town "the time it takes to
smoke two cigarettes" and decided to use the limestone and build a
kiln. At first, he employed an old man, master at the craft, and then
learned the craft himself. Now he employs three men and is able
to earn a regular amount of money every month. Zeynep estimates
that they were lucky to have limestone there, because the income
they would have got otherwise from that piece of land would have
been negligible. They have three children and live in a house
that was left to her by her father, who was a tangerine gardener
and pruner. The house has two rooms divided by a wooden partition,
one being the bedroom and the other the common room. The bedroom has a double bed, mattresses for the children and stacks of
quilts piled up in a corner. But it also has a dressing table with a
mirror. The common room has the usual *sedir* and the sewing
machine. In one corner, a deal table with a cupboard underneath
has been built and a brass Primus stands on it, on which Zeynep
does her "quick cooking". The slow cooking is done in the fireplace.

Zeynep has chickens and, as is the custom, the income she earns
from selling eggs is hers. But the hens do not lay eggs the year round
and are not given feed. They just eat left-over scraps, breadcrumbs
and what they can pick up in the garden. What money Zeynep gets
is for the girl's trousseau, although she is only seven and started going to school this year. The boy has finished primary school and has
been apprenticed to a boat builder. What he earns is his own and

pays for his lunches in town and the cinema. The baby has not yet
been weaned.

Zeynep and her husband may have a middle-class income but they
live very much like peasants, which they are. They spend less than
half their income except in the winter, when prices go up. In the
summer they grow their own vegetables and get their olive oil
from the few trees which grow near the lime-quarry. The husband
does not drink and smokes very cheap cigarettes and he does not
spend time in the cafés, except now and again when he comes
to get supplies or meet a customer. He has to stay by the kilns one
night in four and supervise the three other workers. So he prefers
to stay at home and rest. Zepnep's family has a modest budget:

	(T.L. per month)
Rent	nil
Electricity	16
Kerosene	11
Market	110
Grocer	100
Meat	10
Clothing	45
	292

The grocery bill is high because Zeynep gets flour there, to make
bread and flour dishes of which they have one every day. And the
market bill, higher than what it would be in the summer, is still
fairly high because she buys fruit and likes to have fresh vegetables
every day to make soups for the baby, which is eight months old
and the supply from the garden is not enough. Zeynep, being the
wife of a craftsman, does not go out to work, but takes in sewing now
and again. She gets T.L. 5 to 7.50 to make a duveteen dress for
her neighbours and this money goes into the family budget.

It is interesting to note that a civil servant or a tradesman's
family with a similar income has a budget which takes up all the
income. In such budgets, the clothing and grocer's bill are twice and,
in the case of meat, four times as high. The wives do not work and
there is no additional sources such as hens or home-grown vegetables, but the pattern is urban and not rural. The men get breakfast
in town, their hot lunch is either eaten at home or sent to them, and
the evening meal must have meat in it, in the shape of chunks or
meat-balls, or cutlets. The menus invariably have one "gravy dish"
and one "dry dish", such as meat cooked with vegetables and spaghetti, or rice, or cracked wheat. The meat bill is similar to the meat

bill of the richer group in the community, and the clothing bill just a little lower. The richer group has higher grocery and fuel bills.

If meat is the most expensive item in town, flour is the cheapest. Consequently, meat bills are among the smallest items in a budget, while flour or bread bills are among the highest. A Bodrum person eats half a kilogram of flour a day, in the shape of bread or a flour dish and, on the average less than 50 grams of meat. This may, but rarely is, supplemented by fish or eggs, both seasonal in Bodrum, and available only if the family keeps hens or has connections with the sea or sea-people. Both the Cretan and local communities share the national habit of "filling up on bread". Hence the type of dishes, always cooked with plenty of gravy into which the bread is dipped. Bread is also dipped into honey for dessert, in salad dressing, in olive oil for breakfast, in tea and milk when these are available. When children get hungry between meals, they get bread, when dinner is late, people eat a piece of bread, when they go on a trip they carry a loaf or two of bread "just in case". Children, except when they are very small, eat as much bread as grown-ups and every other day at least a flour soup or a stuffed pastry is put on the table. The pastry is not stuffed with expensive things, but with herbs or with the white fatless cheese which is made after the milk has been skimmed of its fat for butter. Yoghourt is made of the remaining milk, that is skimmed for more fat and what is left is turned into the fatless cheese which is called here "faithless cheese".

The dishes are not varied, except for a few specialities of the region, which are made rarely because they require meat and good cheese. Dried beans and cracked wheat are staples which recur on the menus many times a week. Tea is rarely drunk, and coffee almost never in the poorer households. It can be safely said that the groups below the middle-income level are nourished on bread, dried beans and cracked wheat almost exclusively. Groceries, such as rice and sugar, tea and coffee, matches and kerosene, have fixed prices in the country and cannot be bought cheaper in the countryside or in small towns. Therefore the grocery bills are lower as the income gets smaller, and where it does not, it is because bread is brought at the grocer's not flour. Even at that, the best varieties of dried vegetables or rice are not available in Bodrum, and the price of flour varies too. The cheapest brands of flour are most often bought, even though they are not as productive as the best. Cooking fats are also brand products, selling for a little higher in remote districts, but the Bodrum women cook everything in the local olive oil and thus consume little margarine or vegetable fats.

The following table gives an idea of the prices of foodstuffs, with two sets of figures for vegetables, showing summer and winter prices. The items labelled "at national prices" cost the same every-where in Turkey ,while meat is the same price everywhere except in the 3 largest cities, where it is 50% higher.

Table 21
(T.L. per Kg.)

Items at national prices		Items cheaper in Bodrum	
		Summer prices	Winter prices
Sugar	3.30	Eggs (ea.)	0.40	0.50
Salt	0.50	Beans	0.50	2.00
Tea	40.00	Eggplant	0.40	1.50
Coffee	48.00	Peppers	0.25	1.00
Spaghetti	2.50	Tomatoes	0.25	1.50
Margarine	8.00	Carrots	1.25	1.50
Cooking fat	7.00	Onions	0.50	0.75
Cheese (fat)	10.00	Potatoes	0.50	1.25
Butter	15.00	Fish	1.00-15.00 according to	
Olive oil (in tin)	8.00		kind & season	
Meat	10.00	Olives (local)	3.00 in all seasons	
Olives	8.00	Cheese (fatless)	3.00 in all seasons	
Milk	1.00	Olive oil	5.00 in all seasons	
Yoghourt	1.50	Dried vegetables	2-3.00 in all seasons	
		Loose salt	0.20	
		Loose spaghetti	2.20	

Of the items in the left-hand column, only sugar, tea, coffee and meat are bought by most people. The other items are bought only by the category with an income of T.L. 1000 and above. Fruit is not mentioned because there is virtually none, except seedless grapes, melons and tangerines in season, and again these are bought only by the higher-income groups, such as civil servants and trades-men with no land of their own.

The budgets described above are for families of four, except in two cases, where there are five people. In 1967, the National Bureau of Statistics estimated that it would cost a family of four T.L. 600 a month to have a properly balanced food bill. It has been seen that even the higher income groups barely spend this in a budget which includes fuel, lighting and clothing. Even the highest income

groups, with incomes ranging from T.L. 2,000 to T.L. 7,000, do
not have a meat bill exceeding T.L. 150—just over 125 grams a day
per person—or a grocery bill above T.L. 250, for a family of four.

HEALTH

Most of the people in Bodrum do not eat adequately. The most
balanced budgets, as far as food is concerned, seem to be the budgets
of the T.L. 500-600 monthly income group, the civil servants and
teachers, with a few tradesmen thrown in, who have adopted urban
ways of living, including eating. The result, as we shall see later,
is the basis for emigration from Bodrum or the holding of more
than one job for most people. In spite of this, the Bodrum people
are in good health, visibly so and according to the two doctors in
town, who have worked for many years in other parts of the country
and are therefore able to make comparisons.

They attribute the good health of the inhabitants of Bodrum to
the fact that they eat enough bread to compensate for the deficiency
in proteins deriving from a low-meat diet, that they grow up in a
good climate by the sea and that they consume plenty of olive oil.
The Bodrum breakfast of bread and olives, or bread dipped in olive
oil and eaten with a little "faithless cheese" is healthy and nourish-
ing, and the dishes made with dried beans, lentils and chick-peas
energy-giving. But this diet has drawbacks too. The olive oil has a
high content of acids, sometimes as high as 8% or 9%. Added to the
high content of carbohydrates, this results in some diseases which
plague the people, such as ulcers and high blood pressure. Another
complaint is kidney stones. Doctors attribute this to the fact that
so many marriages occur between relatives that these have become
hereditary, and also to the drinking water in Bodrum, which has
a high lime content.

The people of Bodrum get their drinking water from various
places and either carry it themselves to their homes or buy it from a
man who delivers it to the house on donkey-back at T.L.0.50 a petrol
canful. The water comes from the spring of Salmacis, on the western
side of the town and is brought in by boat, except when there are
storms. This water is supposed to be the best in Bodrum and, in
fact, has the reputation of keeping people eternally young, a quality
which has been handed down from the times of the earliest Dorian
occupation; in fact, the taste of the water appeared so sweet to the

ancients that they gave the spring a reputation for weakening and corrupting manliness. For Samlacis was that very nymph who, being unable to resist the charm of the son of Hermes and Aphrodite, threw herself around his neck one moonlight night and begged the gods to make them one. The gods acceded to the wish of Salmacis and Hermaphroditus acquired that "dual nature which could not be called male or female but seemed to be at once both and neither" as Ovid says. However, Vitrivius, with his solid engineer's sense, refuses to believe the story and offers a more realistic explanation: the barbarians who lived near the spring became civilized, in time, by the invading Dorians and lost their "rough and savage ways to the delights of Greek civilization"! The people of Bodrum, mostly unaware of either the legend or its refutation, still attribute magic qualities to the spring.

There are other sources of good water in Bodrum which are known and used by all. Ancient underwater galleries, connecting subterranean pockets of water with one another and emerging at two or three points in the town have been used from time immemorial. Seljuks and Ottomans built fountains and aqueducts, and some of them are still in use. For water is the main drink in Bodrum and enormous quantities of it are drunk all day by everybody. Only two or three people have gone to the expense of building underground tanks to collect their own rain water. But water, except rain water, always contains an excess of lime.

According to the doctors, who know about every family in town, of the two communities the Cretan is in better health, because they eat more fish and all kinds of sea-food, which the locals will not touch, such as squid and octopus, sea-urchins and pinna, sea-crayfish and crab.

There is no tuberculosis in Bodrum and the TB fund in the municipality has not been touched for years. The town's most popular doctor, Alim bey, attributes this to the sun, air and sea and to the fact that even the poorest children get plenty of all three all year round. On the other hand, many of the older fishermen have chronic bronchitis and the sponge-divers get the dreaded "bends". There is a decompression chamber down near the harbour, but nobody knows how to use it and a serious case of the "bends" has to be taken to Izmir. Because of this, there is a death or two each year in Bodrum but more often than not, the divers become cripples and have to look for other ways of earning a living.

Although there is no sewage system in Bodrum, there are no epidemics of thyphus or typhoid fever. Very few vegetables are eaten raw, since salad is not available and only small quantities of parsley and dill come to the market. The only vegetables which are eaten raw are tomatoes, radishes and green onions. But small children suffer regularly from worms. When one child in the family gets worms, the others catch it immediately since they sleep together on the same mattress. Two years ago, there was an epidemic of hepatitis and almost one hundred children caught it. No child died and the epidemic did not touch children of higher-income groups, as they have adopted the habit of children sleeping in separate beds.

There are few cases of insanity in Bodrum, and for the last ten years not a single certifiable case has been recorded. However, there are a good number of "odd" people, who are designated by the townspeople by the addition of the word *deli* in front of the names of the persons concerned. *Deli* means anything from eccentricity to definitely queer behaviour, but does not apply to neurotics or psychotics. Such is Deli Ali, who is a respected merchant belonging to a respected family, but who sleeps all day and works all night; or Deli Huseyin, who is a sea captain turned *hotelier*, because he shouts at the top of his voice when he speaks, and loses his temper most frightfully a few times a year; or Deli Mehmet who is definitely not right in the head but does not hurt a soul and earns his living as a load -carrier. His latest delusion is that he is going to marry Makarios' daughter, that she is waiting for him in Cos, but that djinns prevent him from going there. There is also Deli Fatma, who reads fortunes and looks and bahaves like a gypsy, and Gogo Ali, who is seventeen and humoured by all, from his mother to his neighbours. Gogo Ali likes to "telephone" Izmir and to look at pictures of pin-ups. He goes to all the weddings and all public entertainments, and the ban against men never applies to him. It is only the "strangers" who look upon Gogo with pity in their eyes and a little fear. The *deli*, for the most part, live normal family lives, have children and are as much part of the town's everyday life as anybody else. Alim bey attributes the large number of *deli* to intermarriage between close relatives.

Mild nervous disorders are more numerous among women and adolescents. Women suffer from suppressed boredom, self-imposed discipline and the consequences of the local habit—which reflects

national practice—of *coitus interruptus*. As many as 85% of the women
have come to the doctor to ask for pills and tranquillisers. "In some
cases", says the doctor, "I call the husband and explain the situation to him. He goes away contrite, but does not change his habits".
As for adolescents, the complaints are of repeated headaches, list-
lessness and such like debilitating uneasiness. When this happens,
the good doctor advises the young men not to wait until they get
married. This kind of nervousness will disappear when the young
man marries, and then it will be his wife who, presumably, will
come to see the doctor.

There are no cases of venereal disease in town and no syphilis, but
in the last two years, a couple of cases of gonorrhea have been reported. Interestingly enough, the males concerned were young tradesmen connected with the tourist trade. They were able to earn money
and run off to Izmir and Milas and go to the bars and cabarets
there. There are no prostitutes in Bodrum, except reportedly one
in the Cretan quarter, and the institution of prostitution, possibly of
vital importance in a society where the sexes are segregated in
adolescence and later, cannot play its presumably catalysing role.

No woman drinks in Bodrum but all men do "when they can find
it". And some men drink regularly. The most popular drinks are
raki, wine and vodka. *Raki* and vodka are a government monopoly,
while the wine comes from the island of Bozcaada, the only Turkish
island where wine is produced. The wine is distributed by "Djange"
Süleyman in Bodrum and throughout the peninsula. He is a modern-
thinking man and had a glass case, illuminated at night, made
to hang over his tourist agency as an advertisement. Since the
agency is right by the mosque, he did not know what to do during
Ramadan and the sign was lighted only one night in three. Although
he fasted and went to the mosque regularly, he did not neglect his
wine-distributing business; because of this, he was heartily teased
by the other men in the market. "Djange" estimates that he sells
something like 18,00 bottles of red and white wine in the town and
that his rivals sell something like 6,000 bottles. The Monopolies
distribute about 1,000 bottles of wine and 12,000 bottles of *raki*.
This does not cover the town's entire consumption, because there
is no liquor sold in the villages, and peasants buy their *raki* and
wine on Fridays, when they come to market. But the overwhelming
quantity is consumed in Bodrum, and in the summer the tourists
bring the consumption up and the locals are encouraged to drink

more, through sheer example. If one deducts the child and female population, this would mean that a little below 1,600 adult men consume something like 17 bottles of alcoholic drink a year each. But in fact, no more than 50 men or so drink regularly something like half a bottle of raki each day or, in the case of wine, a bottle.

The locals drink more than the Cretans and the "drinkers" are well known, since very few men drink in their own home. The locals are better off than the Cretans and less extroverted. But for both local and Cretan, every occasion is an occasion to drink: slack times through idleness, tangerine or sponge harvest-time because there is money, winter-time because it is cold, and so on. In spite of this, there are very few alcoholics in Bodrum. One of the most well known is Ali Dayi the peanut-seller. He is over seventy, a little bent, but in good health. Early in the mornings, at about five-thirty, he goes to the bakery and waits there for the Bodrum bun, the *gevrek*, to come out. He recovers there slowly from the night before and is usually given a glass of tea while he waits. He then carries his baskets all through town, in any kind of weather, and after having sold all his wares, goes to sleep for the day. In the evening, he re-emerges, this time his baskets filled with peanuts, which he salts and roasts himself, and goes from café to restaurant to *meyhane*— the local bars—and sells them. He is offered glasses of drink everywhere and since he likes to sing and dance, people urge him on and give him more drink. He is never sober and in the summer, he is so popular with the tourists that he falls into comas and has to be carried home each dawn, by whoever happens to be passing by. Ali Dayi never loses his courtesy or his balance, never forgets his songs and is always friendly and courteous.

Bodrum does not have a fully fledged hospital but only a Health Centre. The Health Centre is situated on a hill in the western part of town and far from the centre of things, because it was built on a piece of land donated by one of the town's citizens. People who need the Centre in emergencies, such as sponge-divers, fishermen and craftsmen, complain that it is too far and that a man can die a hundred times before he can get help. There are two buildings in the Centre, and a garden; one of the buildings contains the out-patients' clinic, the pharmacy, the doctor's office and the other contains the wards, the nurses' room and the kitchen.

Care is entirely free and most of the in-patients are peasants from the surrounding villages. The townspeople stay at home when they are ill and, if they have to go to hospital, they prefer to go to Izmir. But rich and poor alike come to the Health Centre for minor complaints or in emergencies and when Alim bey is not available. Like any other place of business in Bodrum, the Centre is busiest on Fridays and Mondays. Most of the ten beds are occupied by women from the villages or from the poorest quarters in town who have had a difficult delivery and the government doctor in charge of the Centre estimates that at least five more beds are needed. In fact, the Centre is only equipped to take care of minor emergencies and no surgery of any kind can be undertaken there. The government doctor employs the municipal doctor part-time and both complain that two nurses and two orderlies are not enough to look after the work. A scorpion-bite takes up most of a morning, and a traffic accident will mobilize the whole Centre. Although there is a washing machine and a refrigerator, the Centre does not have an autoclave, an operating table or adequate lighting. It has, however, a jeep which picks up patients and brings them in. Drugs are bought in town and this takes up a large part of the Centre's budget, since the drugs provided by the Ministry of Health are scarce and cover a narrow range.

The doctors and the population would like a hospital similar to the one in Milas, where all services would be available, including dentistry, for there is no dentist in town. There is a man who worked once in Izmir as a dental assistant, and he pulls teeth when necessary. The Bodrum people do not know of any other remedy for an aching tooth. Whenever anyone complains about toothache, "get it pulled" is the immediate answer, given however if all other remedies have been tried and proven of no avail. People are advised to put a clove against the aching tooth and hold it there, or a bit of cotton wool dipped in *raki*, or again to bathe the tooth in sage tea. But if none of these works, then evidently the tooth has to be pulled out. Even so, the Bodrum people estimate that they have good teeth and they attribute this to the water. Nevertheless, the tooth-puller makes a very good income and has a nice little house with a sign saying "Dentist" on it, and not M.D., as he would were he a qualified dentist. He also makes false teeth.

There is another doctor in town and that is Alim Bey. He came here many years ago as a government doctor, and then resigned and began practising on his own. His wife is a school teacher and they are both among the most well-liked people in town. He and his wife

have been able to aquire a tangerine grove and another piece
of land on which they are now building a small hotel. They were also
able to buy a new two -storied house built in the modern way with
a kitchen and a bathroom. Now Alim Bey has his consulting rooms
downstairs, which allows him to take a rest now and again.

Years of practice in Bodrum and its villages have made Alim Bey
the typical country family doctor. He delivers babies, lances boils,
cures pneumonia and whooping cough, knows what to do with the
sand and stones. Although he keeps up with developments in medicine through the medical journals of Istanbul and Ankara, he never
loses sight of the fact that he is dealing with people who live in an
environment which ignores the more modern aspects of civilization
and his prescriptions are therefore simple and can easily be followed
by the patients. Many parents in the villages have given his name
to baby boys which he successfully delivered in difficult cases.

Alim Bey considers that the townspeople are healthier than
people living in other parts of the country, owing to the climate
and the sea, but also because they consult a doctor when they feel
sick. They do not come as soon as they have a cold or a small
temperature and endeavour to cure these with home remedies,
lemon juice and lime tea, or by applying suction cups. But if the
fever persists, they will see the doctor. Especially in the case of
children, they are very careful and bring the child to the doctor
as soon as something goes wrong. According to his experience, the
people with better incomes and a better education than the average
come to him more often because the poor decide in advance that
they will not be able to afford the medicine which he will prescribe.
But it is only the very poor who do not come. Government officials
and tradesmen come more often than fishermen and workers and
the Cretans more often than the locals.

Medical insurance only came to Bodrum in the past year. Alim
Bey has become the Medical Insurance representative and now has
a lot of paper work to do. All the civil servants are automatically
insured and these include the night watchmen and the people who
work at the cold-storage plant. Since most workers are employed
on a short-term basis, employers do not insure them and the workers
have no card. Even if an employer, such as the tangerine cooperative or a fig exporter, deducts medical insurance from his worker's
pay, this does not help the worker, since he has not been informed
about the routine and does not ask for a card where his benefits

can be recorded. Some of the more prosperous merchants and one of the boat-builders have registered their employees with the doctor, but the vast majority of the people still have to pay themselves for medical care.

Modern medicine is not the only method by which people hope to get well in Bodrum. Applying to the *imam*, and often to an old man or woman living in the neighbourhood who has the reputation to heal through prayer, is another way. Warts, for instance, are always cured in this way. Alim Bey himself resorted to this method when his son developed warts and asked an old man with the gift of healing to come and "read over" the warts. The warts disappeared and Alim Bey says that it is just as well that the "reading" works, since there is no cauterizing apparatus in town!

For everyday use in the home, various oils are used. They are sold by an old man who goes around the market every day and in and out of the neighbourhoods. These are the oils extracted from the herbs and trees which grow on the hills. Sage and mint, aniseed and almond, thyme and berries heal a multitude of minor aliments. Thyme oil and sage oil are the most popular remedies. All the mothers of Bodrum use sage oil to cure the stomach-aches of their babies, by applying some to their lips and rubbing their stomachs with it. Quince seeds, dried and steeped in boiled water, are used to cure coughs; poultices of crushed and cooked onion are put on wounds; raw meat, minced, is applied to sprains. Sometimes these remedies are discarded for more drastic ones. Ali the Barber is called in to apply leeches—another of his accomplishments in addition to circumcision. There is a story that one day, when poor Ali Dayi the peanut vendor had to be bled, all the leeches fell back in a stupor, so charged with alcohol was his blood! In cases of simple hepatitis or jaundice, a cut is made between the eyes or under the tongue with a razor-blade. Alim Bey did not deny that the ensuing shock may relax the gall-bladder ducts, and thus help.

The doctor does not discourage people from resorting to such methods as long as he does not consider them harmful. But neither does he encourage them. The case of salting babies is an instance; he fought, together with the midwife, the habit of salting the baby like a fish, but does nor prevent people from putting salt or stones in the water. He believes that these customs are usually harmless and take away some of the strain of being sick. He also believes that we do not know enough about human nature and the human body and that there may be something in such practices as "reading over".

Resorting to "readings" and herb-therapy is shared by all the people in Bodrum, regardless of the level of income or education. The difference shows when the remedies prove useless and when people feel that the situation is serious enough to warrant going to the doctor. Compared to other parts of Turkey, like the East for instance, the Bodrum people are less superstitious and more open to new ways. However, just as in the case of spells, the Cretans are the biggest users of home-made remedies and "readings", while they are, at the same time, the best customers of the doctors.

In everyday life, the townspeople take few precautions. They try to keep out of the north wind and wear as many clothes as possible in the winter, which they never take off, even when they come into a heated room. All the old sailors wear a woollen vest all throughout the year. In the summer they try to keep out of the sun and marvel at the fact that the tourists lie for hours under the sun without getting sick. They fight the damp and when they build a house or have to rent one, the first thing they say about it is "it's protected from the north wind" and "it is not damp". For the people who live along the sea-shore, the sea is their enemy during the winter-storms, sending spray and stones into the very rooms. So that in the winter, the family moves into the back rooms and board up the windows with a view. For the rest, they trust to God. What they dread is a serious illness which may incapacitate or kill a husband or a mother and bring economic disaster to the family. In such cases, only the better-off people can survive as a family. The poor are permanently crippled.

This year another pharmacy was opened in Bodrum and the people were delighted. "Now", they said, "there will be competition and our druggist won't be able to exploit us". This druggist and his wife—she is the one with the pharmacist's diploma—came to Bodrum in 1963 and opened the first pharmacy. Before that, the doctors used to bring drugs and sell them to the patients, not an unprofitable business. While the lady pharmacist stays at home and looks after the children, her husband reads the prescriptions and makes up the medicines, or so the townspeople say. It is true, though, that she is away most of the time. When the writer asked for an interview, it was granted right away but most of the answers were given by the husband.

They confirmed that the townspeople were mindful of their

health but were so poor that they rarely bought all the medicines prescribed by the doctor. Very often, and especially on market days, peasants would walk in, address the husband as "Doctor" and ask for a medicine to alleviate their ills. Very often they ask for natural remedies, lime-flowers, or sage and thyme oil. The towns-people and the peasants alike are very fond of beauty products. Even village women come in and ask for "Dr. So-and So's cream", they forget the brand name but remember the product. They use a lot of "stone" powder, which is talcum and day cream against the "sun and the wind", while the ladies of the town buy all the range of a beauty brand. Although the most sophisticated makes are not available, there were one or two quite respectable products on sale. The pharmacist said that the younger generation, the village women and the Cretan women were their best customers for cosmetics. The local ladies use very little make-up.

The shop gets its goods by telephoning Izmir almost every day and the stuff comes by truck, like all the other manufactured products used in Bodrum. Like all the shops, they have to give credit, and half their business is done that way; out of this amount, 10 to 15% is given on a year-long basis, from harvest to harvest. While they do not like it, they said it was an "economic necessity", to keep the custom. They themselves buy on credit, or with promissory notes, but they have to pay up on much shorter time.

When the writer asked them which medicines sold most, they said that there was a constant demand for drugs against stomach aches, asthma, gallstones and rheumatism. A lot of women ask for sedatives, such as tranquilizers or bromides, which are cheaper. As for contraceptives, a few women, mainly government employees, or their wives have just begun to use the pill. But the pill is expensive and only seven or eight women use it. As for male contraceptives, fifty to sixty men buy them and they cost a lira and a half for a packet of five.

This couple came from Ankara, looking for a good business opportunity and a quiet life and they say they found it. They like the people, who are "civilized", albeit poor, and the children thrive in the clean air and the sea. They have seen many changes in the last seven years, new shops opening, a greater variety of goods coming; "a few years ago you could only buy onions and potatoes, there were no toys, no furniture or household appliances". Tourism has helped, they said, because tourists keep asking for the things they are used to, and the shops order them.

CHAPTER ELEVEN

SOCIAL RELATIONSHIPS

Personal relationships in Bodrum seem, to the casual observer, to by pretty much what they are everywhere else: some people see each other often, some do not; some are liked by everybody and some disliked in the same way; some people have a wide circle of acquaintances and some keep themselves to themselves. Upon closer acquaintance, however, one can see that a great deal of subtlety and a peculiar logic forms all relationships. The reason why this has to be discovered slowly is that the people of Bodrum are fairly reserved about themselves and others and in this they are similar to most Turks. The apparent cordiality which reigns among the shopkeepers in the market, or among the members of the City Club and other circles may disguise deep antagonism. The relations between men from the two main parties are far from being cordial but the antagonism is only apparent when anelection draws near or when a political personality visits the town. Otherwise politics are not discussed in everyday encounters. The Cretan-local relationships are a mixture of indifference and mild but persisting distrust. Those between the townspeople and strangers, townspeople and the civil servants, civil servants themselves, rich and poor, all exhibit different characteristics which do not seem to change with time, or at least have not changed over the last two decades or more, according to most people and the strangers who have settled here.

First of all there are some groups which, as a matter of course, do not mingle with others. Such are the local women and the Cretan women, the higher civil servants and the minor ones, the tradesmen and the fishermen or sponge-divers, the families and the bachelors, the townspeople and the civil servants or strangers generally. There are exceptions to the rule. The sea people have leisure-time contacts with the civil servants, with whom they must be on good terms, such as the harbour-master and the customs officials. But the wives do not meet and more often than not, only know each other by sight. The men meet over an occasional *raki* table, or over a cup of coffee in the cafés. In the City Club, some of the higher civil servants play cards with some—one or two—of the most prosperous tradesmen and boat-owners. The relationship rests there, and does not develop into one where families visit each other. Here again, the wives know each other by sight only, and are not on greeting terms. The school-teachers, who are considered by the higher civil servants as second-class civil servants, meet the towns-people on social terms and visit each other, but only when the school-teacher happens to be a local. Whether they are so or not, they have no social contacts with the higher civil servants, the exception being the Education Director and the Headmistress of the Girls' Technical School. The doctors and especially Alim Bey and the Museum Direc-tor, both popular men, meet and visit all the members of the "upper crust" together with their wives. As for the strangers who have settled in the community, only one of the bank directors and the Museum Director have been "accepted" by everybody and consider-ed as having become "local" and so are able to drink or eat with almost everyone, while their wives will only visit the wives of their "class" and not have contacts with the wives of fishermen or trades-men.

These relationships, however, are superficial. They consist of a few formal visits exchanged by the wives on set days, a few evenings spent, *en famille*, at each other's homes and a meeting or two a month between the men over a "*raki* table", and are rarely in the nature of a close friendship. As for relationships between Cretan and local, they are closely affected by four factors: the closeness of neighbour-hood life, the segregation of women and men, the occupations of men and the level of income.

The seamen, fishermen and sponge-divers, whether they are boat-owners or workers on boats only spend some months of the year on land. When they are home, they spend their evenings at the neighbourhood café, or in the harbour café, and the more prospe-rous may spend some evenings eating and drinking in one or two restaurants in the town. In no case are they ever accompanied by their wives. These visit one another in their homes in their respec-tive neighbourhoods but rarely go to another neighbourhood. Since all the Cretans, with one or two exceptions, live in Kum-bahce, this automatically precludes frequent meetings with women living in other neighbourhoods. Even the wives of wealthy fishermen and sponge-captains do not go into other neighbourhoods. The local women similarly live their social life in their own neighbour-hoods and the men, working downtown day in and day out, auto-matically spend some of their evenings together, leaving the shop for the restaurant without going home first. Their business life is tied to the business life of the other tradesmen and craftsmen: the the supplier of building materials to the builders and carpenters, the yard-goods and general store owners to their partners or relatives in the trading-houses, the shopkeepers to other shopkeepers. These men will not go to the neighbourhood café which is the meeting place of the poorer people, since only tea and sage-tea and coffee are available there, but meet in the more central places, the restaurants in the market and the City Club, places where the Cretan fishermen and sponge-captains come in only when the season is over and when they are flush with money. After a while the Cretan contingent will disappear and either spend the evenings at home or in the neighbourhood café. Also, a considerable number of wealthy Cretans—compared to similarly well-off locals—are more inclined to spend their evenings with the family and their relatives.

THE CONCEPT OF EL

Again, while on closer observation and in respect to certain aspects, such as the care of children, neighbourhood life seems to be an extension of family life, this is really not so. The twin concepts of "family" and "stranger"—in Turkish *el*, meaning anyone not connected by blood ties—govern neighbourhood and, in fact, all relationships. When a gardener or a waiter proves lazy, "what do you expect from an *el*", people will say. When a bride proves spoilt, "why should my son work his fingers to the bone for an *el*'s daughter", mothers-in-law will say. When a craftsman has made something which breaks down, "*el*'s work is like that", everybody will say. to which the immediate sequence is, in all cases, "only you yourself can do a proper job of work" or "if they had married their son to someone from the family, he would not be like that today".

This does not mean that members of a family consider themselves as infallible or particularly able; for from it. The family is well aware of the faults of uncles and aunts, counsins and in-laws, and speak about these freely among themselves. But it is truly believed that someone in the family is always to be preferred to an outsider, no matter what the problem or the job at hand. Worries and annoyances, even shame can be brought upon the family by some of its members, but this is in the nature of things and bearable. They are unbearable and exasperating only when they are caused by *el*.

This is illustrated by a series of misfortunes which befell the Ilter family last year, in quick succession. An Ilter uncle wounded some-one very seriously with a knife in the course of a drunken evening and had to go to prison for it. An Ilter son went to prison for sumggl-ing a few weeks later and finally, an Ilter daughter-in-law was caught with a neighbour's son in circumstances which left no doubt as to that particular relationship. The Ilters are a highly respected family, well in the higher-income bracket, and known for the closeness of their family relationships. In the first two cases they were distraught and unhappy, but in the last they were, in addition, furious. This was shame brought upon them by an *el*'s daughter, by an outsider and not to be borne. While they maintained a dignified silence in the first two cases, they did not mind discussing the last case with something amounting to gusto with anyone who brought the matter up. In the same way, Fureyya accepts the fact that her husband is not an ideal husband and does not mention their relationship too often, but she would freely criticize her sister-in-law.

The attitude towards the *el* is especially marked among the women. Men, who depend on each other for their livelihood are more inclined to judge a man by his abilities but still not very willing to have more than the necessary dealings with strangers, and definitely unwilling to bring strangers within the family circle. This is closely connected, too, with the pattern of family settlement and neighbour-hood life. The immediate neighbourhood of each family contains most members of the family, as has been seen earlier. Within the larger family, constant visiting takes place in the homes and the men can talk about their business with their male relatives, while the women talk among themselves. During the day, women see each other constantly and drop in casually into each other's houses, to borrow something, a tray or a cup of sugar, a couple of eggs or spices, a mortar or the sewing machine. The visits are rarely long-drawn and limited to the usual greetings and the business at hand. It is only women who are close friends who visit one another in the afternoons, bringing their children and their knitting with them. This is a pattern which belongs both to the Cretan and the local neighbourhoods, with this difference that in the summer, the Cretan women prefer to congregate on the seashore rather than in their houses, while the local women sit in their gardens.

However, there are limits to neighbourhood relationships. Food is almost never received or offered, money never borrowed and small children are not left in the care of a neighbour if the mother has to go away. If the child is over four or five years old, he will be entrusted to his father, if smaller to an older brother or sister. Women with babies will only leave the baby to a relative in the neighbourhood, not to a neighbour or a friend. Each woman has her hands full and it is not "right" to burden her further. Within these limits, relationships are easy and cordial and the unwritten rules work fairly well. The same spirit prevails in the men's relationships in the neighbourhood café; if the men concerned are in the habit of spending their spare time there. The neighbourhood *el* is just a little better than other *el*, but not much more so.

In this way, relationships are closest within the family, and get progressively weaker as they proceed from immediate family to extended family, from immediate neighbourhood to the whole neighbourhood and then to the town in general. It is only in the upper levels of income and class that relationships span the family and neighbourhood lines. This also is helped by the fact that in these groups, the immediate family is smaller, many members having left to settle elsewhere and that as far as the strangers and civil servants are concerned, "exile" makes them draw closer to each other. As it is said locally, these people have only one another as *muhatap*, a word meaning someone with whom you speak the same language. Strangers and civil servants are often heard complaining about the fact that they do not have *muhatap* and thus feel forced to fall upon each other's resources.

The general reserve observed in personal relationships in Bodrum is not peculiar to the town. It is a national trait. The society puts a premium on such qualities as silence, reserve, coolness and what is called "face", *yüz*. Spontaneity, lightheartedness, especially in the young and in women are discouraged. The formulas which are exchanged upon each occasion, which are used according to a person's age, sex, position in life are fixed and strictly conformed to. This is relaxed and people find release from these strictures when they drink or, in the case of women, in gossip sessions among small close groups. At other times, the pattern is conformed to, a pattern learnt in childhood and later adhered to as a matter of habit. This way of conducting everyday relationships may have its drawbacks, but it has many advantages. Not being too close, not being "mixed up" as the saying goes, prevents the frictions which are bound to occur when people see each other constantly for long periods of

time and share knowledge of everything, from money transactions
to family secrets. It also prevents quarrels and estrangements. Very
few people in Bodrum put themselves in a position where they would
have to ignore other people in the street or stop having dealings
with others as a result of a quarrel or a misunderstanding. When
a tale is circulated, or a piece of unpleasant gossip is heard by the
subject of the tale or the gossip, the thing to do is to find, a "reasonable" third party and ask them to put matters right. Outright
protest or explanations are almost never resorted to. It is thus
hoped that the spreader of the tale will mend the damage and will
not feel, in this way, that he or she has lost "face". A direct approach
would invariably lead to a quarrel and to a corresponding loss of
face for both parties.

LAW AND ORDER

In the same way, men do not seem to resort to street or café-
brawls. The writer has never seen a street-fight and has been told
that these almost never occur. In fact, people were not able to recall
one. If two men begin to exchange what is considered as offensive
remarks in a restaurant, while drinking, or in a café, the people
around will very soon put a stop to the quarrel and the attacker
will be escorted out by his friends before they start shouting. They
are a few men in the town who are known by everybody to be
quarrelsome or aggressive. When these come into a restaurant in
the evening, people exchange glances and inwardly prepare themselves to face a possible spate of unpleasantness. At the first sign of
trouble, the aggressor will find himself either ignored or, if this
does not work, taken out by his companions. In this way, the reputation of the town among policemen and other keepers of law and
order, such as the judge and the *kaymakam*, is a good one. In fact,
one young policemen complained to the writer that "he would never
learn his job" in this town and that only policemen near retirement
age should be sent here, to end their career peacefully. He soon got
his wish, because he set out to create his own trouble with visiting
tourist girls.

By the same token, night -watchmen estimate that going round
the streets at night is a waste of time. Nothing ever happens except
that they catch colds. What they would like is to draw their salaries
and go to bed, like everybody else, not later than ten o'clock. This

pattern has been changing with the advent of tourism. Then the town fills with "strangers" and "there is no telling what may happen". When someone lost a considerable sum of money last summer, the townspeople kept telling each other, "some stranger must have taken the money", and the Tourism Association people and the police agreed that no local could possibly be involved. This is borne out by the fact that people do not lock their doors at night or when they go away. Most doors do not have a lock, and what locks there are, are broken. It is not unusual to find the two wings of a door held together by a piece of string, tied on the outside, and this is more to keep stray dogs out or a cow from walking into the courtyard than anything else. It also means that there is no one at home. The few cases of theft which occur in a year—a maximum of four in 1965—occurred in the market and involved "strangers" in two instances, young men who had come from another town. When strangers marvel at this, at the open doors, at the shops left untenanted for hours on end, the people are fond of saying, "and who would dare steal anything with all the neighbours' eyes glued to each other's doors?" Baggypants the grocer knows that anybody entering his shop while he is in the café next door of an evening, is bound to be seen by the people opposite—"you cannot prevent women from looking into the streets", he says. In the same way, shopkeepers in the market will leave their shops for long periods, either to get cool or to warm up, according to the season, knowing that an eventual customer will know where to find them. Thus, buying some thread or knitting wool may involve finding oneself eventually sitting in a café and drinking some tea as a prelude to the transaction. Time is not of the essence in this town.

The police *komiser* showed the writer his files to give an idea of the sort of offences which were committed in the town. Many of these end at the police-court and do not reach the court-room, especially those involving quarrels. Thus in 1965, a high point in the committing of offences, only 23 out of 45 offences reached the court-room. This was the year of the elections and the year when Bodrum knew its first large intake of tourists; these two factors may have influenced the pattern. The largest cluster of offences is recorded under the name of quarrels, meaning verbal aggression without blows. Two or three of these quarrels, which do not exceed a dozen a year, end in blows, and knives only seemed to have been used once each year. Although a few people carry arms, such as a gun or a knife, they do not seem to use them much. There are many traffic offences, but of the milder sort, such as failing to pay taxes on licence plates, or driving without a licence. There have been two "political" offences, one man accused of extreme-left propaganda and the other of extreme-right propaganda. Upon enquiry, however, these proved to be mistakes. People jokingly explained that the first case involved a drunken postman who had "insulted" the government and the other involved a very religious old man who was thought to possess books praising the advent of a large Islamic confederation. The books were duly found, but they had been sent from "outside" to the old man, in the hope that he would use them. However, he did not happen to know how to read. Both men were cleared in no time at all. As for what may be termed "sexual" offences, such as rape, bothering girls and such-like offences involving the sexes, there has not been a case of rape in living memory, while there had been two other interesting cases: one in which a young man was reported as "following" a girl wherever she went, and the other in which a young man who had written a letter to a young girl suggesting that they meet. In both cases, the complainants dropped the charge!

An interesting aspect of the verbal quarrels is that as many of them involve men as women and that most of them take place either in the market or in the poorer quarters of town, including the Cretan quarter. In this latter, the women seem to quarrel as much as the men and the quarrels are often an extension of quarrels between children. Coming out on the doorstep to see what the children are quarrelling about, the women will eventually start among themselves. Still, the total number of quarrels is so small and their nature such as to lead to the conclusion that the people of Bodrum are a peace-abiding lot.

Murder is almost unknown in the town. But one murder took place last year, an event which had not happened for twenty-five years at least. The town was shaken to its foundations and the shock was such that the radios could not be heard for a week. The young man who was murdered was well-liked, serious and hard-working. He was a jeep-driver and engaged to be married. His killer is a well-known scoundrel, reported to be of gypsy stock, and worked in a bakery. No one knew the motive, except that everybody believed that it was due to jealousy, not over a woman, but that the baker could not stand the driver and envied his popularity. The two had had words before and one night, the baker hid in the jeep and jumped on the driver when he took his seat. He was wounded in eight places. The knife was found a few paces away and the baker gave himself up, saying that he had "lost control of himself". He got a life sentence, which he is serving in the prefecture prison for serious offenders in Muğla.

Many people in the town say that this kind of peace cannot last, that tourism and films between them will soon lead Bodrum to become "like other towns", with murder and everything. Indeed, these are not empty fears. The younger shopkeepers and craftsmen have begun to earn money and are able to go to Izmir and Milas and drink in the restaurants. They are able to extricate themselves from the strict control of their elders, and the more subtle ones of the community. They have begun to strike up acquaintanceships with the less desirable type of tourist, the kind who looks for free board and lodging, for a spot of smuggling or embezzling. Especially in the summer and in the last three or four years, cases involving them and some young men have come in fornt of the *komiser*, to end in the court-room.

According to the judge, Bodrum is beginning to acquire some "modern" crimes, such as embezzlement, breach of confidence, offences against women. The judge terms these "elegant urban offences", in contrast to the good old-fashioned quarrels ending with either an honest blow or a drink of reconciliation. He expects that in the years to come, cases involving the townspeople will come up in front of him as often as cases among the villagers. For the judge presides over the district court and most of the work involves offences in the thrity-one villages of the district. The great majority of these offences consists of violations of the forestry law and disputes involving the harvesting of olive trees and the boundaries of fields; the carrying of arms without a licence and such-like offences are relatively few and again there seem to be no murders and no serious quarrels. Quarrels in the villages are settled either by the villagers or by the village headman, the *muhtar*.

The court-room in Bodrum occupies an old Greek house with three rooms on each of its two floors. The Clerk and the typists sit downstairs, the prosecutor and the judge have an office each upstairs and the court is the largest room on the second floor, with large windows overlooking the gardens and the hills. Each morning the room is drenched with sun and in the winter a stove is perpetually fed with good logs and not the usual prunings and cuttings. Two small benches at the back are used for spectators and two similar benches are reserved for the accused and the witnesses. The judge and the prosecutor sit on a small platform, with the Clerk just beneath. The whole place is the size of a large bedroom in a country-house. The judge wears everyday clothes—a pull-over with a turtle-neck collar—under his gown, but the prosecutor always wears a collar and tie. Outside on the large landing, accused and witnesses, relatives and friends sit close to each other, chatting in muted voices during the session. Everybody nods to everybody, the two solicitors of the town—political enemies but brothers in the law—flit in and out and the young usher endeavours to maintain the atmosphere of quiet dignity that court-rooms ought to have. Usually this is in vain, and chatting and shufflings go on regardless.

One morning when the writer came into the court-room, the judge interrupted what he was saying to tell me to sit by the fire and to order me some coffee. He then went on with the proceedings which involved some people from a nearby village. It appears that there was an old woman in the village who threatened people and beat up children and generally behaved oddly. The witnesses were a young women, an old man, and the village *gendarme*. The old man could not state his age and a witness was brought it to estimate it. The *gendarme* had difficulty in expressing his thoughts, and the judge had to dictate the story to the typist again, in a more logical sequence. Finally it was decided to send the woman to the district doctor to find out exactly what was the matter with her and the case was dismissed. After that, repeated callings for other offenders by the usher went unanswered and the judge, the prosecutor and the writer adjourned to the judge's room for a cup of coffee. "On cold days like this, the villagers do not come; next session they will have to be brought in by *gendarmes*", said the judge.

In such cases, there are no spectators. But when a case involving a citizen of Bodrum in being tried, then the landing is full to the point of making the boards creak ominously. Such was the case involving "Deli" Salih and "Rich" Hasan, two colourful personalities who had taken each other to court over a matter of olive trees, or the famous "Dolly Case", which involved a tourist girl and no less than seven young men. In this latter case, breach of the peace, drunken behaviour, insults to the keepers of law and order, followed each other in quick succession. It is the "Dolly Case" which started the people of Bodrum on their head-shaking about the future of law and order and the young men. Indeed, it was to be the first of four or five cases in the next two summers involving, as Kasa put it reflectively, "the clash of many different mentalities": the pleasure-bent young tourists, the girl-starved young men, the concomitant good and bad results.

Money is a subject of law-suits in Bodrum. Seven or eight cases against debtors occur each year. Usually the creditor is a wealthy man who can afford the expense of taking the debtor to court. But the majority of the people, who are relatively poor, do not go to court over matters of money. First of all, they have not got the money to lend and if they do lend money sometimes, it is to relatives, whom one cannot take to court if one does not want to lose face. Also, in the very rare instances of debts between two poor men, the creditor can neither afford to go to court nor can he hope to receive his money that way, since all the court can do is to give a seizure order and there is nothing very much to seize. So people prefer to wait and hope that one day the debtor will earn enough money to repay the debt. Many transactions are conducted that way, especially among the smaller tradesmen and craftsmen. They give each other goods on barter and one day the accounts are drawn up. Each hopes to be able to repay the debt in more goods and sometimes, when there is no way of receiving the remainder of the debt in money, the creditor has to buy things he may not need, like wooden planks or roof-covering, lengths of rope or wire, hoping that he may be able to resell them or that they may come in useful one day. "Djange" was owed money by a building materials supplier who also owns a small restaurant. The man brought wine from him but could not pay the bill at the end of the summer, having invested in his materials business. "Djange" waited that winter and come next summer, acquired a stock of tiles with which he was going to cover his roof. He did not have that intention before, but calculated that this was the best investment he could make given the situation. One of the smaller restaurant owners borrowed money from a shopkeeper in town, but could not repay the debt for a long time. He finally offered the shopkeeper free drink and food to the amount of the debt. "Now" says the shopkeeper, "I feel I have to go and drink a few evenings a week, if only to recuperate my money". The shop-keeper's wife thinks that he should recuperate his money, but on a longer-term basis.

Debts are not, however, a matter for quarrelling but for persuasion. No one seems to remember of a case of two men shouting at each other because of money, or fighting about it. Quarrels and fighting occur usually after drinking and are ways of letting off steam. This behaviour is not too severely frowned upon by the community if it occurs rarely. For the rest, the people here behave like everybody else. Generally, they keep "themselves to themselves" and out of the way of trouble-makers; and in the relationships involved in everyday life, they try to maintain a mixture of cordiality and reserve, without allowing intimacy to develop, with all its possible consequence. "Go about your business", says Aunt Zubeyde" and do not mix yourself in 'el's" business', and this is a pretty good summing up.

<h2 style="text-align:center">Associations</h2>

Given these attitudes of mind, it is not surprising to find that the people of Bodrum have difficulty in banding together to get things done. Apart from the Tangerine and Sponge Cooperatives and the Tourism Association, there are sixteen assorted associations in the town, of which some are branches of national Associations, such as the Child Protection Society, the Air Force Association and the Red Crescent. The others are the newly founded Women's Union, the League against Communism, the Truck and Jeep-Drivers' Association, the Wood Products Association and an Aid Association each for the four schools and the Girls' Technical School.

These latter are the only ones which show some activity largely because most of the work is done through the Family-School Association, as the membership of each does not exceed eight people, most of them being on the Board. The membership of the others varies between three and seven members and since dues are not collected, there is no way of knowing how the membership has changed over the years. The Women's Association registered some sixty women, but here again dues are not collected and the board does not really know what it is supposed to do. Soon after the establishment of the Association, the money collected went to pay for the circumcision festivities of eight little boys whose parents were too poor to afford a proper celebration, and there the matter rested. The Association's chairman, however, is always invited to participate in the town's events, such as the visit of some political personality.

The League against Communism is the newest association and was founded by a schoolteacher who is known for his religious conservatism. He has not managed to enrol people in the League and the entire membership consist of the board only. The League is part of the national League, but somehow has not been able to attract people into it, which is not the case for some other parts of the country.

Nor do the townspeople organize themselves for the running of the town. A fairly passive and politically preoccupied municipal organization is not bothered or pushed into activity by the citizens of Bodrum, who remain content with bad roads, lack of proper drinking water, a modicum of garbage disposal and an erratic electricity supply. As was seen earlier, the members of the municipality are considered as part of the political organization and very few people expect them to act as the managers of the town. This does not mean that they are unaware of the situation, but simply that they do not think anything can be done about it. It will be some time yet before the town, like the rest of the nation, realizes that the vote is also—and maybe only—an instrument to get things done, and that this requires a revised version of the *el* concept.

CHAPTER TWELVE

LEISURE

FAMILY ENTERTAINING

Personal relationships and the pattern of work being what they are in Bodrum, it is not surprising to find that leisure and entertainment are closely affected by them. For many people in the town, men as well as women, girls as well as boys, leisure and work are closely intertwined and it is difficult to say where one begins and the other ends. The shoemakers and tailors, who work while the radio is on, who receive their friends in their shops during the day or in the evenings, and sometimes far into the night, obviously consider the shop as a place where time can be passed pleasantly, exchanging gossip and filling in football-pool coupons. The girls and women who go visiting and take their knitting or sewing with them, do not make a strict division between entertainment and work and would not dream of such a division. In the summer, the boys and men who take tourists on swimming and fishing trips do it to earn a living; but they enjoy it as much as the tourists do and if they dive for fish and sponges, it is not only to earn money but also because it is something they like doing anyway. When a tradesman and his wife go out to their tangerine grove of a Friday or a Sunday, taking with them a light lunch and the transistor radio, this is as much a picnic as a work expedition; they would rest under the trees and eat their lunch, pick flowers or herbs for a meal or two, and come back at night to town, tired but satisfied with the day's outing. In the same way, fishermen who sit in the cafés and mend nets enjoy the company of their friends, the radio, and would be hard put to answer if they were asked whether they have been working or not that day. One day, when the writer asked Deli Mustafa if he had been working that day—for he had been making a net— he said, "no, I just went to the café, the weather was not fishing weather". A few days later, the writer said to him jokingly, "Uncle Mustafa, I see you enjoy life, sitting in the café all day", to which he replied, quite shocked, "What do you mean enjoy', I mended my nets all day"!

However, there are many occasions which are purely leisure and

considered as such. A few of these are shared by both men, and
women, while most are segregated. The non-segregated ways of
spending time are the cinema, visiting in the evening and once a
year the play put on by the Youth Club for the benefit of the needy
pupils of the Secondary School.

Evening visits, where one family goes out to visit another, after
having sent someone in the daytime to announce it, are rare occasions; relatives visit one another in the evening unannounced.
But people who do not belong to the family do not. The announcement is made a day before but more often on the same day, and it
is a rare occurrence when the visit cannot take place because the
hosts are otherwise occupied. The townspeople, on such occasions,
pay a little attention to their clothes, especially the women. They
may change their skirt or their blouse and wear shoes instead of
the usual plastic or rubber slippers. But the men will come in their
everyday clothes. Children will come too, but if there is an adolescent boy or girl in the host family, the guests will not bring an adolescent of the opposite sex. When the adolescent is a boy, it is unlikely
that he will stay; he will prefer to join his own friends. But the
girls stay and listen in to the conversation of the women, and only
speak when addressed, unless the guests are very close friends. A
young girl knows that during such visits her behaviour will be
observed and reported upon next day in the neigbourhood, and
she is aware that quietness and modesty are the most prized qualities in a future bride.

After the usual greetings have been exchanged, everybody sits
down and another round of formal greetings is exchanged. People
ask each other in turn how they are and the traditional answer
"Praise be to God, we are well" is given in return. After that,
the atmosphere relaxes and conversation begins. The weather,
especially in the winter, is immediately discussed and compared
to the weather in other parts of the country and even the world.
This is one of the topics which men and women discuss together
but very soon the company splits in two and the men begin to
talk among themselves, while the women move closer to each other
and carry on chatter about the usual subjects, illness and health,
news from children away at school or in the army, neighbourhood
events and a moderate amount of gossip which takes the form of
praise, commiseration or blame as the case may be. After a while,
the hostess or her daughter makes coffee, which is invariably drunk

very sweet, and a dish of sweets is passed around. On such occasions the men are not offered drinks. In the more prosperous or "modern" households, liqueurs may be circulated with the sweets, but here again, hard drink will not be offered. After two hours or so the visit will come to an end; farewells will be exchanged and a promise to return the visit asked for and granted.

These visits, however, are rare occurrences since the men see each other constantly at work and the women during the daytime. They are usually arranged beforehand by the wives, who welcome an occasion to go out in the evening with their husbands and more often than not have a reason. These reasons are many and varied and provide an excuse or an opportunity for visiting. Such are visits paid to a family whose son has gone into the army; the visitors come to wish the parents a happy return of the boy and hope that the time in the army will be easy for him; or upon the announcement of an engagement, visits are made to congratulate the parents and proffer hopes about the future happiness of the couple; or again, when a new house has been bought or an old one renovated, to wish the householders good luck in their new surroundings. More often than not, these special visits will take place in the daytime between the women, while the men will congratulate each other casually in the market streets. It is only in the case of close friends that family visits in the evening will take place.

These occasions are quiet. Nobody expects to be entertained or amused or expects to have "a good time". The visit has to be paid and it is paid. A social obligation has been discharged. It is only when someone in either family is known to be "gay" and can be relied upon to enliven the evening that people really look forward to the visits. There will be jokes and stories, and sometimes a bit of moderate clowning. The women will never tell a joke or a story themselves, but leave their conversation aside and listen and laugh with the men. Some women are known for their humour and their gaiety and they will entertain their friends during the afternoons, but will rarely entertain people at such gatherings.

The second occasion upon which it is usual for men and women to go out together is the play. The play is put on once a year, in the winter, and everybody buys tickets since it is felt that the cause is worthy. On such occasions, the whole family goes, the small children sitting in the arms of their parents, or left to run around during the performance and sit on anybody's knees for a while.

There is a small negro boy who has been adopted by a childless couple and who is petted and loved by everybody in the town. Each time his running around during the play is as much of an attraction as the play itself and nobody minds the disturbance.

The play last winter was a comedy called "Before the Ice Melts" and told the story of a small town in the East which is awaiting the arrival of a new *kaymakam*. But the snows come and the town is completely cut off. Out of the snowy horizon one day comes a man and he is mistaken for the new official. He does not deny the fact and takes up office, and for some time the town knows a fair, just and good administration. All the bogeys which plague the East are successfully fought by the man: feudal landlords, corrupt policemen, selfish politicians are put in their place, to the astonishment and delight of the population. Now and again the man is heard to mutter: "Before the ice melts, before the ice melts, I must do all this before the ice melts". Indeed, after a few months, the ice melts and the roads are opened again and the real *kaymakam* arrives. It is then found out that the man was the inmate of an insane asylum who had escaped and somehow reached the town. The play ends in an anticlimax where everybody agrees that it was too good to last and that the bad old days were here again.

This play had been a great success in Istanbul and the capital and had not its writer been a well-known literary figure, might very well have known troubled days with the censors. It was chosen in Bodrum by some of the members of the Youth Club and one or two of the more educated gentlemen of the town, such as Teoman. Teoman himself directed the play, the Peace Corps girl designed and helped make the décor, and the midwife took charge of the make-up and costumes. For days before everybody was interested and asked members of the team how the play was going and when the opening would come. A week before the opening, the tickets were sold around the town and it became quite obvious that the seats in the cinema would not be enough. Additional chairs were borrowed from cafés in the market and people were told that there would be no seats for children.

Finally the great evening arrived. Everybody hurried home to eat an early supper and the restaurants did a poor trade that night. Two of them had closed anyway to be able to go to the play. When the writer came, she was taken to one of the best seats, and found herself seated between the wives of the *kaymakam* and the doctor.

The front row had been reserved for the officials and the second for the wealthy people in the town who had donated more than the price of the ticket. It was not very surprising to find that not all these seats were filled and before the play started, lesser mortals sat in them. All through this there was utter confusion. Noises of hammering came from behind the curtain, the wireless blared, children shouted, babies cried and everybody greeted everybody else and talked at the tops of their voices. Finally, there were three knocks and the *kaymakam* left his seat and made a speech about the function of the theatre which, from time immemorial, had been "the mirror of man's woes and aspirations". He was heartily applauded and the curtain parted to reveal Ali Dayi the Piper, Ismet and his banjo, Ahmet the policemen and his lute and young Cihat and his wooden spoons. Great applause greeted them and they regaled us with a selection of Bodrum songs and dancing tunes. After that the play began.

The décor and the costumes had recreated for the people the all-too familiar figures of officialdom and its halls. Right away people followed the story with interest, laughing at the immediately identifiable characters, at the way in which official business is conducted, at the bewildered "man in the street" reactions of the *kaymakam's* clerk to anything the mad official proposed. This was rich farce and delighted people who had so often been exasperated and frustrated by officialdom.

During the first interval, one of the prettiest schoolteachers came on stage, dressed in a *temel devren* and recited a long poem with a patriotic flavour. She was loudly applauded and the second act began. All through the people were laughing loudly and exchanging delighted remarks with their next-door neighbours. Throughout the play, watching the predicament of a small community in the far-off East, the townspeople felt identified and elated and, for once, at one in their feelings, without distinction of Cretan and local, rich or poor. This time the enemy was immediately recognizable, the bureaucracy with its unchanging and unalterable ways. During the second interval, the audience was entertained by one of the barbers, a handsome and portly youth, who sang a sentimental love song, accompanied by the lute only. He obliged with two encores and everybody agreed that he was good enough "to go on the radio".

The third act proceeded and suddenly there was a huge roar of laughter. Upon being told that their new and beloved *kaymakam* was noting but a madman, a chorus of townspeople exclaimed "God preserve us from a sane man". It is this remark that brought the enthusiasm of the audience to its climax. All eyes turned to the *kaymakam*, necks were craned to see how he would take it. He took it very well, laughing with the rest. This was the high point in the play and brought the evening to an end.

Such occasions are rare and each year, the Youth Club decides that they should form an amateur company and produce at least three plays, the proceeds of which would finance the school and other activities. But as in everything else, conflicts occur, the boys split on decisions, and the idea peters out. Nowadays the play is produced and acted by a group of young men who may or may not be connected with the Club. This year the choice is to be "Our Town".

If the play and visiting are accidental occurrences, the cinema on the other hand is a regular and popular form of spending leisure time. The Bodrum Cinema is named after a famous Ottoman admiral, reputed to have been born in these parts, though people north of Izmir claim the same honour. It is a tumble-down structure, awkwardly situated in a corner of the old church square. Its wooden boards and balcony shudder as you walk on them and people sit on hard wooden chairs with straight backs, closely packed together. It is never completely dark and the screen is a narrow old-fashioned one, with disastrous results for panoramic films. The projectors flicker and the picture is never black and white but a dirty kind of grey and dark brown. In spite of all this, the cinema enjoys the privilages of a monopoly and is full every other night, when the new film comes on, practically full the next day and always full to bursting point on Saturday and Sunday matinees when the children invade it. At those times, the dialogue is punctuated with shouts and laughter and the continuous small noise of bursting peanuts and water-melon seeds. There is one performance each night, at seven-thirty, which allows the people of Bodrum to go to bed just a little later than usual.

All the children go to the cinema, all the young men, practically all the women and the young girls and a smattering of men. While most of the schoolteachers and officials will accompany their wives to the cinema in the evening, only a small number of men from the town will do so. The older men and women do not go in any case, the religious inclined to think that it is sinful, the others not having patience with "the nonsense". Of the middle-aged men, only about a quarter consider that the cinema is a form of pleasure and prefer other types of entertainment, which they can indulge in while their wives are seeing a film. Still the cinema is the only regular entertainment where wives and husbands can be seen together.

Practically all the films which come to Bodrum are local ones. The few foreign films are dubbed in Turkish and the undisputed favourite is the western. When the French film "Le Gendarme de St Tropez" came to Bodrum, duly dubbed, it was liked for two reasons: one, because policemen were being made fun of and two, because the location was familiar. Promptly, the townspeople decided that there was no reason why Bodrum should not one day become another St Tropez, obviously ignorant as they are of the less savoury aspects of that particular pleasure-ground. They appreciated the beauty of the boats and the cafés and the bikinis of the girls. It was one of the rare non-western foreign films which were talked about in the town.

The Turkish films are preferred because they are a slight exaggeration and simplification of everyday life. They do not vary in subject and always the same protagonists exchange more or less similar dialogue. The moral is always quite clear and there is always a happy ending, for somehow or other the wicked are punished and the good rewarded. In a country which has been witnessing for the last fifteen years the rise of a new business middle class, with all that this implies in terms of conspicuous consumption and "dog eat dog" mentality, the films happily go on spinning the same old tale of honest toil versus ill-earned wealth, of the sanctity of marriage and family life versus *dolce vita*, of the final triumph of the little man pitted against the big city tycoons. Adultery, illegitimate children, orphaned girls and boys, gamblers and courtesans, city slickers, innocents led astray, drunken fathers, succeed each other on the screen with unfailing regularity. For the women, this is another form of the picture magazine strip and a consolation to those who recognize their woes on the screen. For the happy ones, it is an occasion to congratulate oneself and commiserate with less-favoured women. It is understandable that most men are not too keen on the films, except maybe for the ever-present belly dancer.

So it happens that many women go to the cinema every other evening, and most go at least twice a week. It must be said, however, that the popularity of the cinema lies in the fact that there are few other forms of public entertainment for the women and that the cinema reigns, therefore, unchallenged. In the summer, when the cinema moves to its open-air quarters on the sea-shore, the attendance drops. Many people are away then, or too busy with the tourists, but many women, prefer to sit outside or in the only two cafés they can go to on the sea-shore and watch the strangers and the tourists, a favourite and rewarding pastime.

The entrance fee is small, one lira for the seats in the upstairs gallery and 0.75 lira for the rest. But the difference in price is not designed as an economic necessity. It is there to mark a subtler difference; unaccompanied men are sold the cheaper tickets so as to prevent them from sitting with the "families", that is the group of women or the couples. These invariably sit upstairs in the winter and at the back, on a low platform in the summer. No woman or girl would sit in the cheaper seats among the youths and the men, even if they are short-sighted and could see better that way. This is to prevent, as the manager put it, "unpleasantness". In Bodrum, however, such "unpleasantness" can only take the form of general remarks about the actresses, enunciated loudly; no man or youth would dare do anything else. The odd thing is that the remarks are still made and fully audible to the protected groups, but from afar.

WOMEN'S LEISURE

The women have no other opportunities to go out with their husbands. In the summer a few will come down to the harbour café or the Palm Café after dinner and sit with their relatives and husbands, drinking a lemonade and looking at the tourists. Mini-skirts and the free and easy ways of foreigns girls and boys will be observed and commented upon, more in wonder than in criticism—"this is their way", the women will say, "we have different ways". The tourists' children will be admired, for there is a general predilection for fair people and most tourists coming from Northerm Europe are fair. The fact that small children are allowed to run around clad in just a pair of shorts will be commented upon, and the women will wonder at the fact that the children neither catch colds nor get sun-stroke with so little protection. Beauty of face and limb will always be admired unreservedly, by men as well as women, for physical beauty is one of the things that the townspeople feel strongly

about. The fact that foreign women drink will be noted, but no
more. Again, "It's their way" and that's that.

The poorer women cannot afford to go to the cafés in the evenings
and will congregate either on the sea-shore or in a garden overlooking the sea. One of the typical sights of Bodrum is the clusters of
Cretan women seated by the sea-shore in the summer, staring at the
passers-by, while in the local quarters almost no women are visible.

Looking at the street, at people, at events is a favourite pastime.
anyone sitting in a window or a shop may be asked about the where-
abouts of a neighbour and will provide the answer. So-and-so went
down to the harbour, such-and-such has gone into the doctor, yet
another has been down to the market and has come back. Women
sitting in their windows and knitting will remark to each other,
"here is Zubeyde going to congratulate the Ilters", or "here is Gülen
going to the Gokbel's *lohusa*". Any event is immediately known, and
according to its nature, the movements of women in the next few
days are interpreted accordingly.

Mrs. Oral, who is a sensible woman, said to the writer one day,
"births, deaths, engagements, circumcisions, all these are excuses
to go visiting. How else would you be able to leave the house?"
Indeed, visiting remains, for the women, the most habitual way of
passing the time. Now and again, they go to a *mevlut*, and to all the
ceremonies attendant upon births and marriages.

There are enough events of this type to provide two or even three
outings a week. Since they do not require an outlay of money,
all women, even the poorest, can enjoy them. There is no in-
come-bar on these occasions, considered, as they are, as public
events. The women of means, however, have "visiting days", which
are formal occasions. One does not go visiting except on a visiting
day, unless the lady of the house is a relative or a close friend.
The days are announced by each lady at the beginning of the autumn and end in the spring, with the onset of the heat. Some ladies
have one day a month, but most hold two days in one month, such
as the first and third Wednesdays. The writer was taken by Nazime,
a tradesman's wife to her sister's house on one of these days, which
was followed, eventually by many others.

These affairs, called "days", however, involve a ritual which is
almost Far-eastern in its rigidity. The pattern is the same, and the
writer came to recognize it in subsequent visits and to react automatically in the proper manner at every step.

Nazime's sister lives with her husband, who is the owner of a sponge boat and quite well-off, and her three daughters, in one of the old houses in the inner harbour, the local quarter. The house has wooden floors and ceilings, and the walls are made of wooden partitions with doors in them opening on to cupboards. The furniture in the downstairs family room in sparse, a few rugs, muslin bags containing beans and dry lentils or peas hanging from the beams on the ceiling, and two long and low *sedirs* on opposite sides. We were taken upstairs, that day, into the formal drawing-room. We had taken off our shoes at the entrance and given slippers and we walked on carpets. A brazier, or *mangal*, was set in the middle of the room to take the chill off, and we sat on chairs or on a long *sedir* covered in embroidered material, and hung with hand-crocheted lace which was made by the grandmother for the girls' trousseau. A wooden cabinet covered in veneer contained an "art nouveau" oil lamp and decorated tea cups which obviously were never used.

After we sat down, the hostess came round and shook hands quite formally with her sister and the writer; a lady was already sitting on the *sedir* and we greeted her no less formally. She had her knitting with her, and Nazime got hers out. Two or three other women came up, coming from another "day" and they set down and told us their harvest of news. There was little gossip. Most of the talk was about children away at school, the weather—so important to these women with men at sea—and the way the tangerine crop was coming along. After a while, Nazime's sister passed round a bottle of eau de cologne, then some sweets, and then some cigarettes. After that, she disappeared and came back a while later with a tray upon which was one glass of tea and a few biscuits and gave it to the lady who was there before us. When the lady finished, the tray was taken away, and we received our trays; the tea was already sweetened. No one ate more than two buscuits and a second cup of tea was not offered. The writer reflected that a dozen biscuits would see one through a tea-party!

The visit lasts one hour or a little more, and one moves on to another house, where the ritual is the same. In very rich houses, a second glass of tea is offered and, more often than not, accepted. But the ceremony is the same, the conversation identical and the knitting goes on unabated.

The wives of the government employees give teas to each other, and a few of the local ladies are regular guests, but by no means all.

The visiting days follow the pattern of visiting as far as "the upper crust" is concerned, a subtle combination of income and status, with education coming a good third. The mayoress, very active in local politics, does not discrimate in her days, which she obviously considers as useful occasions to communicate political news to the electorate. As for the mayor himself, he invariably sits in the Party's café, opposite the cinema, and conducts the local political life of the town from there.

MEN'S PASTIMES

As is to be expected, occasions for enjoying one's leisure are much more numerous for the men in Bodrum. Although older men do not go swimming—an occupation fit only for young men—they go fishing and hunting, play cards and the pools in cafés and clubs, and drink in the evenings in the two or three *meyhane*—drinking houses—of Bodrum which are ordinary restaurants with a licence to sell spririts and wines.

Fishing is a summer pastime while hunting is a winter one. Few men indulge in both pleasures. The hunters do not fish and the fishermen do not hunt. The Sunday fishermen all have a small boat with a small engine attached and on Sundays they go around the bays and creeks and fish for pleasure. In the winter they stop altogether and fishing is only done by the professionals. The hunters are a more dedicated group. As soon as the cold weather sets in, they begin and will continue until the end of March. They will shut up their shops and other places of work and go hunting for days on end, leaving the house at dawn with the dog and coming back at nightfall. Although there is wild boar in the hills, the religious taboo on pig's meat prevents the hunting of these animals and, by the same token, rabbits not being popular as a food they are not shot except as a pest in the same way as foxes. The Bodrum hunters shoot birds, quail, partridge, woodcock and blackbirds. They also catch small birds with sticks smeared with birdlime. The birds are never shot for sale but for pleasure and, once back in town, if the hunter has bagged a few birds he will adjourn to one of the *meyhane* and enjoy them with his friends, with generous glassfuls of *raki*. The Bodrum hunter is not particularly mindful of rules and regulations or anything remotely resembling fairplay. They shoot in and out of the official season and are not above waiting for the birds to come down to the water to drink, and then shooting them.

There is a Hunting Club in Bodrum which is no more than a very large room with a coffee and tea-making stall in one corner and a large stove in the middle. The Hunting Club does not function as a club at all and although it has a Chairman and a Treasurer, it never meets formally. The Club is just another café in Bodrum with a mixed clientele of neighbours, hunters and fishermen.

There are four restaurants in Bodrum and a number of eating-houses where only the local meat-balls are available. This latter category cater to people who drop in at lunch-time to have a quick helping with large chunks of bread for the price of T.L. 1. The more important function of these small eatingplaces is to provide break-fast—also the meat-balls—for many of the shopkeepers and trades-men who are in the habit of having breakfast in the market. No drinks are available in these places and most close in the evening. But the restaurants are different; they all have a licence for selling drinks and a more or less varied menu. At lunch they cater to very few people, restaurant meals being expensive by Bodrum standards—T.L. 10-20—and most men either go home for lunch or have their meals brought in from home to them. A few schoolteachers, one or two of the museum staff, a passing businessman or travelling sales-man are the usual clientele. In the summer they cater to the tourists and then they are so full that people have to await their turn.

It is in the evenings that these restaurants do their briskest trade. Three of them are situated in the market and one on the inner harbour. The lunchtime customers also eat there in the evenings but in addition there are a good number of those who are called, locally, the "evening-outers". These are men who every evening, after shutting the shop or the office, proceed to one of these restau-rants with their friends and settle down to an evening of *raki* and food. The meal invariably begins with the hors-d'oeuvres that "go" with *raki*, white cheese and melon, cucumber and tomato, small dishes of fried squid and octopus, and slices of *pastirma*, which is beef cured in garlic and spices. The meal ends with grilled fish and the Bodrum fish soup, eaten last of all "to settle the stomach" or, more rarely, tripe soup. A "raki table" is a meal which is eaten slowly; it may last for four hours and rarely do people leave the table under two. Jokes and stories, gossip and deals succeed each other and tit-bits are sent from one table to the other, such as a partridge or, in the summer, grapes and peaches. It is the favourite entertainment for men and the *bête noire* of wives. Only fifty men or so are regular, daily "evenings-outers", going to these restaurants every evening. Most men go once a week, usually on Saturday evenings or in the middle of the week. Such outings are expensive and only the better-off fishermen, sponge-divers, craftsmen and tradesmen can afford to have them. The less well-off go to the cheapest of the four or hold their *raki table* now and again in their shop.

The four restaurants have their *habitués*. The most prosperous and staid citizens go to the one on the inner harbour and to the largest of the three remaining ones, which is run by two brothers. The history teacher and his two dogs and one or two of the wealthiest tangerine-growers, local men, go to the one in the inner harbour, which is located in the richest local district. The poorest fishermen and sponge-divers go to the "Broken Fork", a modest place in the market. But it is Kasa which is the liveliest of them all. Everybody goes there and in the summer it is full of the youngest and more "Bohemian" type of tourists. The two Chief Clerks, the one from the Municipality and the one from the Court go there once a week, the museum staff invariably goes there, and so do the two or three strangers who have settled in Bodrum. A few *kaptans*, one or two boat-builders complete the group. Ali Dayi the Piper makes an appearance every evening and plays his pipe while the rest of the group sings the Bodrum songs over and over again, but always with the same pleasure. At around nine in the evening the dancing starts. Those who dance well and those who like dancing are urged by the others and get up one by one to do the *zeybek* on the saw-dusted floor. In the winter, a small wood stove is lit by whoever happens to be the first comer and then is looked after all through the evening by everybody. People get up and fetch what they need themselves, and often act as waiters for whatever out of town visitors there may be. Kasa himself presides, cooks, sits down and chats and, when he feels very gay, plays the trumpet he acquired when he was in the Navy, in the band. He always plays "Summertime" and when it gets late, "Lights Out". In the summer the place is so full that a pin conldn't be dropped and entertainment is provided by the tourists, who play the guitar or sing songs from their own country. Kasa is well-known by hundreds of people abroad and receives considerable mail which has to be read and translated for him by Teoman, the writer or one or two others in the town, such as the Peace Corps girl. In the winter, however, it is cosier and pleasanter. People say to each other across the tables, come November: "now we are among ourselves", and look forward to many pleasant evenings of this kind.

No women come to Kasa's except the tourists and the wives of the museum staff and the local "strangers". But they do not come too often, and when they do not, their husbands usually rise by eight, to have dinner at home, whereupon the usual teasing about henpecking takes place, to be sheepishly denied by the recipients.

These evenings are, as was said before, the privilege of a few men in the community. But this is not so with the cafés. All the men of Bodrum go to the café at least once a day and those who do not are so few that their names are known. The café is an institution which combines the features of a neighbourhood or professional club with those of a labour exchange, a post office and a shelter. There are twenty-nine cafés in this little town and some do not have more than three or four tables. They are evenly distributed in all the neighbourhoods, except for the market where there are many more. All the cafés, except those which are frequented by fishermen, are not very full in the daytime or after lunch, since people tend to have coffee brought to them. They are full early in the morning and after supper, that is after six o'clock. The remotest ones shut at nine or ten in the evening, and the ones in the market later. Usually the charcoal stove is extinguished around ten, but people are not turned out. Only tea and coffee and lime and sage infusions are served in the cafés. One or two of the largest have begun to serve orange and tangerine juice in the winter and all provide soft drinks in the summer in the form of a cheap carbonated sweetened water. The more expensive brands are only sold in the cafés where tourists go.

The cafés never close on Sundays but some of the smaller ones situated in the poorest quarters do not serve tea or coffee during *Ramazan*, but nevertheless remain open, and the men go there as before. The cafés situated next to the four mosques open very early in the morning to cater to those who go to early prayers and one café opens at four-thirty in the morning, because it is next to the bus station and travellers drink a cup or two before the bus leaves at 5 a.m.

The café is as much a part of neighbourhood life as its houses and streets. Each neighbourhood has one or two small cafés to which all the men of the neighbourhood go and where they can be found by anyone who knows the pattern. Looking for labourers or odd-job men, for men who are not in their shop, finding out when so-and-so will return from the village, all these things are done in the cafés. The café owner is a mine of information. He knows where every man in the neighbourhood is likely to be found, knows all about his children and family, knows who is out of a job and looking for one and freely provides the information. Messages and parcels are left with him, and many letters come to Bodrum addressed care of the café in the neighbourhood. The café owner will deliver the letter to the recipient within the hour, if he is in town. Men at work will come in before starting the day and then come back after supper, "still chewing the last mouthful" as the women put it. And men out of work will wait in the cafés until something turns up. In the cafés which are mostly visited by fishermen, the nets will be made and mended in the café or outside it when the weather permits and piles of nets will be stacked in corners, awaiting their owners. In Yeniköy, the neighbourhood where most casual labourers live, the café is a veritable labour exchange where building contractors and tangerine-grove owners go when they need men. The cafés in the other two poor neighbourhoods, Umurca and Yokuşbaşi, have a similar clientele with a spattering of small craftsmen; the cafés on the harbour are visited by the officials connected with the customs and the harbour-master's office, and a few tradesmen but the majority of those who go there are seamen, who sit and scan the sea, winter as well as summer. The Justice Party people have their own café opposite the cinema where the more politically active members meet each evening to discuss the news, listen to the speeches of the Prime Minister or other party higher-ups and plan and plot strategy. A few years ago, the opposition party also had a café where it met, but the building did not belong to them and had to go to make room for a row of shops, and since then the opposition has scattered.

One or two are known as cafés where the "old men" go. Such is a café on the far side of the inner harbour where bubble pipes can be smoked and where a few old men meet every day, only going home for meals. It is a very quiet and pleasant place but will not be so much longer because a largish—for Bodrum—hotel has been built next door. Another "old man's" café is the one in the market opposite the New Mosque, where old men living in the surrounding streets come. The owners in both places are as old as the customers and drinks are never ordered, since they know who drinks what and bring it to them as soon as they sit down.

The young men have two or three cafés where they congregate

in the evening. They are usually apprentices who have a little money, or idle young men who just come for the company and the talk. Since there is no obligation to order anything, anyone can sit for hours in a café, just passing the time of day. In the winter this is very welcome, since all the cafés have a small wood stove burning.

It is not unusual for people to sit in a café for an hour or two in exchange for a single glass of tea. The smallest cafés do not use more than a packet of one hundred grams of tea a day, which would make fifty glasses, at a quarter of a lira each. The larger cafés, the ones in the harbour and in the market area, use as much as two packets a day. The price includes two lumps of sugar per glass. At this price, the owner of a small neighbourhood café will earn a daily wage similar to that of a casual labourer, while the owner of the larger cafés will earn as much as a qualified worker and a little more, because he will also serve a goodly amount of coffee, which costs just less than half a lira a small cup. Restaurants and eating-houses do not serve coffee and have it brought in from some of the surrounding cafés. The most prosperous businessmen and craftsmen also have a cup of coffee at mid-morning. Most of the café owners own the building and do not have to pay rent. They use charcoal-burners to boil the water and rarely employ a waiter. Only two of the cafés in the market-place have a waiter, who work for a very low wage one getting T.L. 50.- and the other T.L. 30.- per week. For most café owners, life would be very hard if they had no other source of income; as it happens they all have a bit of land and one of them has a prosperous souvenir and antiquities shop and for the latter, the income from the café is negligible. In the summer only two of the cafés are visited by the tourists because they are situated at the water's edge and are favourite viewing points for the cele-brated Bodrum sunsets. In the seasons they employ a couple of boys to help with the service, who are paid T.L. 10-20.- a week, but make more from the tips, an institution reserved to "strangers". The people of Bodrum do not tip and the writer was asked not to start this bad habit when she first arrived, with her city ways!

One other meeting and drinking place in Bodrum is the City Club, situated in the Cretan quarter. At the beginning the City Club functioned properly, with regular meetings and a good restaurant and all the higher civil servants and the more prosperous merchants were members. As time went on, however, card playing took over and the place became the monopoly of gamblers. This is the only place in the town where large sums are lost and won over cards and many members ceased to go to it. Eventually the restaurant was closed, and nowadays about a dozen men go there, to drink and play cards every evening after dinner. Some of the civil servants play bridge, but the majority of those who frequent the Club play poker and are known as hard drinkers. Like almost all organized associations, the City Club has lost its purpose over a period of time. Needless to say no women ever go there and every woman dreads the day when her husband will become a habitué of the Club. The solidarity created by gambling and drinking together night after night has, of course, repercussions in the relationships between some of the civil servants and the more prosperous boat-owners and merchants.

CHAPTER THIRTEEN

OLD AGE

Growing old in Bodrum seems to be less difficult than in larger towns, and old people do not seem to be lonely or neglected. Like very small children, they are known and helped by the whole neighbourhood and feel that after an active and useful life, they have earned their rest.

Before growing very old, they would have helped their children in the raising of the grandchildren, the women minding the baby and knitting for the older children, the men taking the little boys for walks along the sea-shore or for a jaunt down-town to the café. They will run their house unaided for as long as they like, or can, with their children keeping a watchful eye on them, and their daughters or daughters-in-law sending them a meal or two every few days. The old men will continue to go to the café and the old women will become regular attendants at Nedime Molla's Fridays or at *mevlut* meetings. They will be, what is most important, independent of their children, or made to feel so. For the attention and care lavished on the old is both expected and received, but never interpreted as dependence. The old are entitled to respect and care, and they get it, and that is all there is to it.

No one feels very sorry for old women, but when an old man loses his wife, everybody feels sorry and wonders how he will manage. In this way, many old men, once widowed, move into the house of one of their children, but very few old women do so. They feel they want to end their days in their own homes. When they need help—water from the fountain or well, the carrying of something heavy, the sending of a message—all they have to do is to come out on the doorstep and call to the nearest passer-by. The job will be done, the helper blessed and sent on his way and the old one will go back into the house, muttering a prayer.

In the case of the poor, the situation is not very different. The municipality will help with a little money, but it is the friends of the family and the neighbours who will keep the old one in food and clothes. Some of them will attempt to do some work, like old Huseyin who mends shoes, or Ali Dayi the peanut seller. These are the really independent ones, who would feel lost without their tools, and who continue to work because they have always done so. Whey they go to the café, they are proud of the fact that they can buy a friend a glass of sage tea, while many of the other old people do not mind if someone younger treats them; for in their youth, they also treated old people in the cafés.

The very old do not drink and do not play cards. They smoke and talk and observe the sea, the people and the tourists. Many of them, especially among the Cretans, turn religious and go to the mosque three of four times a day "to get their sins forgiven". The rest of the time they talk to each other and recall the old days of sailing, when being a sailor really meant something. But the locals have no such epic memories, and are content to sit and exchange news about the neighbourhood and pass remarks about the crops. The very old live from day to day, without thought of the future, for the future has become something very near.

This is not so for the nearly-old. They are still young enough to be active, but not so young that they do not feel the passage of time. So they complain about old age creeping on, and can joke about death and boast about their powers to each other.

Who will bury who first? The question was debated on evening in Kasa's, with Ahmet Kaptan and Basri Kaptan as the main protagonists. "I will bury you first", said Ahmet Kaptan, and hic-cupped hugely; "and what's more, I'll put a bunch of flowers on your tomb and get the Milas Band to come and play". "I will bury you first", replied Basri Kaptan, "and put a bottle of *raki* on your tombstone". The Town Clerk remarked, in his usual serious way, that he "had been on the other side and did not like it", referring to a serious illness which had stricken him some years earlier. Kasa himself put to an end to the argument and got silence by blowing his trumpet and then announcing, "we shall all go down below, captain and crew, for death and military service are both inevi-table".

The rest of the audience were laughing so much they had tears in their eyes, for the argument had been going on for some time and all the familiar jokes had been made. All the same, there was a serious undercurrent, for the winter had been harsh and many of the oldest people had died in quick succession. "God is cleaning the place up, making room for new ones", said Aunt Zubeyde, "we are all fellow travellers on the same road".

The road meanders through the gardens and fields of the Umurca quarter and ends up in a field, which at first sight does not differ from the others. The same trees and grasses, and the same hedge of prickly branches. It is only after a second look that the cemetery becomes apparent. There are very few tombstones made of marble or good stone and engraved with the name of the buried, and most of the stones do not differ very much from ordinary slabs of rock, standing upright, which they are. On many tombs, simple slabs of wood, simply indented on the edges, mark the site of the grave and there are no inscriptions of any kind. The tomb is known by the fact that each time it is visited. children are taken along and come to know the place in time, to show their own children later. Something which strikes the visitor is that most of the marble tombstones have been installed in the late fifties, a sign that there was money then to spend on this sort of thing. The overwhelming majority of the townspeople sleep peacefully in this garden, unknown to any but their relatives.

The people of Bodrum die old, much older than people in other parts of the country, even if the people who have emigrated and live away from town are taken into consideration. The largest number of deaths occur between the ages of seventy-five and ninety, with half a dozen deaths or so over that limit. The number of deaths each year reaches about sixty on the average, including the infant deaths. In 1966 only, eighty-one deaths occurred—through the cold, people said—but actually because of extreme old age. In the winter of 1967 and 1958, the deaths were fewer.

Over half the deaths occur through natural causes and heart failure, which may be another "natural cause" in the case of very old people. A third of the remainder occur through haemorrhage of the brain or stomach. Cancer of the lungs is a new killer which took away five people in 1966 and three in 1967. One death and at the most two occur through tuberculosis. In this respect, Bodrum presents a different picture to the rest of the country and the region. The national expectancy of life is fifty-five years and the main causes of death in the region are tuberculosis, diseases of the respiratory tract and malignant stomach growths. On the other hand, Bodrum presents the same picture as elsewhere, inasmuch as many more men than women die each year.

Death, like birth and marriage, is attended by conventions and ceremonies which are scrupulously observed. While customs are changing fast and variations are being freely introduced in the case of birth and marriage, the death ceremonial does not alter and always follows its prescribed course. It is also an event in which the various steps do not vary, except for one or two small details, from what is done in other parts of the country, or as between Cretan and local.

When someone dies, the first thing to be done is no notify the government doctor, and then get a grave dug. The depth of the grave varies according to whether the deceased is a man or a woman. Men's graves are dug to a depth equivalent to that of the stomach, and women's graves to that of the breast "women, being more sinful, must be buried deeper" say the people half in jest. Actually this corresponds to the prayer position, in which men pray with their hands crossed over their stomach, and women with their hands crossed over their breast. The body is then measured for the shroud, and after the body has been washed—in the case of a man, by one of the *imams*, or in the case of a woman, by two old women who have done so for years—it is wrapped in the shroud and awaits burial. The first pouring of the water is always done by an immediate relative, "to help them understand that the end has really come". All the while, the *imam* has been reading the death prayer over the minaret's microphone and the town learns of the event in that way, and people begin to come to the house: "the house of the dead is visited for three reasons; to steal, to make fun of the dead and to cry" it is said in Bodrum. For at this stage, the deceased's clothes and shoes are distributed to the poor and it is thought that a coin or two may have been forgotten in the pockets; if the dead person had enemies, now is the time for them to rejoice, while those who loved the deceased will come and share in the family's grief.

Only the richest families in Bodrum have a coffin made by one of the carpenters. Most people get the coffin from the mosques, a simple affair of unpainted wood in all cases. When the coffin is closed, a rug or an embroidered cloth, preferably green—the colour of Islam—is thrown over it and the deceased is ready to leave the house. By this time, the yard and the street have filled with people, the men remaining outside, the women joining the women of the family inside the house. Two ranks are formed and the coffin is passed from hand to hand, as a last homage before it leaves the house. At this stage, the *imam* in charge addresses the people in these terms," renounce the world, all of you, this man is leaving".

The coffin is always carried on shoulders to the mosque, each follower asking for the honour in turn, and when the mosque is reached, the coffin is placed outside on the "funeral stone", the "last throne" on earth. This part of the ceremony always takes place after the midday or the afternoon prayer, and then the prayer for the dead is read, different for each sex and age. Since the cemetery is not very near, it has become the custom in Bodrum of late to carry the coffin by jeep. Once there, the body is taken out of the coffin, laid slightly on its side "so that rising will be easier" and a roof of planks is made, over which the earth is put, each follower throwing a shovelful. No women, ever, go to the cemetery, or participate in the prayers for the dead, just as they do not participate in *Bayram* prayers.

After the burial, verses from the Koran are read and the *imam* is left alone with the dead. He will then call to the dead, addressing him or her by name and quoting the deceased's mother's name and remind it of the fact that "your book is the Koran, your Prophet Mohammed, your religion Islam".

On the evening of the death and for the two or three days following, neighbours will bring food to the house. The Cretans "who have to have everything fancy", bring pilaf and meat on the first day, *helva* on the second and pastry on the third. But the locals bring anything. For the following days, the family will be visited by friends and neighbours, the women secluded in one of the rooms. On the seventh day, prayers will be read, on the fortieth a *mevlut* meeting held, on the fifty-second day, pilaf will be cooked and distributed. In the meanwhile, notification of the death has been communicated to the *muhtar* of the neighbourhood, who will inform the Registry Office. From now on, at every *Bayram*, the grave will be faithfully visited and branches of wild laurel placed thereon. Another stone will be added to the cemetery a year after the death, with or without an inscription. People will show each other the tombs of relatives and friends, and invariably shake their heads over one of them, which belongs to a young man who died of unrequited love, having set his heart on a married woman. He asked his people to commemorate the event, and visitors to the Bodrum cemetery can now read this inscription, put well in evidence:

> "Passers-by, read my story and
> think about my end; madness
> overtook me; my heart burned;
> how was I to know that this

> Was a hopeless love; how was
> I to know that destiny would
> strike me; my only hope is
> now in resurrection."

The carving is crude and the spelling erratic. But it is the only death in Bodrum which occurred through love.

A NOTE ABOUT BODRUM IN 1971

Two years have passed since completion of this study. In the interim I have settled in Bodrum and become one of the "strangers" who have chosen it as a permanent home.

I have not brought the study up to date for two reasons: one is that the time which has elapsed has been too short for any significant evaluation in terms of social change and too long for continuous study; the other is that I have begun to lose my objectivity. Living here, I share the problems of the local inhabitants and have come to display some of the the same reactions. However, I am attempting a short enumeration of the most obvious changes.

What is striking now is a great increase in building activity and in the number of shops. Two more banks have opened and these provide jobs for three girls who have returned after their studies in Izmir and half a dozen young men. The girls seem to consider that their stay is temporary and the young men know that they will be promoted one day away from Bodrum.

Tourism has had effects which are both good and bad. The number of tourists has greatly increased. Two private hotels have been built, a dozen or so small pensions have been started and the municipality has received assistance from the central government and built a large hotel. The Tourism Association no longer gives help to those who want to convert their house into a "pension". The need seems to have disappeared, the prospective "pension" owners finding the funds they require elsewhere. All the touristic establishments, including three more restaurants and three more eating-houses do a brisk trade from June to August, but the more expensive ones, such as the restaurants of the larger hotels, close down for the winter.

Another touristic innovation is the chartering trade. Foreigners, Turks from other cities and the townspeople themselves are having pleasure boats built and these are chartered out to tourists in the summer. There are now twenty-three such boats, sleeping from six to twelve people. Their numbers have increased rapidly and, as a result, three more boat-yards have opened and the older boat builders have begun to pay taxes and have had to learn to keep books, pay social security to their workers and draw up contracts.

A further effect of tourism has been that land and houses have been sold and each holiday and summer season are periods when considerable amounts of property change hands. A few Europeans, but mainly people from Istanbul and Ankara, are investing in a house or a plot to be used as a holiday home, or for retirement in the future. The price of land has rocketed to incredible heights— twenty, forty and sometimes fifty times what it was in 1966. Very few properties are still available on the sea-shore and the demand for land has enriched many a poor fisherman or worker who has sold part of his field or a disused *dam* in the corner of his garden. The richer merchants of the town have not followed this trend, content to watch values rise.

As a result of these activities, the "onion and garlic months" have become a memory for many of the inhabitants. But the poorest people have become poorer. The devaluation which took place last summer and the rise in prices which preceded and followed it in the last two years have brought the costs of food up by 50% and sometimes more. Labour has also gone up. Male labour has increased by 60% and female labour by 25%. These wages are the same as are demanded in larger cities such as Izmir. But the labour force has decreased, with more men going to Germany and other European countries to work, taking their families with them, and thus less labour is available for agricultural work, labourers preferring to work in building or on the charter boats. A number of them are working on two new government projects. One is the measuring of the land and the establishment of title-deeds for all the land owners of the town, and the other is the building of a yacht harbour on the western side of the inner harbour. As a result, the price of land around the site of the yacht harbour has reached levels which makes the price of land similar to that in a large city such as Ankara or Izmir.

The Sponge Cooperative has closed down and the Tangerine and Fishermen's Cooperatives are idle. An enterprising trader, one of the family of K's, has established a sorting plant and conveys the whole of the Bodrum crop to Europe through the intermediary of a firm of exporters in Izmir. The tangerine growers are thus spared the fluctuating prices of the old method and receive a steady price for their crop all though the season. They also are spared the packing and transport expenses. The great majority of growers are therefore willing to take a smaller price, but one that does not change and a way of selling their crop, which they find easier to operate. The fishermen send most of their catch to Izmir, and so do the people who raise cattle for meat. Prices are much higher in Izmir, and as a result, meat and fish have become scarce and very expensive. Fish which used to be thrown back into the sea or given away because of its poor quality now commands prices which are not far below that of the best. These two facts are reflected in the diet of the poorer people, who now eat even less meat and fish, cheese and other milk products.

The butchers have left their old quarters in the inn and have moved into shops built by the municipality, which have running water. They all have refrigerators and have gone on strike twice this year in order to secure increases in the prices of meat. When they did not get them, they sent most of their meat to Izmir. It is expected that the tourist seasons will see an increase in the amount of meat available, with a concurrent rise in prices.

The grocers have now begun to sell fancy goods, canned food, biscuits and many different makes of sweets, not only in the summer for the tourists, but throughout the year. More refrigerators, bottled gas ovens and lamps and even washing machines are being sold. As for the tailors and shoe-makers they have started making resort clothes and shoe-ware, leather necklaces and head-bands, suede suits and even peace emblems for the younger groups of tourists.

Since 1967, the number of trucks and jeeps has increased. During the school holidays and summer, the Bodrum bus company runs as many as four trips a day to Izmir. Women who used to carry their baskets home after shopping in the Friday market, now band together and hire a jeep which takes them and their heavy loads home.

To summarize, it can be said that following the general trend of the country, prices and wages, and opportunities for investment have risen in Bodrum, but without a concomitant redistribution of incomes. The gap between the highest and the lowest incomes seems to have grown wider, not narrower. This development is not unexpected and reflects the development in other small towns of the Aegean and Mediterranean which have become, or are becoming, popular tourist resorts. It is the people who deal directly with the tourists, or those who are connected with tourist activity indirectly, who have benefited. Some extraneous factor, such as an epidemic of cholera or an adverse development in foreign politics, may upset the present situation and end in a considerable amount of hardship for these people. Only a healthier economic basis, one which will rest on the real natural resources of the area, can achieve a fairer and more lasting economic development. In a country such as Turkey, the initial impulse for such a development can only come from the central government.

Again, following developments in the capital, parties in Bodrum, have gone through a crisis. When some members of the Justice Party in the National Assembly split and set up a new party, strongly reminiscent in flavour and membership of the outlawed Democrat Party, the split was followed in Bodrum immediately. The new branch of the new party has set up the best political office yet to be seen in Bodrum, and the members have rallied around the old mayor again. Two professional men and a retired civil servant, all three from other places, have founded a branch of the Turkish Labour Party. The executive committee contains only one local man, and he from a neighbouring village. While no members from Bodrum have registered as members, there seems to be some sympathy towards this party, which may be reflected in the next elections. On the other hand, the people who have split up from the Justice Party and joined the new party consider the setting up of the Turkish Labour Party as nothing short of treason on the part of strangers whom they had "taken to their hearts".

However, these new political developments do not reflect a change in the power structure of the town. The holders of economic power hold their peace and continue to operate their trading houses, their private money-lending activities and their network of small favours and benefits. Those who were members of the People's Republican Party contemplate the upheavals in the ruling party with nothing more than what seems distaste to the observer.

In the present atmosphere, I doubt whether I would have been able to conduct this study. For one thing, there has been a rapid turn-over of such important officials as the *kaymakam* and the Director of the Agricultural Bank. Two *Kaymakam* and no less than four Directors of the bank have succeeded one another in Bodrum. Two national banks have opened branches, not because of increasing economic activities— which the Agricultural Bank could have handled easily enough—but as a public relations policy established in their Head Offices. There has also been a perceptible stiffening of attitudes among the townspeople. A more exploitative, more impersonal, more competitive climate prevails in professional and personal relationships. This attitude is even reflected in the dealings which take place between the members of the same family, let alone strangers. Small shopkeepers and craftsmen and the merchants no longer have much time to talk and laze in their shops. The distinction between work and leisure is emerging, which is deplored by many, although it is one of the best indicators of the fact that urban characteristics are gaining on rural ones in the town.

Another emerging characteristic is increasing specialization, both among the male and female labour force and among the craftsmen. The town seems to have reached a level of development nowadays which makes it possible for another doctor, a properly qualified dentist, two architects' offices and even a lawyer's office to operate. It must be stated, however, that most of the people who make use of these services are people who used to go to Izmir for them or bring someone from Izmir to perform them. Now, people who were content to use a master builder for a new house, or have their teeth pulled out by the local man without further ado, apply to the architects and the new dentist.

At the moment it is difficult to foresee what the future of Bodrum holds. Unless there are important changes in the policies of the central government, Bodrum would seem to be going the way of many other small towns: loss of the younger, better educated and more dynamic groups, a somewhat chaotic and feverish touristic development and the settling there of retired couples in search of a quieter and more natural life are its main characteristics. These factors have already begun to operate changes in some of the social attitudes of the inhabitants, changes which were not difficult to predict. But it is too soon to determine whether or not, in the long run, there will be changes in the basic attitudes. Workers who return from Germany after a few years there, or people from Bodrum whom I have met in Izmir and Ankara, do not seem to have changed basically. They have learned, it is true, to manipulate the institutions of larger communities and have acquired the desire for material comforts, as well as the means of achieving these. But in their basic attitudes, to the family, to neighbours, to the community or to the nation at large, they are still provincial and peasant. Therefore, it is difficult to say that the people of Bodrum will eventually change in this or that way. There are rapid changes here, as in the rest of Turkey. But here, as in the rest of Turkey, it is much too soon to engage in predictions.

INDEX

adolescents, 16, 149-61; employment of young men, 149-51; leisure, 151-4; relations with parents, 154-5; attitudes to religion, 155-6; 160, and politics, 156, 160; and marriage, 156-8, 160-1; girls' restricted life, 158-60; and further education, 186-7; nervous disorders, 209-10; cafés, 244-5

Agricultural Bank, 27, 42, 47, 66-70, 72, 76, 78, 256

agriculture, irrigation, 33, 34, 68; non-mechanisation of, 34-5; labour-landlord relations, 35-6; cultivation of olives, 36-40; figs, 40-1; tangerines, 41-4; rain-prayer, 44-5

alcohol, alcoholism, 210-11

antiquities, smuggling of, 46

Artemisia I, Queen, 3

Artemisia II, Queen, 4

associations, 228-9

Atatürk, Kemal, 72, 76, 100, 131, 139

bakers, 25

banks, new, 253, 256; *see also* Agricultural Bank

barbers, 59-60

boat-building, 11, 25, 53, 62, 63-4

Bodrum Castle (St Peter's), 5, 6, 13, 26, 73, 75, 85, 105

Bodrum Post, 93-5

butchers, 25, 56-7, 255

cafés *see* leisure

carpenters, 11, 25, 53, 62-3, 64; family budget, 201-3

cattle-raising, 34, 57, 255

cemetery, 249, 251-2

children, 184; Republic Day parade, 71-4; illnesses, 209, 213; *see also* education; infants

cinema *see* leisure

circumcision, 124-8, 180

civil servants, 27, 55, 75, 204, 207, 217, 218

CKMP (Republican Peasants' National Party), 80

climate, 14-15

credit, 27, 54; for fishing and sponge-diving, 47; purchase of goods on, 52, 55, 58, 59; for tourism, 66; agricultural, 66-8, 78; commercial, 68; repayment of debts, 227-8

Credit Cooperatives, 68

Cretan community, historical background, 7-8, 10-11; flair for commerce, 10-11, 25-7; different living styles of local quarter and, 17-19; population, 21; size of families, 22; smuggling, 46; tourism, 65-6; political affiliations, 78-9; casting of spells, 113-14; children, 118, 119, 120, 121, 129, 138; education, 131, 140, 141; attitudes to marriage, 162-5, 188-9; housekeeping, 195; social relationships with locals, 218-19

Cretan massacres (1897), 7, 8-10, 26

Cyprus crisis, 65, 74, 93

death, 248-51

PLATES I-XV

PLATES I–XV

PLATE I

Fig. 1. Castle of St. Peter (*courtesy David Tombs*)

Fig. 2. Street in the Cretan quarter

PLATE II

Fig. 3. The Myndus-Mylasa Road

Fig. 4. A water-cistern

PLATE III

Fig. 5. An inner courtyard

Fig. 6. A Tangerine grove

PLATE IV

Fig. 7. The Friday market with the Castle in the background (*courtesy Tourism Association*)

PLATE V

Fig. 8. The 18th century inn, until recently the Butcher's quarters

Fig. 9. Draper's store on a Friday

PLATE VI

Fig. 10. Olive Press with waste on the floor (*courtesy Foto Barut*)

Fig. 11. Stringing dried figs

PLATE VII

Fig. 12. The grocer-cum-chandler (*courtesy M. Asatekin*)

Fig. 13. Loads drawn by men in Bodrum

PLATE VIII

Fig. 14. Boat-building (*courtesy M. Asatekin*)

Fig. 15. I. O. the tailor

PLATE IX

Fig. 16. Uncle Hüseyin the cobbler

Fig. 17. The barber-cum-souvenir shop

PLATE X

Fig. 18. Mr. & Mrs. Oral in front of their hotel

Fig. 19. Drawing water

PLATE XI

Fig. 20. Ismet prepares to dive

Fig. 21. A "local" family

PLATE XII

Fig. 22. Ahmet Kaptan, a cretan

Fig. 23. "Local" types

PLATE XIII

Fig. 24. Children at play

Fig. 25. Children's matinee at the cinema (*courtesy Foto Barut*)

PLATE XIV

Fig. 26. "Cretan" women relaxing by the sea-shore

Fig. 27. A fishermen's café

PLATE XV

Fig. 28. Kasa and Ali dayi the piper

Fig. 29. Old men enjoying the winter sun